International Relations Theory of War

International Relations Theory of War

OFER ISRAELI

Praeger Security International

BLOOMSBURY ACADEMIC
NEW YORK · LONDON · OXFORD · NEW DELHI · SYDNEY

BLOOMSBURY ACADEMIC
Bloomsbury Publishing Inc
1385 Broadway, New York, NY 10018, USA
50 Bedford Square, London, WC1B 3DP, UK
29 Earlsfort Terrace, Dublin 2, Ireland

BLOOMSBURY, BLOOMSBURY ACADEMIC and the Diana logo
are trademarks of Bloomsbury Publishing Plc

First published in the United States of America by ABC-CLIO 2019
Paperback edition published by Bloomsbury Academic 2025

Cover photos: Red green blue and sand military camofl age background;
(Blackroom/Dreamstime. com); UH-60 Black Hawk helicopter, Kandahar Air Field,
Afghanistan. (AP Photo/Rahmat Gul); Soldiers Rush the Beaches of Normandy.
(National Archives and Records Administration)

Bloomsbury Publishing Inc does not have any control over, or responsibility for,
any third-party websites referred to or in this book. All internet addresses given
in this book were correct at the time of going to press. The author and publisher
regret any inconvenience caused if addresses have changed or sites have
ceased to exist, but can accept no responsibility for any such changes.

Library of Congress Cataloging-in-Publication Data
Names: Israeli, Ofer, author.
Title: International relations theory of war / Ofer Israeli.
Description: Santa Barbara, CA : Praeger Security International, [2019] |
Includes bibliographical references and index.
Identifiers: LCCN 2018058594 (print) | LCCN 2019001304 (ebook) |
ISBN 9781440871351 (ebook) | ISBN 9781440871344 (print : alk. paper)
Subjects: LCSH: War (Philosophy) | International relations—Philosophy. |
Balance of power. | Military history, Modern.
Classification: LCC U21.2 (ebook) | LCC U21.2 .I775 2019 (print) |
DDC 355.0201—dc23
LC record available at https://lccn.loc.gov/2018058594

ISBN: HB: 978-1-4408-7134-4
PB: 979-8-7651-3687-4
ePDF: 978-1-4408-7135-1
eBook: 979-8-2161-0393-6

Series: Praeger Security International

To find out more about our authors and books visit www.bloomsbury.com
and sign up for our newsletters.

To Eden

To everything there is a season, a time for every purpose
under heaven: . . .
A time to love, and a time to hate; a time of war, and a
time of peace . . .

—Ecclesiastes 3:1, 8

Contents

Preface

Grateful acknowledgment is due to the Institute for Policy and Strategy (IPS), Lauder School of Government, Diplomacy & Strategy, Interdisciplinary Center (IDC) Herzliya, Israel.

I particularly wish to thank Professor Alex Mintz, Maj. Gen. (res.) Amos Gilead, Professor Boaz Ganor, Professor Shaul Shai, Professor Ely Karmon, and Professor Benny Miller for their encouragement and, in many forms, their support. Finally, I wish to thank my beloved kids, Nitzan, Guy, and Oren, and especially my dear wife, Eden, for her constant support, cheerful disposition, and understanding.

Introduction: International Relations Theory of War

This book deals with the *International Relations Theory of War*. The realist theory, which is also known as political realism, emphasizes the competitive aspects and conflicts of international politics, and it is usually at odds with political idealism or liberalism, which tends to emphasize cooperation. This book is based on research that deals primarily with the development of a theory and an analytic model for predicting the results of wars. The theory that has been developed is a systemic theory of international policy systems,[1] known as the *international relations theory of war*. It deals with factors that determine international outcomes—in other words, the consequences of political policy in an international forces system. Outcomes are a result of the conduct of a certain political force and are distinct from its conduct in and of itself.

In *international relations theory of war* terms, the political forces system that prevailed in 1992–2016 was a system consisting of a sole polar power, a hyperpower with a democratic regime—the United States. A unipolar system headed by a democratic hyperpower will tend to war more than a bipolar system in which one of the two superpowers is a dictatorship, such as the bipolar system of 1946–1991, in which the Soviet Union was a regime of that kind. Similarly, the behavior of a country acting toward achieving territorial expansion by war, such as Germany in both world wars, may be in complete contrast to its behavioral outcomes. In other words, offensive behavior, whose purpose was expansion, paradoxically led to Germany's territorial contraction at the end of these two wars.

This book tries to answer two key questions. The first is why certain periods are more prone to war than others. The second is why certain wars that involve polar powers end with their territorial expansion, whereas other wars end in their contraction or maintaining their territorial status. In conclusion, it is asked whether the polarity of the system affects these two outcomes and, if so, how.

The book attempts to make good the dearth of structural theory of international political systems that focuses on an explanation and outcomes expectation, while expanding existing knowledge about the war institution and developing tools that may reduce its damage.[2] Even 2,400 years after the Thucydides's study of war, the war institution remains a significant man-made threat to human well-being,[3] and for more than 300 years, international history has been woven with the rise and fall of great powers and the formation of international systems on the ruins of their predecessors.[4] In view of the foregoing, the importance of structural theoretical research about the war institute is perfectly understandable. Studies of wars and their results still pose a significant scientific challenge that may help reduce and even prevent them in the future.[5]

The study presented in this book is primarily a practice of international relations theory. It is not a historical study that describes the events with which it deals in detail. It is not an attempt to present an exact description of diplomatic history and of the bilateral and multilateral relations between the polar powers in the 200 years that the study covers, 1816–2016.

The study analyzes two key international outcomes. The systemic international outcome deals with the stability of the three possible international system models and may assume three main values: a destabilized, stable, or partly destabilized system; the intrasystemic international outcome deals with the degree of territorial expansion of the polar powers at the end of wars in which they participated. This outcome may assume three main values: territorial expansion, territorial contraction, or maintaining the territorial status quo ante bellum.

The theory explains the two international outcomes resulting from one of the three system polarity models, which are defined according to the number of polar powers operating in the system at any point in time. These are multipolar systems, in which there are three or more great powers; bipolar systems, in which there are just two superpowers; and unipolar systems, in which there is a single hyperpower.

In the three possible polarity models, the polar powers constituting the system have a similar degree of power, which will be significantly greater than the power that the remaining actors in the system would possess. In order for a country to be defined as a polar power, it must have material power consisting of military and economic power and long territorial power, meaning control of areas of geostrategic importance for their time. These would include trade route regions in the Eurasian continent in the 19th and 20th centuries, areas in the Persian Gulf region today, and probably areas in Southeast Asia in the future.

In the international system, two opposing significant transhistorical forces constantly act irrespective of the strategic environment or changes in the distribution of power in the system. The *anarchy* principle, in the sense of a lack of common regime, *motivates* the players, primarily the polar powers constituting the system, to tend always to *expansion* and to establish a hegemony that they are to head.[6] A rise to hegemon status in the system grants its possessor great security, and no challenging factor can pose a significant existential threat to the hegemon.

The *homeostasis* principle, in the sense of a system that resists change, *dictates* to the players, primarily the polar powers, to tend always to *stagnation* and maintain the system as is, because polar powers cannot control the character of a change that may undermine their status in the system instead of benefiting them and improving their status.

These two constant forces pull in opposite directions—the *anarchy* toward expansion and the *homeostasis* toward stagnation. The intensity of their effect is not necessarily identical, and the distribution of the capabilities in each of the three polarity models will cause a change in the power of both forces relative to each other. The presence of just two polar powers in a bipolar system will result in anarchy having low influence, whereas homeostasis will be highly influential. The presence of three or more polar powers in multipolar systems will result in anarchy having great influence, while that of homeostasis will be lower. The presence of a single polar power in unipolar systems will lead to the influence of anarchy and homeostasis being more or less equivalent.

The tension between these two forces will lead the players, according to their status of polar powers, great powers, or small countries, to employ one of four key action strategies: *balancing*—an action for retaining the existing distribution of power; *bandwagoning*—joining a strong power instead of resisting it; *buck-passing*—avoiding taking any action with the aim of shifting the burden of resistance to another country; and *catching the buck*—assuming the burden of resistance that has been transferred to the risk taker by another player in this system. This will lead to significant differences in the values of the two international outcomes that the study deals with, as will be shown below.

THE SYSTEMIC INTERNATIONAL OUTCOMES— STABILITY OF INTERNATIONAL SYSTEMS

Research in the field of systemic international outcomes assesses the stability of international systems and belongs to studies that examine the causes of the outbreak of wars. The stability of international systems is defined based on four parameters: the number, frequency, duration, and lethality of wars in which the polar powers are involved in the three polarity models. The stability of an international system is defined through three values: destabilized system, stable system, or partly destabilized system.

The multipolar systems will be the most destabilized or the most inclined to war. The benefit of one of three or more powers that will operate in these systems will not necessarily be at the expense of the other great powers in the system. *The flexible game* that will unfold between the great powers will lead to multipolar systems becoming the least stable or most destabilized. The strengthening of one of the great powers will not necessarily threaten the homeostasis and will not lead to breaking of the balance of the system. Therefore, in the case of regional powers, multipolar systems will *increase* their constant aspiration for expansion stemming from the anarchy principle. They will embark on expansionist wars regardless of preservation of the homeostasis. Therefore, in multipolar systems, the great powers will wage more wars than the other two systems.

Bipolar systems will be the most stable or most peaceful. The gain of one of the two superpowers operating in these systems will inevitably be at the expense of the other superpower in any given system. *A zero-sum game* that will occur between the two superpowers will lead to bipolar systems having the greatest stability. The strengthening of one of the two superpowers will inevitably threaten the homeostasis and may lead to breaking of the balance of the system. Bipolar systems will *suppress* the constant expansionism of powers stemming from the anarchy principle, and they will wage wars primarily in order to maintain the homeostasis. This means that in bipolar systems, the two superpowers will wage very few wars relative to the other two systems.

Unipolar systems will be partly destabilized and will find themselves between the two other systems. The gain of one of the players acting in the system will always manifest at the expense of the sole power, or the hyperpower, constituting the system. *A one-side-loses game* on the part of the sole hyperpower in the system will lead unipolar systems having medium stability or being partly destabilized. The strength of other players acting in the system at the expense of the hyperpower will inevitably threaten the homeostasis and may lead to breaking the balance of the system. Unipolar systems will *allow* for the constant tendency of powers to expand following the anarchy principle. They will wage wars only when their leadership is at risk, in order to maintain their homeostasis. This means that in unipolar systems, the hyperpowers will wage more wars than in bipolar systems and fewer than in multipolar systems.

Multipolarity—1849–1870 and 1910–1945—was found to be the least stable of the three systems. Bipolarity—1816–1848, 1871–1909, and 1946–1991—was discovered to be the most stable of the three systems. Unipolarity—1992–2016 (unipolarity was measured until the end of the study at the end of 2016 but may persist into the future)—has been discovered to be more stable than multipolarity and less stable than bipolarity.[7]

THE INTRASYSTEMIC INTERNATIONAL OUTCOMES— TERRITORIAL EXPANSION OF POLAR POWERS

The second family of international outcomes that the theory assesses includes intrasystemic international outcome, or the degree of territorial expansion by polar powers at the end of the wars in which they have participated; this family is assessed in studies dealing with the causes of the outcomes of wars. The theory defines territorial expansion as occurring when one of the following six options applies, as long as they occur at the end of the war rather than while it is still being fought: conquest, annexation, cession, secession, unification, or mandated territory.

The theory defines the degree of territorial expansion by polar powers at the end of wars in which they have participated through three values: territorial expansion, territorial contraction, or territorial status quo ante bellum.

The conclusion arising from the theory is that unipolar systems will *dictate* the territorial expansion of the sole hyperpower; bipolar systems will *lead* to a territorial status quo ante bellum of the two superpowers; and multipolar systems, alternatively, will *dictate* territorial nonexpansion (status quo ante bellum or territorial contraction) or will *allow* territorial expansion of the great powers.

The conclusions of the book concerning the degree of territorial expansion of the polar powers at the end of the wars in which they fought correspond with its basic assumptions. In all three instances of bipolarity— 1816–1848, 1871–1909, and 1946–1991—all wars involving the polar powers, or the two superpowers that constituted each of the instances, ended with a territorial status quo ante bellum. In the single instance of unipolarity, in 1992–2016, all wars in which the polar power—the sole hyperpower constituting that instance—was involved, ended with territorial expansion of the hyperpower. In the two instances of multipolarity—1849–1870 and 1910–1945—two different territorial outcomes of the polar powers, or the great powers constituting the system, at the end of the wars were yielded. When the territorial outcome of expansion of the great power would not have the potential for positioning the expanding power as a hegemon in the system, the system permitted the expansion of the great power at the end of the war. When the territorial outcome of the expansion of the great power had the potential of positioning the expanding power as a hegemon in the system, the system prevented the expansion of the great power at the end of the war and eventually forced the reduction of the war.

Failing to understand the factors that determine the two international outcomes may be fatal for small countries and for polar powers alike. For example, in the First and Second World Wars, Germany—one of the great powers constituting the multipolar system of 1910–1945—failed to understand that systems in general, including multipolar systems in which these two wars were fought, did not allow for expansion whose outcome would position the expanding power as a hegemon in the system. Germany's two attempts to ascend to hegemony in the system resulted in it being heavily penalized. Unlike Germany, Libyan president Muammar Gaddafi understood that unipolar systems could dictate to individual hyperpowers heading them the removal of any threat or provocation, and he reversed his policy of provoking the United States. Unlike him, Iraqi president Saddam Hussein failed to understand this and continued his provocative conduct toward the United States, resulting in the Iraq War (2003) breaking out, leading to the occupation of his country and his personal downfall. Similarly, the leaders of Afghanistan headed by the Taliban regime failed to understand the forces operating in unipolar systems. The outcome of their provocative behavior toward the United States, which included hosting the Al Qaeda organization that carried out the terrorist attacks on September 11, 2001, on U.S. soil, was fatal to them—the United States embarked on a war against Afghanistan (2001), occupied it militarily, and overthrew the Taliban regime.

In these cases, the leaders of countries erred in evaluating the constraints that international systems imposed on all players in the system and led their countries to tragic results. Leaders who were aware of the constraints imposed by international systems, such as Libya's leader, Gaddafi, in the early 2000s weathered the international storm while keeping their countries' territories intact.[8]

According to the *international relations theory of war*, the system does not determine all outcomes occurring in it and does not affect them categorically, but influences only the important outcomes, two of which are comprehensively assessed in this study. Therefore, the theory does not provide any explanation, forecast, or prediction of other key phenomena despite their great importance in the field of theoretical research of international relations. For example, it does not engage in the manner in which polar powers act in international crises, as this is not a theory of foreign policy at the individual or state level. It also does not deal with the factors that lead to the outbreak of wars or factors that lead to the occurrence of other significant events in the international scene, such as the collapse of the Soviet Union or the end of the Cold War,[9] inasmuch as the theory does not purport to predict the behavior of individuals or countries that cause international events to occur. To paraphrase Paul Kennedy's book,[10] it does not predict the timing of "the rise and fall of international systems" and does not engage in the reasons behind it,[11] as it is not intended to explain the factors that lead to change in international systems, but the outcomes inside them after the formation of those systems.

The theory contends with two of the arguments made against realism: its inability to explain change and its inability to predict change.[12] The theory attempts to explain why in those international system models the two outcomes to be assessed will have similar values, whereas in different international system models the two outcomes assessed will have different values. These two phenomena, primarily stability of international systems, have been expansively discussed in theoretical research of international relations. However, to date, no comprehensive theory expansively dealing with the effect of the three possible international system models on these two international outcomes has been undertaken in the manner in which the *international relations theory of war* does.

The *international relations theory of war* is based on the systemic analysis level that examines international relations from the broadest viewpoint. It attempts to conduct comprehensive reality analyses, maybe to too extreme a degree, and provide a broad mapping of international phenomena and outcomes, sometimes at the price of neglecting details. The theory acts at the international system level, and according to it, the polarity of the system is the factor that provides the best possible explanation for the various models of global outcomes. The two principles of transhistorical order, *anarchy* and *homeostasis*, have remained as two constant systemic properties over the years, because the international system always remains without any supreme authority over the legitimate use of force. Countries have also remained homogeneous over the years. Therefore, according to the book's conclusions, the changes in global outcomes throughout modern history, primarily since 1816, have resulted from the difference in the polarity of the system. This means that two outcomes of the three possible international system types assessed in the study may be identified.

INTERNATIONAL OUTCOMES: PRIMARY DISPUTES AND COPING

The *international relations theory of war* contends with five key questions that have been expansively discussed in the theoretical research of international relations in recent decades. The first question is does the international system encourage expansion of territory and influence or maintaining the status quo?[13] The two key approaches in the debate that this question has generated are neorealism and offensive realism, theories that constitute contemporary realism.[14] The second question is what level affects the manner of conduct of the international system—the levels of the individual, the state, or the international system? The debate that this question has generated takes place between neorealist theories and the various realistic approaches that criticize them.[15] The third question is what international systems exist?[16] The fourth question is what international systems are stable and which are destabilized,[17] or in other words, which systems tend to peace and which tend to war?[18] The fifth question is what is the factor that affects the conduct of the international system—the system or the players constituting it?[19]

WHY DO WARS BREAK OUT? STRUCTURAL THEORETICAL RESEARCH

The forces that cause powers to wage wars and influence the territorial results of wars in which they are involved also affect the security of individual countries and that of the entire system.

For individual countries operating in the international system, these two forces determine both the lethality of wars and the number of wars in which they will be involved, according to their standing in the system—polar powers or countries or powers that are not polar powers. In addition, they determine the territorial results of the wars in which they will participate. According to the theory, in bipolar systems, the territorial outcomes of wars in which two superpowers constituting the system will be involved is preservation of the status quo ante bellum preceding the outbreak of the war. In this context, one can treat the wars of the two superpowers, the United States and the Soviet Union, during the bipolar system of the 20th century, 1946–1991: the wars of the United States against Korea, Vietnam, and Iraq (1991), and the Soviet invasion of Hungary and war against Afghanistan. All these wars ended with a return to the territorial status quo that preceded the outbreak of the wars.

At the same time, the factors that affect the territorial outcomes of wars may shape the entire international system. The formation of certain international systems greatly depends on the extent to which leaders understand the forces acting on the system. Bismarck, who correctly assessed the extent to which the multipolar system of 1849–1870 would allow him to expand territorially, led Prussia to unite with the German states in three wars,[20] and the result was the formation of the united German state based on Prussia, its predecessor. The outcome of Bismarck's conduct was the formation of the bipolar system of 1871–1909, headed by Great Britain and Germany as the two superpowers of the system. In the same manner, the collapse of certain international systems closely depends on the extent to which leaders, primarily the leaders of the polar powers, understand the forces acting on the system; the leader of Nazi Germany erred when he assumed that the multipolar system of 1910–1945 would allow him to expand territorially. Owing to that mistake, he led his country to defeat, which to a great extent caused the collapse of the multipolar system and the formation of a bipolar system on its ruins.

The current study's extensive occupation with the war institution continues an existing trend.[21] Historians have tended to present the causes of war as unique to each individual case. Thus, for example, it has been argued that countries joined the First World War out of concern that the other countries in the unstable European continent of those years would attack first; others argued that the Nazi ideology and the personality of Germany's leader were what caused the Second World War.[22] In the same manner, historians tend to present the causes of the results or outcomes of wars as unique and limited to each case. According to some researchers, the United States had to withdraw its forces from Vietnam because of domestic pressures.[23] In the same manner, it has been argued that the United States abstained from occupying Iraq in the Gulf War (1991) because of the objections of its fellow coalition members. The current book has no intent of rejecting the unique explanations of these and other cases. Alternatively, the book presents a transhistoric systemic explanation of the phenomena that it examines, through the *international relations theory of war* that is developed in it.

The *international relations theory of war* presents a number of significant innovations. The argument that there is a unipolar system represents a kind of innovation relative to other systemic theories—such as Kenneth Waltz's *Theory of International Politics*[24] or John Mearsheimer's *Theory of Great Power Politics*[25]—which both argue that a system of that kind is not possible. The argument that unipolar systems will be less stable than bipolar systems and more stable than multipolar system provides new insights relative to other theories that argue that unipolar systems are the most stable ones, such as A. F. K. Organski's and Robert Gilpin's *Hegemonic Stability Theory*[26] or William Wohlforth's study.[27]

The theory presents another innovation, namely that in international politics, *behavior options are given and the key outcomes are known*. That is to say, according to the theory, there is a clear distinction between the behavior of countries and the outcomes of their behaviors, and moreover, there is no direct relationship between them.

According to the theory, different international systems cause different international results or outcomes, whose dependence on the aspirations of the country (the aspiration for sufficient security according to Waltz or the aspiration for maximum security according to Mearsheimer) or the manner of conduct of countries (Waltz's status quo or aggressiveness according to Mearsheimer) is misled. The latest innovation is the argument that polar powers have the ability to choose among various behavior patterns—such as balancing, bandwagoning, buck-passing, or catching the buck. In other words, the polar powers can choose to behave in a manner that opposes the systemic dictate, but this will have two main possible results. One is penalization of the country. Germany, for example, was punished after the First and the Second World Wars, two cases in which Berlin failed to understand that international systems would *dictate* to the players acting in the system to counter a country that was aiming for hegemony. The other is the collapse of the existing system and the formation of another system in its place. Two prominent examples of this are (1) the collapse of the multipolar system of 1910–1945 due to the absolute defeat of Germany and Japan at the end of the Second World War, which was caused by the reaction of the allied powers to their aggressive behavior, and (2) the collapse of the 1946–1991 bipolar system due to the Soviet Union's economic exhaustion that was caused by overutilization of its economic resources that were intended to preserve its standing as one of the two superpowers in the system.

The theory also provides innovation in the way in which it defines the polarity of the system. Most of the other theories in the realistic paradigm define great powers, which are referred to in the current study as polar powers, only according to their material power, which consists of military power and economic power. The *international relations theory of war*, in contrast, adds the territorial power of countries to this definition.

The theory presents a novel argument that holds that the stability of unipolar systems is somewhere between that of the other two systems—greater than that of multipolar systems but less than that of bipolar ones.

THE STRUCTURE OF THE BOOK

The first chapter is devoted to explaining the manner of action of the two dependent variables: *systemic international outcome*—the stability of the three possible international system models and *intrasystemic international outcome*—the degree of territorial expansion of polar powers at the end of the wars in which they will participate. In this chapter, a distinction will be made between *stability* and *durability*, which in other theories are both known as *stability*. In this chapter, the six possible manners of territorial expansion or contraction are also defined: conquest, annexation, cession, secession, unification, or mandated territory.

The second chapter presents the *international relations theory of war* and its key assumptions. In this chapter, a clear differentiation will also be made between the theory that the book presents and contemporary systemic realistic theories, primarily from neorealism and offensive realism.[28]

The third chapter precisely defines the distribution of power in the system, which is represented using the existing polarity model at any point in time. Within the examination, material power, military power, and economic power are examined using a combined index of these two power components of all strong countries in the system in the period that is being assessed in the study, 1816–2016.

The fourth chapter will empirically examine the two key phenomena that the theory deals with. The first part of the chapter examines the degree of stability of the three possible international system models (i.e., multipolar, bipolar, and unipolar systems, and their six instances). The second part of the chapter examines the degree of territorial expansion of polar powers at the end of the wars in which they participated, in the six instances of three international systems, as described above.

The fifth and last chapter presents the book's conclusions by examining the theoretical assumptions of the *international relations theory of war*. This chapter also presents a conceptual and empiric summary based on the theory explaining the events unfolding in the international system from the end of the Cold War to the present.

CHAPTER 1

War—Theory and Analysis of Results

The *international relations theory of war* does not attempt to explain the behavior of countries but to provide a retrospective causative-systemic explanation and predict, or forecast from the outset, *the outcomes of their behavior*. The theory discusses two of the most important international outcomes in international relations research in general and the field dealing with research of the war institute in particular.

The stability of the three possible international system models is the *systemic international outcome* that is assessed in studies that deal with the causes of the outbreak of wars. It is defined by the number, frequency, duration, and lethality of wars in which the polar powers that constitute the system in the three possible polar models are involved. This outcome may assume three values: stable systems, destabilized systems, or partly destabilized systems.

The degree of territorial expansion of polar powers at the end of wars in which they have participated is the *intrasystemic international outcome* that is assessed in studies dealing with the causes of outcomes of wars. It manifests in one or more of the following six possibilities, as long as they occur at the end of the war rather than while it is being fought: conquest, annexation, cession, secession, unification, or mandated territory. This outcome may assume three values: territorial expansion, territorial contraction, or territorial status quo ante bellum.

The *international relations theory of war*, as a systemic theory, is based on an examination of wars in which polar powers are involved. These types of wars form the basis of the theory because the international relations theory is defined by them. The polar powers are the main contenders in the international system. Their actions, primarily their wars, have great influence on the international system, much more than wars in which great powers or small countries are involved have.[1]

ON POWERS AND WARS

International systems influence international outcomes in different ways, particularly in the case of the two international outcomes that are assessed in the study. Different terms describe systems in general, including powers acting in each of the three international systems: the term *polar power* is used as a general term to describe the powers constituting the different poles in each of the three possible systems. To differentiate *polar powers* operating in each of the three international systems that the book discusses, specific terms are used. Multipolar systems consist of three or more *great powers*; bipolar systems consist of two *superpowers*; and unipolar systems have a single *hyperpower*.

The polarity of the system is defined in the following manner. A *unipolar system* consists of one polar power, a single hyperpower, which enjoys absolute superiority over other countries operating within the system; this superiority will manifest in a combination of its material, economic, and military power, along with its territorial power, which is defined by holding of territories of geopolitical importance at that point in time. *Bipolar systems* are when there are just two polar powers, or superpowers, which have absolute economic and military superiority alike, combined with territorial power, which is defined as holding of territories of geopolitical importance in the given time. *Multipolar systems* are when three or more polar powers, or great powers, have absolute superiority over other countries operating in the system; this superiority manifests in a combination of their material, economic, and military power and their territorial power, which is defined as holding of territories of geopolitical importance at that point in time.

In the international system, three main families of wars involving countries can be defined: *interstate wars* (wars between countries), *extrastate wars* (wars between countries and nonstate players), and *intrastate wars* (wars that are fought within countries).[2]

Interstate wars in general and those that involve polar powers in particular are divided in this book into three main categories. *Central wars* are the broadest of the three war types, and all polar powers constituting the system are involved in them. Central wars may occur in multipolar systems. In bipolar systems, central wars and major wars are identical because both involve the two superpowers constituting bipolar systems. Central wars cannot occur in unipolar systems because there is just one polar power acting in them—a single hyperpower.

Major wars are of low intensity relative to central wars and of greater intensity than those of minor wars, and they involve more than one polar power but not all. Major wars may occur in multipolar systems. In bipolar systems, central wars and major wars are identical because both involve the two superpowers. Major wars cannot occur in unipolar systems because, in systems of this type, there is only one polar power—a single hyperpower.

Minor wars are the smallest type of wars out of the three possible families involving a single polar power fighting against a country or countries that are not polar powers. Minor wars may occur in any of the possible three polarity models—multipolar, bipolar, or unipolar.

SYSTEMIC INTERNATIONAL OUTCOMES

In theoretical research of international relations, it is common to consider the term *stability* as describing the stability of international systems and the durability of international systems alike. Wohlforth defines stability as peacefulness and durability.[3] Waltz merged these two meanings[4] but later defined stability through durability only.[5] The *international relations theory of war* avoids the ambiguity by making a distinction between two components: (1) *international systems durability*, which is defined as the time that a single polarity model has remained in place until being replaced by another polarity model, and (2) *international systems stability*, which is defined through the combination of four components of war: the number, frequency, duration, and lethality of wars in which the polar powers are involved in the three polarity models.

I shall briefly discuss the durability of international systems in order to assert the difference between it and the stability of international systems while avoiding drawing any erroneous conclusions.

SYSTEMIC FACTORS AND INTERNATIONAL SYSTEMS DURABILITY

The durability of international systems is defined as the time for which a given polarity model stays in place until being replaced by another polarity model. A change in the durability of international systems may occur in two main ways. One is a change of the system through a transition from its current anarchic structure to a hierarchical structure. This phenomenon did not occur in the past and will probably not occur in the visible future.[6] The other is a change within the system manifesting in a change in the existing polarity model in the system. This phenomenon has occurred in the past and will almost certainly continue to occur in the future too as long as the anarchic structure of the international system remains in place.

To paraphrase Alexander Wendt,[7] "The polarity of the system is not determined by policy," and international systems do not rise and fall because of the will or lack of will of countries or individuals.[8] Rather, the polarity of the system changes following the transhistoric systemic constraints that are always imposed on the powers constituting international systems.

The first transhistoric systemic principle is *anarchy*, which causes the international system to *spur* the polar powers constituting it to tend always to form hegemonies that they will head. The systemic dictate that is persistently imposed on polar powers to form their own hegemony because of the existence of anarchy leads them to take the main course of action, which may lead to replacement of the existing polarity model.

One model of action is a gain of economic strength by medium powers to the point of rising to polar power status in the system. Two medium powers of their times whose economic gain led them to polar power status, resulting in the changing of one polar arrangement to another, may be mentioned. The economic gain of Germany in the mid-19th century led to strengthening of its military, which helped it win three wars—the Second Schleswig-Holstein War (1864), the Seven Weeks' War (1866), and the Franco-Prussian War (1870–1871). The last war was one of the causes of the change of the multipolar order of 1849–1870 to a bipolar order of 1871–1909. Another example is the rise in the United States' economic strength in the early 20th century, which was one of the causes of the replacement of the bipolar order of 1871–1909 to a multipolar order of 1910–1945.

Another model of action is exploitation of opportunities and waging a war that may develop into a change in the polarity of the system.

These two patterns of action may lead to the economic or military collapse of the polar powers. Two wars that led to a replacement of one polar order by another may be mentioned. The Franco-Prussian War (1870–1871) led to the replacement of the multipolar order of 1849–1870 by the bipolar order that formed in its wake of 1871–1909; and the Second World War (1939–1945), which led to the replacement of the multipolar order of 1910–1945 to the bipolar order that followed it in 1946–1991.[9]

The other transhistoric systemic principle is *homeostasis*. It leads the system to *dictate* to the polar powers to act persistently to preserve the existing polarity model through two main courses of action, which may lead to the replacement of the existing polarity model with another.

One course of action is taking negative and positive feedback actions to maintain their standing in the system. This course may lead them to exhaust their economic resources, a move that could lead to their fall and replacement of the existing polarity model with another one. One example of this is the collapse of the Soviet Union. The realistic argument states that the collapse of the Soviet Union was a result of its faltering economy and inability to contend with the United States' technological developments.[10] One may therefore conclude that its collapse stemmed from the systemic dictate that was applied to it to preserve its standing in the system. That dictate caused it to exhaust its economic resources to the point of loss of its standing as a polar power in the system. The fall of the Soviet Union led to the collapse of the bipolar system of 1946–1991 and to formation of the unipolar system of 1992–2016 in its place. Similarly, unipolar systems will dictate to the hyperpower heading them to preserve its status as the sole polar power in the system, even at the price of exhausting its economic resources. An example of this is the forecast that the United States may lose its current status as the sole hyperpower in a unipolar world following its efforts to preserve its status in the system, which may exhaust its material resources.[11]

Another course of action is taking negative and positive feedback actions to prevent the formation of hegemonies by the other powers. These actions may lead to destruction of the homeostasis, which will lead the polar powers to act to balance out other polar powers by engaging in total war against a potential hegemon. This action will lead to their fall and replacement of the existing polarity model with another one. An example of this is France's and Great Britain's decline from polar power status due to their economic exhaustion at the end of the Second World War. Their fall from their standing stemmed from their attempts to prevent the rise of Germany to hegemon status in the system. In other words, it involved taking negative feedback action that was intended to preserve the homeostasis in the system.

This book assesses only one systemic international outcome, the stability of three possible polarity models of the international system, which I discuss expansively below.

SYSTEMIC FACTORS AND INTERNATIONAL SYSTEMS STABILITY

The term *international systems stability* has been given different definitions in theoretical international relations research. Harrison Wagner makes a distinction between stability and peace. According to him, an international system will be defined as stable if the independence of all players is maintained, but when one or more countries are removed, this system will no longer be defined as stable. In his opinion, peace is defined as an absence of war. An international system may be defined as stable even if there are frequent wars in which many countries lose significant parts of their territory, as long as they continue to be part of the system.[12] Like Wagner, Randall Schweller argues that the meaning of systemic stability is that no player in the system is destroyed.[13] Waltz defines stability as an absence of change in the number of poles,[14] but elsewhere he recognizes that stability is an absence of war between the great powers.[15] Mearsheimer states that stability is an absence of wars and major crises.[16] Jack Levy defines stability as the absence of a major war.[17]

The book assesses the stability of each of the three possible international systems relative to the two other international systems. The stability of international systems is defined through four components of war: the number, frequency, duration, and lethality of wars in which the polar powers constituting the system are involved, in the six instances of the three possible polarity models. The assessment was done by examining each interstate war in which the polar powers participated, in the way they are defined in the book, in each of the six instances of the three system models in 1816–2016. The stability of international systems is defined according to four parameters.[18]

The first is *the number of the three war types*, a parameter that examines the number of each of the three types of wars in each of the three systems. The variable will be examined by adding up the three types of wars separately: (A) *central wars*—which involve all polar powers constituting the system, (B) *major wars*—involving only some of the polar powers, and (C) *minor wars*—in which one of the polar powers fights against a country or countries that are not polar powers.

The second is *the frequency of wars*, a parameter that examines the frequency at which wars of the three types broke out in each of the three systems. The parameter will be examined by calculating the length of each of the three systems in years, or the three polarity models, including the total number of instances of them, by calculating the number of years of war of each of the systems, and by finding the percentage of years in which the three types of wars occurred out of the total number of years in which the system being assessed existed.

The third is *the average duration of wars*, which assesses the average duration of the wars in days in each of the three system types. The variable will be assessed by calculating the total number of days of all wars fought in each of the three systems or the three polarity models and dividing this result by the total number of wars fought.

The fourth is *the severity or lethality of the wars*, which assesses the total number of casualties in battle of the subject wars in each of the three systems being assessed. This variable will be assessed by calculating the number of casualties in battle in each war and totaling the number of battle casualties of all wars fought of the three types of wars in each of the three systems.

Three values will be used for describing the stability of each of the three possible polarity models relative to the two other polarity models. *A system will be considered destabilized* when the values of the four parameters—the number, frequency, duration, and lethality of wars involving the polar powers constituting the system, primarily the *frequency of wars* parameter—are very high relative to those of the two other systems.

A system will be considered stable when the values of the four parameters—the number, frequency, duration, and lethality of wars involving the polar powers constituting the system, primarily the *frequency of wars* parameter—are very low relative to those of the two other systems.

A system will be considered partly destabilized when the values of the four parameters—the number, frequency, duration, and lethality of wars involving the polar powers constituting the system, primarily the *frequency of wars* parameter—are very low relative to those of a destabilized system and very high relative to those of a stable system.

An examination of the systemic international outcome or stability of international systems is conducted in research using an objective test, which examines the number, frequency, duration, and lethality of wars involving the polar powers constituting the system. According to the *international relations theory of war*, on the one hand, in different instances of the same polarity models, the stability of the system will be similar and consistent with the way in which the theory expects it to be; on the other hand, in various instances of different polarity models, the stability of the system will be different and will be consistent with the way in which the theory anticipates it.

INTRASYSTEMIC INTERNATIONAL OUTCOMES

In theoretical international relations research, it is common to consider the term *expansion* for describing the actions of acquisition of territories and for describing the increase in economic influence and control. The current study avoids this ambiguity by making a distinction between the two components.

Expansion of influence in the case of polar powers is defined as a comprehensive action to expand economic influence and control, which manifests in most cases in an activist foreign policy that includes paying attention to international events, expanding diplomatic missions, and participating in the diplomacy of powers. Based on this definition, Fareed Zakaria states that the Soviet Union expanded its influence in the 1970s, although for practical purposes it did not occupy any parts of Africa or central Asia.[19]

Territorial expansion is defined as an action that pertains only to territorial expansion of states, and in the current study, territorial expansion of polar powers at the end of the wars in which they participated.

Although the intrasystemic dependent variable in the study is territorial expansion of polar powers at the end of the wars in which they have participated, I have chosen to discuss briefly the additional dependent variable, that of expansion of influence. Through this discussion, I shall avoid the predisposition of theoretical international relations research to treat these two terms as one, which would distort their meaning and could lead to erroneous conclusions. I shall briefly discuss the expansion of influence of polar powers to assert the difference between it and territorial expansion of polar powers to avoid drawing the wrong conclusions.

SYSTEMIC FACTORS AND EXPANSION OF INFLUENCE OF POLAR POWERS

The expansion of influence of polar powers is defined as a comprehensive action for expanding economic influence and control, which in most cases manifests in an activist foreign policy that includes paying attention to international events, expansion of diplomatic missions, and participating in the diplomacy of powers. This action may also occur other than follow- ing in a war, unlike merely territorial expansion, which according to the current study can result from war only. According to the study, the expan- sion of influence of polar powers may occur in two main ways. One is *colo- nialism*, which means cultural and technological takeover of territory that is not Western owned overseas by advanced Western powers in order to exploit the residents and the many unutilized resources existing in them. The other is *imperialism*, which means a nation taking over other countries for establishing colonies while enforcing its rule on them and exploiting their natural resources.

In addition to the two main manners of expansion of influence men- tioned above—*colonialism* and *imperialism*—a number of other key man- ners of expansion of influence may be mentioned.

Formation of regions of influence. Powers will tend to establish regions of influence in their "backyards" or in nearby regions. The United States established a region of influence in the Caribbean and Central America in the early 20th century. Great Britain formed a region of influence in parts of the Middle East from the 1920s to the 1950s. Germany aimed to create a region of influence in southeastern Europe in the 1930s. Japan aimed to create a region of influence in East and Southeast Asia from the late 1930s to the mid-1940s. The Soviet Union formed a wide region of influence in Eastern Europe after the Second World War.[20] In the last decades, China has been quickly expanding its influence in three nearby regions of Cen- tral, South, and Southeast Asia. It is focusing on these regions peacefully in accordance with the demands of the neighboring countries, which are eager to enjoy the proceeds of China's economy and sometimes appear more enthusiastic than China itself in forming this trend. In addition, the military component of the Chinese territorial expansion in this region is delicate and indirect.[21] Recently, Beijing has extended its influence to Africa too. Russia is strengthening its standing in Asia through new pres- ence in former Soviet Union states and through expansion of its role in Asia, in the Pacific region, and in the Korean Peninsula, as a supplier of energy to China and Japan, and as a supplier of arms to other countries.[22] Recently, Moscow has extended its influence to the Middle East as well, primarily to Syria.[23]

Establishing security and economic international regimes. After the United States' (and allies') great victory over Germany and Japan in the Second

World War, it turned to expanding its influence in the international context. Following two major disasters that occurred in its recent past, Washington has learned two significant lessons. From the great economic depression, the United States learned that the great American economy could prosper only through an open international economy, even one in which its former enemies, Germany and Japan, participate. From the Second World War, it learned that maintaining its own security and that of the Americas—North, Central, and South—depended on no single great power controlling Europe or Eurasia. The strategy for achieving these goals was very sophisticated. The United States planned and led new international organizations that were intended to consolidate the open international economy and contain any potential European or Eurasian hegemon. The United States' influence-expansion project has had two major achievements. While in the United Nations, the U.S. leadership was sometimes subject to criticism manifesting in the form of vetoing the Soviets, it was the international organizations that helped it establish and develop the international economy, particularly the International Monetary Fund, the World Bank, and the General Agreement on Tariffs and Trade. When the United States turned to solve the problems of European security, it established NATO in order to contain the Soviet threat. It also added the Organization of European Economic Cooperation (OEEC) to help it implement its economic aid plan for Europe, the Marshall Plan. Through NATO and OEEC, the United States combined its concept concerning international organizations with its preconception concerning local regions of influence.[24]

Globalization. This is the process of integration of countries through increased contacts, communication, and trade, which form a complete global system in which the change process binds people to each other increasingly to form a common fate. Many voices have indicated increasing dissatisfaction with globalization, which is a means of noncolonial expansion of influence.[25]

Great importance is attributed to the geographic component, which serves as a basis for land power, inasmuch as land power is one of the three components of the definition of polar power by which the independent variable of system polarity has been established. This fact has led to the assessment of the degree of territorial expansion of polar powers at the end of wars in which they participated. I shall therefore turn to discuss this variable.

SYSTEMIC FACTORS AND EXPANSION OF INFLUENCE OF POLAR POWERS AT THE ENDS OF WARS

The territorial expansion variable assesses the degree of territorial expansion, contraction, or status quo ante bellum of polar powers at the end of wars in which they have participated. This assessment is done with a distinction between the three possible polarity models that have taken place in the subject period of the study, 1816–2016: multipolar, bipolar, and unipolar systems, in each of the six instances that are discussed below. The quantitative assessment is undertaken by examining all wars between countries in the three models: central wars, major wars, and minor wars, in which the polar powers constituting the system have been involved.

By definition, territorial expansion occurs when one or more of the following six options occur at the end of a war: conquest, annexation, cession, secession, unification, or mandated territory.[26]

Conquest is territorial expansion that fulfills five conditions simultaneously:[27] (1) the conquest is achieved by war, (2) the main territorial change agent is military force, (3) military forces of one nation seize part or all of the territory of another nation,[28] (4) the conquered territory is under the authority of the conquering military either directly using its military forces or indirectly using local military forces that answer to the occupying military, and (5) the conquering state's control over the territory of the conquered state is temporary and does not claim rights of permanent sovereign control of that territory. Territorial expansion will not be considered as conquest primarily in the case of wartime occupation[29] because it may differ from the final territorial result of the war, which may involve withdrawal or territorial contraction of the occupying power; secondly, in the case of UN presence (UN forces are usually welcomed by the conquered population, and the multinational character of the occupation reduces the pressure on the occupying powers to end the occupation); thirdly, in the case of short-term involvement in which the occupying power exerts limited political influence on the territory in which it has intervened. Therefore, short-term involvements of polar powers in other countries, such as the U.S. involvement in the Dominican Republic (1965), Panama (1983), and Haiti (1994),[30] are not considered conquests.[31]

Annexation means acquisition of territory belonging to another country, or not belonging to any country, and permanent unification with the territory of that annexing country. This is usually a unilateral action whose key change agent is diplomacy, even if it involves an implicit threat of use of force. This action includes application of full sovereignty by the new controller and applying an exclusive judicial and control system to the territory. Annexation differs from military occupation, although military occupation may stem from it.[32]

Cession occurs when part of a political entity is given to another political entity through a referendum, purchase,[33] or compensation agreement, or following hostility.

Secession or withdrawal from territories refers to detachment from an existing border to the existence of another entity living in it for that entity to form a new independent entity.

Unification refers to the building of a new political entity from two or more previous entities.

Mandated territory refers to a territorial unit that has been assigned to control by another political entity by the League of Nations or the United Nations.

The description of territorial outcomes of polar powers at the end of wars in which they have participated is defined through three values:

(A) *Territorial expansion* occurs when the polar power acquires territories at the end of a war through one or more of the six options described above: conquest or annexation of territory of a vanquished state by the polar power, cession by the vanquished state of territory to the polar power, secession or withdrawal of the vanquished state from the territory that the polar power has taken over, unification of territories of the vanquished state with the polar power territory, or assuming control of the territory of the defeated state as mandated territory by the polar power.

(B) *Territorial contraction* occurs when the polar power loses territories at the end of a war through one or more of the six possibilities described above: conquest or annexation of territory of the polar power by the victor state, cession of territory by the polar power to the winning state, secession or withdrawal by the polar power from the territory taken over by the victor state, unification of territories of the polar power with territory of the victor state, or receipt of control over territory of the polar power as mandate territory by the victor state.

(C) *Maintaining the territorial status quo ante bellum* occurs when the territorial borders that predated the outbreak of the war are maintained after its end, without any of the six territorial expansion or contraction options described in the two previous sections having occurred.

Examination of the intrasystemic international outcome or territorial expansion of polar powers at the end of wars in which they participated is conducted using an objective test that assesses the degree of territorial expansion or contraction of polar powers at the end of the wars in which they were involved. The *international relations theory of war* states that on the one hand, as long as wars involving polar powers in the same polarity model occur without their disrupting the homeostasis or collapse of the existing polarity model, it will be possible, with a great degree of precision, to predict the territorial outcomes of the wars examined. In such a state, the territorial outcomes of these wars will be consistent in the vast majority of cases with the theoretical expectations. On the other hand, when wars that involve polar powers violate the homeostasis or cause the existing polarity model to collapse and the formation of a new polarity model in its place, it will not be possible to predict the territorial outcomes of the wars examined.

CHAPTER 2

International Relations
Theory of War

The question of what the reality in the world is and what the nature of innovation in it has been engaging philosophers for thousands of years and manifests in two opposing philosophical ideas. The Ecclesiastes verses "What has been will be again … there is nothing new under the sun" express continuity.[1] On the other hand, "You cannot step twice into the same river," said Heraclitus, for in the interval between your first and second steps, the river has changed and you have changed.[2] These ideas express different principles of systemic theories. According to the first argument, which expresses a deterministic view, changes are almost impossible. The second argument corresponds with the view that the complexity of the international system does not allow us to predict future events.

The *international relations theory of war* presents a combined view that the complexity of the international system and the close interrelations occurring between the players acting in it led to any change made inside it by one player or more influencing the other players acting in the system. This close interdependence between the players stemming from the system's complexity leads international systems to resist change. Because the players cannot control the character of the change that may diminish their standing in the system, they have to act to preserve the existing state. The fact that the system resists change does not mean that international systems will prevent players constituting them from acting, but that international systems will resist their own changes. Therefore, international systems will dictate the outcomes of the overall behavior of players and not the behavior of individual players.

The current chapter discusses in depth the *international relations theory of war*.[3] The first part deals with the theory and its basic assumptions. The second part presents the hypotheses of the theory concerning the two international outcomes—the stability of the various international systems and the degree of territorial expansion of polar powers at the end of the wars in which they have participated. The third part develops the two transhistorical order principles of anarchy and homeostasis and the way in which they affect the two phenomena explained in the book. The fourth part deals with the influence of the polarity of the system over the two phenomena explained in the book. The end of the chapter summarizes the key assumptions of the theory and shows its main conclusions concerning the international scene in general and the values of the two international outcomes in particular.

BASIC ASSUMPTIONS OF THE THEORY

According to the *international relations theory of war*, in an international system, *everything is permissible but the key outcomes are known. Everything is permissible* means that the principle of anarchy and sovereignty of states stemming from it allow each of the individual players to act as it sees fit, theoretically at least, and choose various strategies such as balancing, bandwagoning, buck-passing, or catching the buck. *The key outcomes are known* means that the homeostasis principle that dictates the preservation of the existing state leads to the overall outcomes of the behavior of countries, and primarily the stability of the various international systems or the degree of territorial expansion of polar powers at the end of the wars in which they participated, to be largely known and predetermined, being a result of the polarity model of the system.

Each of the three models of the possible international systems will dictate certain patterns of the two international outcomes: systems of the same type will dictate similar outcomes and systems of different types will dictate different ones. From this one may conclude that identical behavior of the same players in different models of international systems will lead to different outcomes and different behavior of different players in the same international system will lead to identical outcomes. Therefore, the two international outcomes may be predicted despite, and possibly because of, the complexity of the international system and the existing interrelations between the players constituting it. The theory shows that owing to the great importance of the two subject outcomes, the system will influence them according to the polarity model existing in the system at any time. The polarity of the system manifests in three main states—multipolarity, bipolarity, and unipolarity. The system determines the values of the two outcomes according to the relationship between the transhistorical order principles of *anarchy* and *homeostasis*.

HYPOTHESES OF THE THEORY CONCERNING THE TWO INTERNATIONAL OUTCOMES

After discussing the general principles of the theory, the two dependent variables that the *international relations theory of war* explains are now discussed—stability of international systems and the degree of territorial expansion of polar powers at the end of wars that they have fought.

STABILITY OF INTERNATIONAL SYSTEMS

The first family of international outcomes that the *international relations theory of war* assesses is the stability of the three international systems, which is assessed in studies that deal with the causes of the outbreak of wars. The stability of the system is measured according to the number, frequency, duration, and lethality of wars in which the polar powers are involved in the three polarity models.

The theory defines systemic international outcome using three values. A system will be considered *destabilized* when the value of the four parameters—the number, frequency, duration, and lethality of wars, with emphasis on the *frequency of wars* parameter—are very high relative to the other two systems. A system will be considered *stable* when the values of the four parameters—the number, frequency, duration, and lethality of wars, particularly the *frequency of wars* parameter—are very low relative to the two other systems. A system will be considered *partly destabilized* when the values of the four parameters—the number, frequency, duration, and lethality of wars—are very low relative to a destabilized system and very high relative to a stable one.

The theory is based, as set forth, on the existence of two transhistoric order principles. One is the principle of *anarchy*, the absence of a common regime that *spurs* the players, particularly the polar powers, to tend always to expansion or to form hegemonies headed by them. The other is the principle of *homeostasis*, a property of the system that resists change, causing the system to *dictate* to players, particularly the polar powers, to tend always to stagnation or retention of the system in its existing state. Despite the constant presence of these two order principles, the current study does not predict uniformity in the number or lethality of wars over the years.

Each of the three different polarity models will apply certain forces, or *constraints*, *restraints*, and *restrictions*, to the players in the system that distinguish it relative to the other two polar models. These forces will be a result of the influence of each of the three polarity models on the values of the two order principles of *anarchy* and *homeostasis*. These forces will lead to each of the three international system models *dictating* identical systemic international outcomes whereas different polarity models will *dictate* different systemic international outcomes.

Therefore, it may be concluded that each of the three possible international systems will *dictate* different stability in the following manner. *Multipolar systems* will be the most destabilized or the most war prone. The gain of three or more of the powers that will operate in these systems will not necessarily be at the expense of the other great powers in the system. *The flexible play* that will occur between the great powers will give multipolar systems the least stability or render them the most destabilized. The strengthening of one of the great powers will not necessarily endanger the homeostasis and will not lead to violation of the system. Multipolar systems will therefore *increase* the tendency of powers to expand owing to the anarchy principle; they will wage expansionist wars irrespective of preservation of homeostasis. Owing to this, in multipolar systems, the great powers will fight more wars relative to the other two systems.

Bipolar systems will be the most stable or the most inclined to peace. The gain of one of the two superpowers that will operate in these systems will always be at the expense of the other superpower in the system. *A zero-sum game* that occurs between the two superpowers will confer to bipolar systems the highest stability. The strengthening of one of the superpowers must endanger the homeostasis and may violate the balance of the system. Bipolar systems will *suppress* the expansionist aspirations of powers stemming from the anarchy principle, resulting in their waging wars primarily for retention of homeostasis. This means that in bipolar systems, the superpowers will engage in very few wars relative to the two other systems.

Unipolar systems will be partly destabilized and will be between the other two systems. The gain of one of the players acting in the system must be at the expense of the sole polar power, the hyperpower constituting the system. *A one-side-loses game* by the sole hyperpower occurring in the system will lead to unipolar systems having medium stability or being partly destabilized. The strengthening of other players operating in the system at the expense of the hyperpower must endanger the homeostasis and may lead to violation of the balance of the system. Unipolar systems will *allow* the tendency of the powers to expand because of the anarchy principle. They will wage wars only in response to a threat to their leadership and the need to maintain homeostasis. Owing to this, in unipolar systems, hyperpowers will engage in more wars than in bipolar systems and fewer wars than in multipolar systems.

Table 2.1 concentrates the key assumptions of the theory concerning the *dictates* that each of the three possible polarity methods imposes—multipolar, bipolar, or unipolar systems—on the stability of the system.

Table 2.1

Constraints of the System and Their Influence on the Degree of Stability of the Three Possible Systems

	Multipolarity	Bipolarity	Unipolarity
The Number of Polar Powers Constituting the System	Multipolar systems will have three or more *great powers* powering in them	In bipolar systems just two *superpowers* will operate	In unipolar systems just one *hyperpower* will operate
Characteristics of Each of the Polarity Models	In multipolar systems the gain of one of the key players operating in the system need not be at the expense of all the other players, or all the other *great powers*, constituting the system	In bipolar systems the gain of one of the key players operating in the system must be at the expense of the other player, or the other *superpower*, constituting the system	In unipolar systems the gain of one of the players operating in the system must be at the expense of the polar power, or the sole *hyperpower*, constituting the system
	The relations among the players operating in multipolar systems are represented as a *flexible game* that occurs among the *great powers*	The relations among the players operating in bipolar systems are represented as a *zero-sum game* held between the two *superpowers*	The relations among the players operating in bipolar systems are represented as a *one-side-loses* game on the part of the sole *hyperpower*
Values of the Systemic Dependent Variable, or the Stability of Each of the Systems	**Low stability, destabilized system:** In multipolar systems the strengthening of one of the *great powers* will not necessarily threaten the *homeostasis* and will not lead to violation of the balance of the system	**High stability, stable system:** In bipolar systems the strengthening of one of the two *superpowers* must endanger the *homeostasis* and may lead to violation of the balance of the system	**Medium stability, partly destabilized system:** In unipolar systems the strengthening of players at the expense of the *hyperpower* must endanger the *homeostasis* and may lead to breaking of the balance in the system
	Multipolar systems will *increase* the aspiration of the *great powers* to expand. They will go to expansionist wars irrespective of maintaining the *homeostasis*	Bipolar systems will *suppress* the aspiration of the *superpowers* for expansion. They will start wars primarily for maintaining the *homeostasis*	Unipolar systems will *permit* the aspiration of the *hyperpowers* to expand. They will start wars only in response to a risk to their leadership and for maintaining *homeostasis*
	As a result of this, the *great powers* will go to war more often than the other two system types	Following this, the two *superpowers* will go to wars very rarely relative to the two other systems	Following this, *hyperpowers* will go to more wars than bipolar systems and fewer wars than multipolar systems

DEGREE OF TERRITORIAL EXPANSION

The second family of international outcomes that the theory assesses is the intrasystemic international outcome or the degree of territorial expansion of polar powers at the end of wars that they have fought.

Territorial expansion occurs when one or more of the six following options apply during or at the end of a war: conquest, annexation, cession, secession, unification, or mandated territory. The theory defines the degree of territorial expansion of polar powers at the end of the wars they have fought using three values: territorial expansion, territorial contraction, and maintaining of territorial status quo ante bellum.

According to the theory, there are three possible war models involving polar powers in the international system. *Central wars* are defined as wars involving all polar powers constituting the system. These are the broadest wars out of the three possible families. They are more intensive than major wars and much more so than minor wars. Central wars may occur in multipolar systems. In bipolar systems, central wars will be identical to major wars, inasmuch as both involve all the polar powers constituting the system or its two constituent superpowers. Central wars cannot occur in unipolar systems because systems of this kind have just one polar power, a sole hyperpower.

Major wars are defined in the theory as wars that involve more than one polar power out of those constituting the system, but not all. These are wars of less intensity than those of central wars and greater intensity than those of small wars. Major wars may occur in multipolar systems. In bipolar systems, central wars will be identical to major wars. Both involve all the polar powers constituting the system, the two superpowers. Major wars cannot occur in unipolar systems because systems of this type have just one polar power, the sole hyperpower.

Minor wars are defined in the theory as wars in which just one polar power out of those constituting the system fights against a country or countries that are not polar powers. These wars are the smallest of the three families—both relative to major wars and all the more so relative to central wars. Minor wars may be fought in all three polarity models—multipolar, bipolar, and unipolar.

The constant existence of the two order principles of anarchy and homeostasis does not predict uniformity in the degree of territorial expansion at the end of the three war models—central, major, and minor wars—in which there will be polar power involvement. Each of the three different polarity models will apply certain forces, or *constraints*, *restraints*, and *restrictions*, to the players in the system, distinguishing it from the other two polarity systems. These forces will be a result of the manner in which each of the three polarity models influences the values of the two order principles. These forces lead to each of the three international system models *dictating* identical intrasystemic international outcomes whereas different polarity models will *dictate* different intrasystemic international outcomes. Each of the three possible international systems will *dictate* different territorial outcomes at the end of the three war models involving polar powers.

Territorial Outcomes under Unipolar Systems

Unipolar systems will dictate territorial expansion of the sole hyperpower. In unipolar systems, central wars and major wars cannot occur because in these systems there is a single polar power, a sole hyperpower. However, there may be minor wars. Unipolar systems will dictate territorial expansion of hyperpowers at the end of all minor wars in which they are involved because any other result would undermine their superiority as the sole hyperpower of the system and might lead to collapse of the entire system—a result that the homeostasis principle dictates to players to act to prevent.

The only unipolar system that has existed during the study's subject period, 1816–2016, is the unipolar system of 1992–2016. Under it all minor wars in which the United States was involved as a sole hyperpower ended with a territorial result consistent with the study hypotheses: the unipolar system dictated to the United States to expand territorially at its end—the U.S. invasion of Afghanistan (2001) and the U.S. invasion of Iraq (2003).

The constant territorial expansion of hyperpowers in unipolar systems at the end of minor wars in which they participated stems from the way these systems influence the values of the two transhistorical order principles that always act in the international system. While the principle of *anarchy* will *spur* hyperpowers to tend always to expansion through their enormous capabilities, any other result (i.e., contraction or preservation of territorial status quo) would contravene the other order principle, of *homeostasis*, inasmuch as any preservation of or decrease in the ground strength of hyperpowers at the end of wars that they have fought may lead to a collapse of the system—a result that the homeostasis principle *dictates* to players to act to prevent. Therefore, in unipolar systems, the two transhistorical order principles will dictate to their sole constituent hyperpowers to expand territorially. The two other territorial outcomes, territorial contraction or preservation of territorial status quo ante bellum, are not an option at the end of minor wars occurring in unipolar systems. *Territorial contraction* of hyperpowers in unipolar systems at the end of minor wars in which they have participated may undermine the homeostasis. A decrease in the land power of the hyperpower that loses territory will always lead to a decrease in its total power. This will violate the equilibrium and the homeostasis will be threatened. This is an outcome that may impair the polarity of the system, a phenomenon that the homeostasis principle dictates to players to act to prevent. *The territorial status quo ante bellum* of hyperpowers in unipolar systems at the end of the wars they have fought may also infringe upon the homeostasis. An absence of an increase in land power of the hyperpower that does not expand territorially effectively undermines the homeostasis principle, which dictates to the sole hyperpowers in unipolar systems to act according to their standing as the leading powers in the system and eliminate players that challenge them.

Territorial Outcomes under Bipolar Systems

Bipolar systems will dictate a territorial status quo of two superpowers. In bipolar systems, major wars will always be identical to central wars because each war involving more than one polar power will effectively involve the two superpowers; in bipolar systems, instigating a central or major war will result in the collapse of the system and the formation of another type of system in its place. In the period assessed in the study, 1816–2016, there have been three bipolar systems, 1816–1848, 1871–1909, and 1946–1991, and there was no central or major war in which both superpowers constituting the system fought. However, minor wars may occur in bipolar systems.

Bipolar systems will dictate to the two superpowers to act to preserve the territorial status quo at the end of all minor wars in which they will be involved because any other outcome will raise the expanding power to the status of a potential hegemon in the system and might lead to the collapse of the system—a result that the homeostasis principle dictates to the players to act to prevent.

Under all three bipolar systems that existed in the subject period of the study, 1816–2016, all minor wars involving superpowers ended with a territorial result corresponding with the study hypothesis. In other words, the bipolar systems dictated to the two superpowers to maintain the territorial status quo preceding the war: in both bipolar systems that occurred in Eurasia in the 19th century, 1816–1848 and 1871–1909, Great Britain had to preserve the territorial status quo ante bellum that preceded its two wars against Afghanistan. In the bipolar system that occurred in the second half of the 20th century, 1946–1991, both superpowers constituting the system, the United States and the Soviet Union, had to preserve the territorial status quo ante bellum preceding all wars in which they were involved—the wars of the United States against Korea, Vietnam, and Iraq (1991), and the Soviet invasion of Hungary and war against Afghanistan.

A constant territorial status quo of superpowers in bipolar systems stems from the way in which bipolar systems influence the values of the two transhistorical order principles that constantly act on the international system. The principle of *anarchy* will *spur* the two superpowers to tend always to expand territorially through their tremendous capabilities, whereas any other result—territorial expansion or territorial contraction—will oppose the other order principle of *homeostasis*. This is because any increase or decrease in the military strength of one of the two superpowers at the end of wars they fight may lead to the collapse of the system—a result that the homeostasis principle dictates the players to act to prevent. The two other territorial outcomes—territorial contraction or territorial expansion—cannot happen at the end of minor wars fought in bipolar systems. *Territorial contraction* of superpowers in bipolar systems at the end of wars in which they will participate may impair the homeostasis, inasmuch as a decrease in the land power of the superpower that loses territory will inevitably lead to a decrease in its total power. This will result in violation of the equilibrium and a threat to the homeostasis. This outcome may impair the polarity of the system, a phenomenon that the homeostasis principle *dictates* to players to act to prevent. *Territorial expansion* of superpowers in bipolar systems at the end of wars in which they will participate may also damage the homeostasis, as an increase in the land power of the superpower that acquires new territory must lead to an increase in its total power. This will result in violation of the equilibrium and a threat to the homeostasis. This outcome may infringe on the polarity of the system, a phenomenon that the homeostasis principle *dictates* to the players to act to prevent.

Territorial Outcomes under Multipolar Systems

Alternatively, multipolar systems will dictate territorial nonexpansion—status quo ante bellum or territorial contraction—or territorial expansion of the great powers.

Under multipolar systems, all three possible war models may occur: central, major, and minor wars. These systems will *dictate* two key territorial outcomes, according to the model of the war. Multipolar systems will *dictate* a sole territorial outcome of the great powers constituting them at the end of all *central wars* in which they are involved—prevention of territorial expansion, which will manifest in a status quo or territorial contraction, as any other result may lead to a rise of the expanding power to the status of potential hegemon in the system and may lead to a collapse of the system, a result that the homeostasis principle dictates to the players to act to prevent. In multipolar systems, great powers will also be *penalized* if they act to expand territorially at the end of central wars and will be *forced* to contract territorially at the end of these wars.

In the period assessed in the study, 1816–2016, there were two multipolar systems, in 1849–1870 and 1910–1945, during which there were two central wars. These were the First and the Second World Wars that took place in the late multipolar system of 1910–1945. At the end of these two wars, the great powers that aspired to expand territorially in the war had to contract territorially or maintain their territorial status quo preceding the war. Germany had to contract territorially at the end of the two world wars, and Japan was forced to contract territorially at the end of the Second World War.

The prevention of territorial expansion of great powers at the end of central wars stems from the way in which multipolar systems affect the values of the two transhistorical order principles that constantly act in the international system. The *anarchy principle* will *spur* the two superpowers to tend always to territorial expansion, owing to their tremendous capabilities, whereas the opposing result—territorial expansion of a great power at the end of central wars in which it will participate—may lead to the collapse of the system, a result that the *principle of homeostasis dictates* to the players to act to prevent.

The other territorial outcome, territorial expansion, cannot occur at the end of central wars that are fought in multipolar systems. *Territorial expansion* of great powers in multipolar systems at the end of central wars in which they participate may impair the homeostasis. A rise in the land power of a great power that acquires a new territory at the expense of another great power must lead to an increase of its total power. Following this, the equilibrium will be violated and the homeostasis threatened. This outcome may impair the polarity of the system, a phenomenon that the *homeostasis principle* dictates to players to act to prevent.

Multipolar systems will *permit* the expansion of great powers at the end of *major* or *minor wars* involving them, inasmuch as the territorial expansion of great powers will not raise the expanding power to potential hegemon status in the system and cannot cause the system to collapse—a result that the *homeostasis principle* allows to occur.

In the period assessed in the study, 1816–2016, there have been two multipolar systems, 1849–1870 and 1910–1945, and many major or minor wars were fought in them. At the end of these wars, the system allowed for the territorial expansion of the great powers. The multipolar system of the 19th century allowed Prussia to expand territorially in its unification wars, and the multipolar system of the 20th century allowed Italy to expand in its war against Ethiopia (1935–1946).

This outcome—territorial expansion of great powers at the end of major or minor wars in multipolar systems—stems from the manner in which multipolar systems affect the values of the two transhistorical order principles that constantly act in the international system. Thus, while the *anarchy* principle will *spur* the great powers to tend always to expand through their tremendous capabilities, this result will not conflict with the other order principle of *homeostasis*, inasmuch as a rise in the land power of great powers at the end of major or minor wars may not cause the system to collapse—a result that the *homeostasis principle* does not resist and therefore allows to occur.

Table 2.2

The Constraints Dictating the Territorial Results of Wars in Which Polar Powers Are Involved

	Multipolarity	Bipolarity	Unipolarity
Central wars involving **all the polar powers constituting the system**	Multipolar systems will *prevent* the territorial expansion of the major powers at the end of central wars	In bipolar systems a major war will be identical to a central war as both involve all the polar powers constituting the system	Central or major wars do not exist in unipolar systems, because in systems of this type just one polar power acts—the sole hyperpower
Major wars involving **more than one polar power out of those constituting the system but not all of them**	Multipolar systems will *allow* the territorial expansion of the major powers at the end of major wars	The outbreak of a central or major war in bipolar systems will *cause* the collapse of the existing bipolar system and the formation of a new multipolar or unipolar system in its place	
Minor wars in which **a single polar power fights against a country or countries that are not polar powers in the system**	Multipolar systems will *allow* the territorial expansion of the major powers at the end of minor wars	Bipolar systems will *prevent* the two superpowers from expanding or contracting territorially at the end of minor wars; they will *dictate* the preservation of the status quo that prevailed before the war	Unipolar systems will *dictate* to the hyperpower to expand territorially at the end of minor wars

THE TRANSHISTORICAL PRINCIPLES

According to the *international relations theory of war*, since the formation of the modern international system after the Peace of Westphalia in 1648 to this day, there are always two transhistorical order principles in the system. The *anarchy principle*, in the sense of the absence of a common regime, *spurs* the players, particularly the polar powers constituting the system, to tend always to *expansion* and form hegemonies that they head. The *homeostasis principle*, in the sense of a system resisting change, *dictates* to the players, primarily the polar powers, to tend always to *stagnation* and to maintain the status quo ante bellum.

The international system *encourages* the players constituting it to act in manners that stem from the two transhistorical order principles. I shall therefore turn to examining these two order principles and their effect on multipolar, bipolar, and unipolar systems in detail.

ANARCHY AND THE TENDENCY TO HEGEMONIES

Anarchy, the first transhistorical order principle, in the sense of an absence of a sovereign rather than an absence of order, has always existed in the modern international system, since being formed after the Peace of Westphalia in 1648 to date.[4] Anarchy leads the international system to be a self-help system, which lacks a provider of security, or another model of political authority, in international politics. Owing to this, the international system will *spur* the players constituting it, primarily the polar powers, to have an intrinsic aspiration to revisionism. The purpose of revisionism is maximization of power for achieving hegemonic standing in the system. This standing gives its possessor great security because no challenging element may pose a significant existential threat to the hegemon.

The rest of the chapter consists of two key parts. The first part will discuss the term *anarchy* in the theoretical research of international relations, presenting the way in which constructivism, neoliberalism, and neorealism describe the influence of anarchy on the key players operating in the international system. The second part will be more focused presentation of the manner in which three of the key theories in the field, constructivism, neoliberalism, and realism, relate to anarchy and its effects on international relations.

Anarchy in the Theoretical Research of International Relations

In recent decades, the anarchy assumption has regained its position as a central assumption in international relations theory.[5] Both neorealist and neoliberal theorists have pointed out the anarchic nature of the international system as the most prominent, central, and important property in international relations,[6] even if their conclusions concerning this assumption are completely different. Anarchy has been assigned many definitions in the theoretical research of international relations, two of which are more central and prominent than the rest.

The first definition describes anarchy as *chaos* or lack of order and corresponds with traditional realism. According to this definition, international relations represent a pure conflict between states, international activity that characterizes international relations is the war itself, and the international system is a chaotic scene of everyone fighting everyone.[7] Waltz argues, in contrast, that when the equilibrium principle has a proper effect, it grants order to the system by preventing war.[8] Robert Tucker also argues that the history of the international system is a history of inequality and unequal distribution of power to northern and southern countries forms a hierarchy of relations that leads to an orderly system.[9] Hedley Bull argues that order in the international society template has always existed in the modern international system because the effect of common interests, laws, and institutes has never ceased.[10] Studies that deal with international regimes also state that the principles of order and society characterize international politics and argue that international regimes also state that the components of order and society characterize international politics and assert that international regimes dictate and guide the behavior of countries according to common norms and laws, and through the common norms and laws they result in obedient behavior.

According to another definition of anarchy, international politics lacks an entity with central authority that is above individual countries, a body that has sufficient power to pass laws and settle disputes, and which can protect each of the countries from the others.[11] In the opinion of the supporters of this definition, countries may assume obligations and agreements, but no sovereign force can promise that they will follow them or penalize their violators. Therefore, *the absence of supreme power* is the meaning of the anarchic environment of international politics. This formula of anarchy indicates nothing concerning the means that the important players constituting the system have when they try to advance their goals. It only indicates that there is no supreme power that can prevent them from using these means.[12]

The definition of anarchy as a lack of a central government in the international system is more consistent with structural realism or neorealism and is shared by most prominent contemporary realist theorists in international relations research.[13]

Whereas there is consensus among researchers that anarchy is an absence of regime or authority, there is no consensus concerning the question of the meaning of a regime or authority. Waltz associates anarchy with a lack of a regime, and to him regime represents a monopoly of legitimacy of using force.[14] For Martin Wight, the meaning of regime is the existence of institutions and laws to maintain order rather than the use of force. In his view, the absence of a regime means an absence of laws, of the permission to write them, of the judicial right to enforce them, and of the executive ability to administer them.[15] Others emphasize the institutions and power more than the force as a key component of a regime.[16]

The Way Constructivism, Neoliberalism, and Realism Relate to Anarchy

The constructivist discussion of anarchy offers a different interesting view of the term and its implications. In the opinion of neorealism, the anarchic structure leads to the self-help principle irrespective of process. In contrast, according to constructivism, the structure has no existence or causality separate from the process, and the reason we find ourselves in a world of self-help today stems from a process rather than a structure. From this, the constructivist theory concludes that self-help and power politics are institutions rather than inherent properties of anarchy and there is no concept of anarchy that is separate from the habits that form and demonstrate one structure of identities and principles more than others.[17] Thus, Wendt argues that countries can think of anarchy in multiple ways, and that "anarchy is what states make of it."[18]

Like neorealist researchers, neoliberal researchers have also assumed that the international system operates under anarchy. However, in contrast to neorealism, they have concluded that cooperation may occur under anarchy.[19] The argument concerning the possibility of cooperation under anarchy appears in many neoliberal sources. Robert Keohane describes the international environment as devoid of central authority and argues that even in that environment countries may cooperate through acting in a manner that corresponds with their own narrow interest.[20]

The comparison of hierarchy to anarchy poses the question of whether an anarchic system is better than a global empire. Formal international theory has usually objected to the existence of a global state, arguing that it would be too large to be efficient. According to that theory, through the balance of powers, it allows for the division of humankind into free countries, not only into countries but also into individuals acting inside them.[21]

Although consensus exists between the two key contemporary realist theories, neorealism and offensive realism, concerning the existence of anarchy, they are divided with regard to its effects. According to neorealism, anarchy leads the powers to tend to a status quo, whereas according to offensive realism, anarchy pushes the powers to revisionism.

After a review of the current theories concerning the effects of anarchy on the players acting in the international system, I shall turn to reviewing the conclusions of the *international relations theory of war* concerning the effects of anarchy.

Status Quo, Revisionism, and Aspiration for Power

The strength and parsimony of realism stem primarily from its traditional view that countries have fixed preferences.[22] This view releases realism from the reductionist temptation of seeking the reasons for the behavior of countries in domestic processes; the traditional temptation of expecting ideas to influence the material structure of global politics; the utopian temptation of believing that each given group of countries has natural, harmonious interests; and the legal temptation of believing that countries can overcome power politics by leaving the handling of disputes to shared laws and institutions.[23] However, while most contemporary realists agree with the assumption that the preferences of countries are predetermined, they dispute the question of whether the inherent aspiration of countries is to status quo or revisionism.

The terms *status quo powers* and *revisionist powers* are vague and not theoretically developed. According to Hans Morgenthau, the status quo policy is intended to preserve the distribution of power as it existed at a certain moment in history.[24] According to Organski's and Kugler's *power transition theory*, status quo countries take part in planning the "rules of play" and aim to benefit from them. In contrast, revisionist countries express general dissatisfaction with their status in the system and aim to rewrite the rules by which the relations among nations are managed.[25] Schweller argues that status quo powers seek self-preservation, protection of the values that they already advocate, and preserving their resources. They aim to maximize their security and not their power. For them, potential gains from uncertain expansion are offset by the costs of war. They may aim to disseminate and widen the influence of their values in the international scene but will not exercise military means to achieve that goal. Therefore, their interest in developing military power varies with the level of the threat to their values. Revisionist powers, in contrast, seek to expand their resources. They estimate what they covet more than appreciating what they possess. They will wield military force to change the status quo and expand the influence of their values in the international scene. For them, the gains from uncertain expansion exceed the costs of war.[26]

The preferences of countries, or their degree of tendency to revisionism or status quo, are represented in theoretical research using two main groups. The first attributes the degree of revisionism that countries aspire to at the state level based on three main aspects. *Revisionism only*—according to traditional realism all countries are revisionist. According to it, countries have an ongoing aspiration to achieve greater power and expand, and every country will expand until opposing pressure stops its progress.[27]

Morgenthau argues that countries wage an incessant struggle stemming from their innate animalistic dominance and the struggle reflects the human urge to control others.[28] *Revisionism or status quo*—Morgenthau, like early realist researchers who worked after the Second World War, makes a differentiation between imperialist powers and status quo powers. Realists consider revisionist countries to be the main motive forces of the international system. Status quo countries in contrast are perceived by them as responding and as having a secondary function in theory. *A sequence between status quo countries and revisionist countries*—Schweller's *balance of interests theory* makes a distinction between four types of countries: lions, lambs, jackals, and wolves. They are on the sequence between status quo countries, which he refers to as satisfied countries, and revisionist countries, which he refers to as hungry countries. Each of them will be willing to pay different prices for increasing its values in accordance with its degree of revisionism or status quo.[29]

The second group indicates international anarchy as being the factor affecting the preferences of countries. The harsh dispute between neorealism and offensive realism concerning the logical conclusions of anarchy is the strongest factor representing this group.[30]

According to Waltz's *neorealism*, the security motivation of countries is based on structural causality.[31] Countries will tend to a moderate strategy as a means of achieving security, and in most cases, a strong country in international relations will in turn adopt a restrained foreign policy—military, diplomatic, or economic.[32] According to Waltz, the search for power and security is limited. In the anarchic international system, security is the supreme goal. If survival is guaranteed, countries will be able to attempt to achieve goals such as quiet, gain, and power in a safe manner. The primary concern of countries is not maximizing their power but maintaining their status in the system.[33] Neorealism represents an optimistic view regarding international politics, whereby countries act to maximize their relative security and not their relative power, and the international system provides incentives for expansion and aggressive strategies only under very restrictive conditions.[34]

According to Mearsheimer's *offensive realism*, the security motivation of countries is based on structural causality, but unlike neorealism, the search for power and security is never-ending.[35] According to him, anarchy encourages expansion. Powers maximize their relative power and are constantly contending for power.[36] However, unlike Morgenthau, Mearsheimer claims that the motive for this contention is not the lust for power inherent to human nature but the quest for security and the anarchic structure of the international system is what causes it.[37] This model assumes that all countries aim to maximize their power relative to other countries because only the strongest country can ensure its survival. According to him, countries will pursue an expansion policy when the benefit from such action will exceed its cost. Countries under anarchy face the constant threat of other countries using force to attack or conquer them and have to increase their relative power.[38] Offensive realism also assumes that anarchy encourages countries to look for opportunities for weakening potential enemies and thus prove their relative power standing.[39]

The book argument that international politics has order does not deny the assumed existence of anarchy in the international system in the sense of a lack of a central government, since its formation in 1648 to date. This argument is broadly supported by theoretical research in the field.[40]

According to neorealism and offensive realism, the existence of anarchy in the system does not lead to the conclusion that the system is devoid of order. However, their assumptions concerning the existing order principle differ. According to neorealism, the balance principle causes countries to tend always to prevention of hegemonies,[41] whereas according to offensive realism countries always aim to form and head hegemonies.[42] The current study rules out this possibility and argues that realism, as a systemic theory of international politics, must make a few general assumptions concerning the preferences of countries, otherwise it will be impossible to assess the degree to which the international system shapes, pushes, or compels countries and the outcomes that realists are trying to explain. Therefore, the *international relations theory of war* rules out the possibility of the existence of status quo countries or revisionist countries in the international system. Because of the anarchic state that always prevails in the system, the theory differentiates between priorities of countries, which remain constant, and the action strategies of countries, which change with circumstances. Therefore, the theory states that the preference of all polar powers acting in the system remains constant and is always revisionist. It is not possible to tell apart less aggressive and more aggressive ones. In effect, there is no room in the theory for status quo countries.

In addition to this, the theory states that while revisionism of polar powers will always occur, the action strategies that the polar countries choose will be influenced by the system's polarity. Unlike anarchy, which remains constant, the theory states that each of the three different polarity models will have a different effect on the degree of revisionism of the polar powers. *Multipolar systems* will *increase* the revisionism of the three or more great powers constituting them. *Bipolar systems* will *suppress* the revisionism of their two constituent superpowers. *Unipolar systems* will *permit* the revisionism of the sole hyperpower constituting them.

According to the *international relations theory of war*, all polar powers are inherently revisionist and capabilities shape intentions.[43] Therefore, a country whose capabilities increase significantly will inevitably adopt a policy of expansion, irrespective of its political structure. Its abilities, and not just its regime model, are what will shape its intentions.[44] However, the reason that we do not observe a constant expansion spree of powers is that certain polarity models prevent some players constituting them from acting to expand or suppress their constant expansionist aspirations.

Analysis of the basic assumptions of the *international relations theory of war* may catalog it near offensive realism, inasmuch as according to the theory the aim of polar powers is to maximize their relative power in order to realize their constant aspiration of achieving hegemony in the system. The theory argues that the anarchic structure of the international system is what *dictates* the constant aggressiveness of polar powers, but the theory also argues that the degree of aggressiveness or revisionist tendency of countries is a result of the polarity model in the system. As stated above, each of the three polarity models will *dictate* a different degree of aggressiveness to their constituent polar powers. *Multipolar systems* will *increase* the inherent revisionism of the three or more great powers constituting them. *Bipolar systems* will *suppress* the revisionism inherent in the two constituent superpowers. *Unipolar systems* will *allow* the inherent revisionism of the sole hyperpower constituting them. In conclusion, according to the *international relations theory of war*, the polarity of the system prevents international relations from being in a state of constant war, but the international system is a scene in which the war option is always in the background.

HOMEOSTASIS AND PRESERVATION OF THE SYSTEM

According to the *international relations theory of war*, the second principle of transhistoric order, *homeostasis*, has always existed in the modern international system from the time of its formation after the Peace of Westphalia in 1648 to this day. Homeostasis, in the sense of a property of the system that resists change, leads to the international system tending to preservation of equilibrium. Homeostasis will therefore dictate to each of the polar powers constituting each of the three possible international systems to tend always to stagnation (i.e., take actions that will lead to preservation of the system in its existing state or preservation of the existing polarity model). The aim of this tendency is restoration of the system to its previous state or its state preceding the change (status quo ante) because the players cannot predict the character of the change that will occur with a high degree of certainty, which may harm them instead of improving their standing or security in the international system, and they cannot control or influence it.

The tendency to homeostasis or preservation of the existing state stems from two conditions that always occur in the international system and that characterize it relative to other systems. The *interdependence principle* leads to any action of one of the players inevitably affecting all other players in the system. This fact applies particularly to the polar powers constituting each of the three possible systems. For example, a local conflict in the Middle East, such as the conflict between Israel and the Hezbollah in July–August 2016, had a definite effect on the sole polar power in the unipolar system, the United States, the only hyperpower of the system. That dependence led the United States to be involved in the crisis and act to solve it militarily or diplomatically. The *uncertainty principle* is the other condition that leads to the results of the changes occurring in the system not being predictable and having the potential of improving the state of the country compared with the state that preceded the occurrence of the change or worsen it.

The existence of the *interdependence principle* and the *uncertainty principle* leads to international systems having a property that resists change, or homeostasis.

Homeostasis in the International System

Unlike the term *feedback*, which is borrowed from cybernetics, the term *homeostasis* has not been successful in entering the field of international politics analysis.[45]

Homeostasis, a term that was developed in psychology,[46] is defined as a physiological equilibrium that is achieved by balancing of functions and chemical composition within organisms.[47] Homeostasis conceptualizes the way in which an organism preserves its environment and continues to exist in it. In cybernetics, this goal is achieved by the transfer of information concerning the environment relative to the goals that the organism has set and through adoption of appropriate behavioral models. Because according to the principles of cybernetics information enters the system constantly, homeostasis itself is a continuous process.[48]

The existence of homeostasis means constant movement and not remaining static surrounding the equilibrium point. The result of that dynamism is that in all models of the systems, including international systems, it is possible to find a kind of *stability range*, a certain range in which limited changes or gentle positive feedback actions occur, which do not cause the shifting of the system from its equilibrium point because sooner or later most of these changes have opposing effects, such as negative feedback actions that restore the system to near the equilibrium point.

In ecosystems, one may find periodicity in the number and decrease of prey and predators. When predators proliferate, prey dwindles. However, this positive feedback, which may impair the homeostasis and violate the equilibrium of the system, reaches an end when the number of predators increases very significantly and leads to a decrease in the amount of prey, which in response leads to a significant decrease in the number of predators because of a shortage of available food.[49] One may therefore see that fluctuations in the numbers of predator and prey in ecosystems always range around the equilibrium point while maintaining the homeostasis of the system.

Homeostasis in International Systems: Historical Examples

A number of international systems provide us historical examples in which the *stability range* in the system was maintained. The systems ranged around an equilibrium point and did not lead to destruction of the homeostasis. In the bipolar system of 1946–1991, the United States and the Soviet Union fought a number of wars, and the *stability range* of the system was preserved in all of them. These were the wars of the United States against Korea, Vietnam, and Iraq (1991), and the Soviet invasion of Hungary and war against Afghanistan. In the unipolar system of 1992–2016, the United States took part in a few wars and maintained the *stability range* of the system in all of them. These were the U.S. invasion of Afghanistan (2001) and the U.S. invasion of Iraq (2003).

Certain consequences of actions may exceed the *stability range* of the system or the homeostasis. In such a state, the system destabilizes and becomes a system of another type. An unstable transition period may occur between one system and another, but after the formation of a new system, there will again be a balance between the various parts constituting it. In international politics, there are a number of examples of situations in which certain actions have led to the *stability range* being exceeded followed by the formation of a new system. Prominent ones are the multipolar system of 1849–1870. The strengthening of Germany following the Franco-Prussian War (1870–1871) led to the end of the preceding multipolar system and the beginning of the bipolar system that was formed after it in 1871–1909.[50] In the multipolar system of 1910–1945, the First World War (1914–1918) led to the end of one multipolar system and the beginning of a new multipolar system in its place.

In the multipolar system of 1910–1945, the defeat of Germany and Japan in the Second World War (1939–1945), alongside the exhaustion of France and Great Britain following that war, led to the end of the multipolar system that preceded the war and the beginning of the bipolar system of 1946–1991.

Homeostasis and Feedback Models

One cannot understand the effect of homeostasis without discussing the term *feedback*. Feedback means the return of part of the output to the system as an input. This is a term that originates from information theory. Using the feedback mechanism, the organism reacts to its environment and vice versa—the organism's environment reacts to it. Feedback allows the organism to increase the odds of achieving a certain goal through proving that a certain behavior model may or may not lead to the intended goal; feedback may be negative or positive.[51]

Negative or self-correcting feedback allows organisms to adapt themselves to their environment and maintain their stability through adjustment or homeostasis. A homeostatic equilibrium depends on negative feedback, if *learning* is achieved.[52] Feedback is negative when the signals from the target are used for limiting outputs that under other conditions would cross the target.[53]

Feedback is defined as possible if the output value that returns to the object is of the same value as the input signal. One may therefore say that positive feedback increases the input signals and does not correct them.[54]

The International Relations Theory of War and Homeostasis

According to the *international relations theory of war*, the homeostasis principle and feedback models in various systems affect the outcomes of the international system.

According to the theory, homeostasis in international politics is a property of the system that resists change. Homeostasis leads the system to *dictate* to the key players constituting it, primarily the polar powers, that their number defines the polarity model existing at any time and to make the necessary adjustments for restoring the system to the state it was in before the occurrence of the change (status quo ante).

The theory states that after the formation of international systems, these systems, like other systems such as biological, mechanical, or social systems, tend to remain in homeostasis. Similarly, in international politics, in each of the three possible polarity models—multipolar, bipolar, or unipolar systems—there will be a *stability range* or *equilibrium* between the various parts constituting each of the three possible system models. While positive feedback actions of players may violate the equilibrium, they will activate negative feedback actions, which are intended to restore the former situation. This process of restoring the equilibrium inside the system with constant motion around the equilibrium point is known in general systems theory as homeostasis.

The theory states that the tendency to homeostasis or maintaining the existing state of the international system stems from two conditions that occur in the international system distinguishing it from other systems. One is the *interdependence principle*, which leads to any action of one of the players inevitably influencing the other players in the system. The other is the *uncertainty principle*, which leads to it not being possible to predict the results of changes that occur in the system or their outcomes, and alternatively they may improve or worsen the state of the country. The existence of both these conditions leads to international systems having a property that resists change, or a tendency to homeostasis. Following this, each of the three possible international system models will *dictate* to the key players in the system, in accordance with their standing as a polar power or small power, to operate according to the three key principles of homeostasis. The rationale of these three principles is maintaining the standing of the international system or maintaining the equilibrium of the system.

According to the first principle, international systems will *encourage*, and in certain cases, also *dictate* to the key players operating in them to take negative feedback actions in response to positive feedback actions that other players may take and may violate the equilibrium of the system when the homeostasis, or equilibrium, is at risk. The purpose of these actions is to strengthen the homeostasis and maintain the equilibrium of the system. According to the second principle, international systems will *prevent* the key players operating in them from taking positive feedback actions that may lead to disruption of the homeostasis and violate the equilibrium of the system. The aim is to prevent the collapse of the system. According to the third principle, international systems will *allow* the key players operating in the system to use either of the two main feedback models, negative or positive, when these do not pose a significant threat to the homeostasis and do not disrupt the equilibrium of the system because in such a state the system will not be at risk.

The following cases may be enumerated among prominent examples of the three principles shown above. The multipolar system that existed in Europe in the 19th century, 1849–1870, *allowed* the players to take moderate positive feedback actions that did not lead to disruption of the homeostasis and that could not lead to violation of the system's equilibrium. Here one may state the wars for the unification of Italy and of Germany. These wars were positive feedback actions, but their intensity was low and they did not threaten the homeostasis of the system and did not lead the system to *dictate* to the other players to take negative feedback actions for restoring the former situation. In the multipolar system of 1910–1945, there were extreme positive feedback actions, such as the First and the Second World Wars, in which Germany tried to rise to hegemon status in the system and led the system to *dictate* to the other key players in the system to respond by taking strong negative feedback actions. The aim of these actions was to preserve the homeostasis of the system and prevent the violation of the equilibrium. In both these cases, the positive feedback actions that were applied were very extreme and led in response to extreme negative feedback actions. Following this, the homeostasis was not achieved, but instead the equilibrium that occurred in them was violated and both systems collapsed, to be replaced by other systems. The result of the First World War was the formation of a new multipolar system on the ruins of its predecessor; the result of the Second World War was the formation of the bipolar system of 1946–1991.

Under the bipolar system of 1946–1991, the United States and the Soviet Union were the two polar powers of the system. As such, positive feedback actions on the system that could have harmed their leaders, such as the awakening to democracy in communist countries in Eastern Europe from the 1950s to the 1980s (in East Germany in July 1953; in Poland in October 1956; in Hungary in October 1956; in Czechoslovakia in October 1968 [the

Prague Spring]; and the Solidarity crisis in Poland in August 1980), led the system to *dictate* to the Soviet Union, one of the two superpowers at the time, to take negative feedback actions in order to restore the homeostasis and preserve the equilibrium of the system. However, at the same time, the system prevented the USSR from expanding its involvement in those countries because of its fear of American involvement. The expansion of the Soviet Union's involvement in those countries would have made the negative feedback, whose purpose was to maintain the homeostasis, into positive feedback, which in itself could have led to disruption of the homeostasis and violation of the equilibrium of the system.[55] In the unipolar system of 1992–2016, the United States served as the sole hyperpower of the system. The fact that the United States abstained from acting as expected of it as a leader of the system in the 1990s led the system to *dictate* to the other players in the system to take positive feedback actions.[56] Here the attack on the U.S. embassy in East Africa in 1998, which resulted in 224 deaths, of whom 12 were Americans, and about 5,000 injuries; the attack against the *USS Cole* on October 12, 2000, in which 17 sailors were killed; and the most prominent, the terrorist attack on September 11, 2001, on U.S. soil, may be mentioned.[57]

I shall now turn to examining the independent variable "polarity of the system" and its influence on the two international outcomes examined in the study.

POLARITY OF THE SYSTEM:
THE INDEPENDENT VARIABLE

Realism is characterized by a prominent degree of parsimony that is based primarily on its assumption that the assignment of power in the system is the only variable that may explain differences in international politics. This assumption distinguishes it from competing explanations—liberal, epistemic, or institutional. These expect internal sources of resources and interaction between countries to lead to change not through control of material resources but because of the preferences and beliefs of countries and the information available to them.[58] This simple concept has allowed Morgenthau and Waltz to eliminate consistently the influence of ideas, local institutions, economic interests, psychology, and other resources over the preferences of different countries. For these realist theoreticians, the material resources form an extreme reality that has an extrinsic effect on the behavior of countries irrespective of what they are seeking, believe in, or are asking to build.[59]

According to the *international relations theory of war*, like the classic realistic theories that sanctify the distribution of capabilities—and in complete contrast to a number of contemporary realist theories that have

relinquished this core principle, resulting in their becoming liberal, epistemic, or institutional theories[60]—the three values of the independent variable, manifesting in the three polarity models of the system, are the factors
that influence the two international outcomes: the degree of stability of
international systems and the degree of territorial expansion of polar powers at the end of the wars in which they participate.

The rest of the chapter has five main parts. In the first part, the state is
presented as the most important player in the international system because
the polarity of the system is defined in research through the number of
strong countries that constitute it. In the second part, the manner in which
theory relates to the term *polar power* will be defined. In the third part, the
common definitions in research of the term *great power* will be examined,
and the term *polar power* as a replacement term will be suggested. In the
fourth part, the three possible polarity models—multipolarity, bipolarity,
and unipolarity—are discussed. In the fifth and last part, the way in which
the polarity of the system affects the international outcomes occurring in
it will be presented.

THE MOST IMPORTANT PLAYER IN THE INTERNATIONAL
SYSTEM: THE STATE

In the past, countries did not always control the regulating of violence
in the international scene as they do today. In premodern times, countries
in Europe competed with two other organizational models—city-states
and metropolises. Outside Europe, they competed with other models.
The alternatives to the state disappeared, but states continued to struggle
to strengthen their monopoly over violence, confronting the challenge of
mercenaries and pirates in the 19th century and with terrorists and guerilla groups in the 20th century. Under certain pressures, countries have
also failed.[61]

Today, the state is commonly held as the dominant model of political
order that is capable of executing independent foreign policy,[62] and it is
the political authority with monopoly over the legitimate use of organized
violence. Therefore, the focus must be the state when the regulation of violence in the international scene, which is one of the fundamental problems
of order in the social world, which extensively influences the aggregate
of other social relations, is discussed.[63] The relations between states differ
from other models of social interaction and involve primarily alternatives
of peace and war.[64]

The realist theory assumes that nation-states are the only significant
players in global politics. In recent years, an attempt has been made to
expand the theory and extend it to nonstate players too, such as multinational corporations, nongovernment organizations, or crime syndicates.
However, to date, these organizations have operated in the economic or

social field and have not been perceived as having significant security influence.[65] According to neorealism, the units are states and the theory objects to nonstate players, such as individuals, transnational social movements, and multinational corporations.

Neorealism attempts to explain the behavior of these units through the international system and objects to relying on the personality of decision makers or local political structures in foreign policy. Waltz was one of the first to deal with the state system project systematically, and its influence on the neorealism theory that he developed was extensive.[66] The hypotheses of the international states system significantly shape and indeed restrict the way in which we think about global politics.[67]

The 9/11 attacks in 2001 caused "superempowerment" of weak nonstate players that were minor in every other respect, allowing them to threaten great nation-states.[68] If nonstate players are also capable of causing damage to such a catastrophic degree, then many of the concepts on which the security policy of the last 200 years has been based—such as balance of power, deterrence, or buffering—lose their relevance, insofar as the deterrence theory depends on the wielder of weapons of mass destruction having a "return address" with tangible assets on its side that may be threatened with destruction in response.[69]

GREAT POWER OR POLAR POWER

The terms *great power*, which is common in international relations research, and *polar power*, which the current study uses, have received various definitions. Schweller argues that to define a state as a polar state it must have more than half the resources of the strongest power in the system, whereas the rest of the powers will be defined as medium powers.[70] Mearsheimer argues that the polarity of the international system is frequently defined in a broad manner that is out of the context of a specific region: to be defined as a pole in the global or regional system, the state must have a reasonable chance of defending itself against the leading country in the system.[71] Morgenthau, the traditional realist, and Waltz, the neorealist, agree that great powers must excel in all aspects of physical power. The power status of a country depends, according to Waltz, on the manner in which it succeeds in all the following components: size of population and territory, natural resources, economic ability, military force, political stability, and diplomatic skill.[72] Waltz adds that under bipolar systems, no third power can challenge the first two powers.[73]

POLAR POWER IN THE CURRENT STUDY

The *international relations theory of war* uses the term *polar powers* to describe the strongest powers in the system. These powers are the ones that serve as poles in each of the three possible polarity models. The theory distinguishes the term *polar powers* from the term *great powers* that is common in international relations literature and argues that under that system both polar and great powers or minor powers may act at the same time. According to the theory, each polar power is also a great power, but not every great power is a polar power. For example, in unipolar systems, there is just one polar power—the sole hyperpower constituting the system—but in parallel to it there may be other great powers. According to the theory, to be defined as polar powers in the system, the powers should have two families of power that have three key sources, whose importance is greater than that of the other power components that countries possess. The first family, *material power*, has two components: *economic power*—the polar power must have significantly greater economic power than those of the other powers, which are not polar powers, operating in the system; *military power*—the polar power must have significantly greater power than those of other powers that are not polar powers operating in the system.[74] The second family is *land power*. The polar power must have significant land power, which is defined in the research as direct or indirect control of territories of geostrategic importance for their times.[75] An example of this is the Eurasia continent of the 19th and 20th centuries, the Persian Gulf region today, and probably the East Asia region in the future.

According to the theory, holding only these power components—material, economic, and military power combined, and land power—will raise a country from great power status to polar power position in the system. Economic power and military power are quantitative components that may be assessed by comparing the material data of countries. In contrast, the third component, land power, is qualitative and may be understood through the age-long argument between the supporters of sea power and those supporting land power.

Between Sea Power and Land Power

The years around 1900 are perceived as "the age of seas." The most influential study on this subject in those years was written by Alfred Mahan, who believed that control of the sea was essential for every country that was aspiring for global leadership: "Without sea power, a country can only be a second-rate nation."[76] A number of West European countries, such as Portugal and Spain initially, followed by the Netherlands, France, and particularly Great Britain, effectively adopted the support of sea power. These countries discovered the Americas and increased their control of the Mediterranean Basin, India, and later the Far East. The British Empire, for example, conquered Southeast Asia, Egypt, Cyprus, Singapore, and Hong Kong, and also pushed its informal control into the Ottoman Empire, the Persian Gulf states, and upstream in China's great rivers.[77]

According to the realistic view, conquest pays off.[78] According to this plea, in addition to material power, meaning economic power and military power combined, to rise to polar power status in the system, the state must also have land power. In other words, it must control extensive territories in regions of geostrategic importance for their time. This approach is supported in literature on the subject of international relations. Peter Liberman states that in modern times, occupations have paid off for occupiers.[79] Halford Mackinder, one of the strongest supporters of land power, argues that the concept of global issues based on sea power is wisdom belonging to the past and that the balance has returned to land power. In a classic article dating from 1904, Mackinder stated that control of land, or land power, was of great importance in the past and remains so to this day.[80] Mackinder stated:

> Who rules East Europe commands the Heartland.
> Who rules the Heartland commands the World Island.
> Who rules the World Island commands the World.[81]

German dominance in Europe in the Second World War led Nicholas Spykman to rewrite Mackinder's assumption as follows:

> Who controls the rimland rules Eurasia;
> Who rules Eurasia controls the destinies of the world.[82]

The United States' attitude to the Eurasian Continent testifies to the importance of land power. The American realistic plea to join the war against Nazi Germany was based on the view of Spykman that control of territory allowed for the full utilization of its material and human resources besides national loyalty.[83] That plea was strengthened particularly after the fall of France in the summer of 1940, which focused attention on the geopolitical meaning of Nazi dominance of Europe.[84] After the war, Stalin's dominance raised in East and Central Europe the concern that he had supplanted Hitler as a competitor over European hegemony.

The assumption that the Soviet Union could drive occupied industrial economies to a war against the United States, which assumption was supported by the advocates of containment, led the United States to the conclusion that it must ensure that no single land power could control Europe, become a land and sea power, and expand overseas through the enormous resources of Eurasia in a manner that would be hostile to the United States.[85] Containment, in the manner that the United States acted in its involvement in the war against Hitler, was also driven by moral and economic motives. However, even at the end of the Cold War, the ultimate goal of containment, in the words of President George H. W. Bush, was "to prevent any hostile power or group of powers from dominating the Eurasian land mass."[86]

That focus on the importance of the enormous territory of the Eurasian continent, from Mackinder in the early 1920s to President George H. W. Bush toward the end of that century, stems from the geopolitical assumption that the more geopolitically important the territories that a state holds, the more power it will achieve. However, great criticism was also expressed against the argument that territorial occupation added power to the occupiers. Certain researchers denied the assumption that gross national product (GNP) could be transferred between capital cities like the transfer of money between banks. Adam Smith states that the costs attendant to seizure of colonies and protecting them from potential enemies usually exceed the low revenues collected from them, whereas writers of the 19th and 20th centuries argue that even cheap occupation without resistance among modern countries is not worth it.[87]

The current study presents a number of assumptions. Firstly, a power of high but not absolute economic material power, which will also have significant land power, will rise to polar power status in the system. For example, I argue that the Soviet Union rose during the bipolar system period of the 20th century in 1946–1991 to polar power status in the system despite its material capabilities being only half those of the United States for most of the period, because during that time it had high land power. Throughout that period, it controlled very extensive areas in the heart of the Eurasian continent, which were of very high geostrategic importance. Secondly, a power, regardless of how great its material power is, if it has low land power (i.e. a power lacking control of territories of geostrategic importance for their time) will not be able to rise to the status of a polar power in the system. For example, the rise of the United States to superpower status in the bipolar system of 1945–1991 was made possible because of the presence of hundreds of thousands of its soldiers in the Cold War in bases in the heart of Europe. Thirdly, a polar power of high material, military, and economic power combined, which is able to achieve significant land power, will become a sole hyperpower in a unipolar world. For example, had Germany succeeded in the two world wars to achieve significant control of the heartland, it could have risen to hyperpower status in a unipolar world. In the same manner, the departure of the Soviet Union from extensive territories in the heartland and its withdrawal from former communist countries from mid-1991 to its end during that year, alongside the entry of the United States into territories at the edge of the country after the first Gulf War (1991), the U.S. invasion of Afghanistan (2001), and the U.S. invasion of Iraq (2003), led to the system becoming a unipolar one headed by the United States as a sole hyperpower. Fourthly, a sole hyperpower in a unipolar world that loses its foothold in a heartland will gradually lose its status and the system will become multipolar or bipolar headed by more than one polar power. For example, if the United States withdraws its forces from lands of contemporary geostrategic important territories that it controls today overseas—for example Iraq, Afghanistan, or Southeast Asia such as Japan and South Korea—it may lose its sole hyperpower status in a unipolar world, resulting in a new unipolar system leading with other polar powers such as China, or be replaced with multipolar or bipolar world.

POSSIBLE POLARITY MODELS

Theoretically, in a state of anarchy, all sovereign countries are legally equal, but in practice this is not the case. Because of the absolute or relative abilities of one country compared with others, countries have differing importance and influence in the international system. Therefore, according to the current study, in the anarchic international system, there may be three polarity models. A *multipolar system*—a system that has three or more *polar powers*.[88] In such a system, the *great powers* constituting the system will have higher status than that of the other powers and the states that are not *polar powers* in the system. A *bipolar system*—a system that has two *polar powers*. In such a system, the status of the two *superpowers* constituting the system will be greater than that of the other powers and the states that are not *polar powers* in the system. A *unipolar system*—a system in which there is one *polar power*. In a system of this kind, the status of the sole *hyperpower* constituting the system will be higher than that of the other powers and states that are not *polar powers* in the system.

The polarity of the system may therefore change according to the increase or decrease of the number of strong countries operating in it, but this change does not lead to loss of its anarchic properties. The question of which country is to be defined as a polar power in the international system may seem meaningless, but for studies of the realist school and the current study as well, the polarity of the system is of supreme importance.[89] The polarity of the system affects not only *the behavior of countries*, but more important, it affects *the outcomes of their behavior*. However, in the theoretical study of international relations, it is not always clear what the distinguishing characteristics of the polar powers compared with countries that are not considered as players in the balance of power system are.[90]

Usually, it is not exactly understood how polar powers are to be distinguished from other countries, and well-defined criteria for defining the polar powers in the system are missing. For example, there is no consensus whether the 19th century was characterized by hegemonies, bipolarity, or multipolarity, or some combination of these three structural conditions. This long debate proves that unlike the opinion of certain researchers, common sense cannot serve as a sufficient basis for evaluating the number of poles,[91] and that as long as a number of researchers try to base themselves on a more careful estimate of the number of polar powers in the system, disagreements will continue to arise concerning the way in which

the polarity of the system is defined and the way in which it is possible
to measure or operate it. Moreover, researchers who only enumerate the
number of poles for evaluating the division of power assume that great
powers that are not polar powers do not affect the system's structure.
According to most neorealist criteria, the meaning of this is that we must
ignore for example the importance of China, France, and Great Britain in
any systemic study of international relations, from the end of the Second
World War to today, because these countries are not defined in this period
as polar powers.[92]

POLARITY OF THE SYSTEM AND INTERNATIONAL OUTCOMES

The determinations of the two basic assumptions underlying the *international relations theory of war*—*anarchy* and *homeostasis*—may raise against
it the argument that it cannot explain the changes in the values of the two
outcomes that it tries to explain. Against this criticism, the theory argues
that the polarity of the system is what affects the values of the two international outcomes: *the systemic*—stability of international systems; and, *intrasystemic*—the degree of territorial expansion of polar powers at the end
of the wars in which they have participated. The polarity of the system is
represented by the division of the total power between the polar powers
constituting the system—multipolar, bipolar, or unipolar systems. According to the theory, this is the proportion of power in the international system that each country controls, and this variable has a greater influence
on the likelihood of international conflicts or cooperation occurring than
structural restrictions on which defensive realism is based. Waltz argues
that once the international system is formed, like the market, it becomes
a force that units cannot control. It dictates their behavior and positions
itself between their intentions and the outcomes of their actions.[93] Just
as economic outcomes change when the market structure changes from
a duopoly to an oligopoly or perfect competition, argues Waltz, international outcomes also change according to the degree of centralization or
decentralization of capabilities in the international system. In other words,
the international system is defined according to the question of whether
there are in the system multiple powers—multipolar system; two powers—bipolar system; or a single power—unipolar system. He argues that
the market structure is defined by counting economic companies, whereas
the international political structure is defined by counting countries,
and in this count, the distinction is made relative only to capabilities,[94]
in a similar manner as far as the *international relations theory of war* goes
between the three possible polarity models. According to the theory, a
multipolar world that has a number of great powers is very different from
a bipolar world that has two superpowers, and both are different from a
unipolar world in which there is one hyperpower.

A multipolar world consists of three or more polar powers of similar strength. It allows for change in alliances and a transition between coalitions that usually lead to preservation of the system's equilibrium. However, the multiple options for countries to link up sometimes imbalances the system. This world does not cause constant hostility toward any of the great powers constituting it. *A bipolar world* consists of two polar powers of similar strength. It does not allow for a change of alliances and a transition between coalitions between the parties and usually leads to a balance of power in the system. This world tends to focus the fears and hostility in the system on the two superpowers constituting it. *A unipolar world* consists of a single polar power that is much stronger than the other powers in the system. It reduces the possibility of formation of effective military alliances against the sole hyperpower constituting it but tends to focus the fears and hostility of the world against the hyperpower.

Polar powers can disrupt and also destroy the existing polarity model actively by waging a broad war, or passively, by their economic decay. However, the polar powers have almost no ability to influence the polarity model that will form after the crumbling of the existing polarity model. However, the theory argues that once the polarity of the system stabilizes, the two order principles that always act in the system—*anarchy* and *homeostasis*—cause the three polarity models to affect the behavior of polar powers acting in them in the following manner: *multipolar systems* in which three or more polar powers operate will *increase* the lust for power of the great powers constituting them; *bipolar systems* in which two polar powers operate will *suppress* the lust for power among the superpowers constituting them; *unipolar systems* in which one polar power operates will *allow* the lust for power of the sole hyperpower constituting them.

According to the theory in the three possible polarity models, the polar powers constituting the system will act based on two constraints. The systemic dictate that is imposed on polar powers to achieve hegemony in the system will lead them not to suffice with their current status and tend always to expand by investing great economic resources in increasing their military power and by exploiting opportunities for territorial expansion. The systemic dictate that is imposed on polar powers for homeostasis will lead them to act to preserve the system by initiation of actions for preserving the existing polarity model and through actions for reacting against changing the existing polarity model.

According to the theory, each of the three possible polarity models imposes on the powers constituting it constraints that distinguish and differentiate it from the two other polarity models that affect the way in which the polar powers behave. For example, the theory expects that each hyperpower that will act in a unipolar system will be forced by the system to respond to extreme threats or risky provocations made against it. In the unipolar system of 1992–2016, the United States could not fail to respond to provocations made against it by the Al Qaeda organization, which was hosted in Afghanistan, and could not fail to respond to the provocations of the president of Iraq. The actions of these two players challenged its supremacy in the system and required Washington to act to remove them. The United States, which did not act for expansion immediately upon its rise to the position of the sole hyperpower in a unipolar world, effectively underwent "a systemic socialization process," acquiring the behavior required of its status in the system, which forced it to act in that manner, even when perceived by many American decision makers as being against the interests of their country. Following this, the United States started to act according to those constraints: it initiated wars against Afghanistan (2001) and Iraq (2003) and expanded territorially at their end.

However, the theory, as a theory dealing with international outcomes, presents a stronger plea. It attributes little importance to the way in which countries behave or the action strategies they choose. The theory argues that behavior patterns that will be ostensibly different from the way in which the theory anticipates them will not change the results or outcomes that it anticipates. In *bipolar systems*, revisionist behavior of the two super-powers will not affect the international outcomes, and in most cases, they will maintain the existing status quo. For example, in the bipolar system of 1946–1991, the wars involving the two superpowers constituting it did not lead to expansion—the wars of the United States against Korea, Viet-nam, and Iraq (1991), and the Soviet invasion of Hungary and war against Afghanistan. The intrasystemic international outcomes at the end of those wars *remained* maintaining of the territorial status quo preceding their out-break. In *unipolar systems*, in the vast majority of cases, balancing attempts of small and medium powers against the sole hyperpower will end with-out success. For example, in the unipolar system of 1992–2016, the bal-ancing actions of France, Germany, and Russia toward the United States before the Iraq War (2003) had no effect whatsoever on the intrasystemic international outcome—the instigation of war by the sole hyperpower of the system, the United States, and its military victory and territorial expansion at its end.

From the argument that each of the three polarity models has a dif-ferent effect on the two international outcomes assessed, it may be con-cluded that once the polarity model changes, the outcomes will change too. This means that the following conclusions may be drawn: the same polar power will adopt a different policy or strategy under different polar-ity models and as the theory anticipates—the United States as a status quo power in the bipolar system of 1946–1991 and as a kind of revisionist power in the unipolar system of 1992–2016; the policy or strategy of polar powers and of nonpolar powers under the same polarity and as the theory anticipates: in unipolarity, the hyperpower, such as the United States, will act as a kind of revisionist power. In contrast, the great powers that are not polar powers will act as status quo countries—for example, Russia,

France, and Germany, which acted energetically to restrain the steps of the sole hyperpower in the system, the United States, and prevent its instigation of the Iraq War (2003).

SUMMARY OF THE PRINCIPLE OF THE MODEL

Models, owing to their simplicity, allow for differentiation of certain factors from other factors while keeping the other factors constant. They allow for isolation of the influence of certain factors in a manner that historical events allow only rarely. The *international relations theory of war* isolates the effect of the two transhistorical order principles that constantly exist in its view in the international system, *anarchy* and *homeostasis*, on the two variables assessed on the study. The theory does so by differentiating the independent variable of the study, the polarity of the system, which may assume three different values—multipolarity, bipolarity, and unipolarity—a variable that affects the values of the two independent variables that it assesses— systemic international outcome, or international systems stability; and the intrasystemic international outcome, or the territorial expansion of polar powers at the end of wars in which they participate.

Based on Jeffrey Legro and Andrew Moravcsik,[95] it may be determined that the *international relations theory of war* that was presented in the current chapter is a realistic theory. Firstly, because it assumes that countries are individual political units operating under conditions of anarchy. Secondly, because it assumes that the character of the preferences of countries is constant and tends to conflict. Thirdly, because it assumes that the structure of the international system, or the polarity of the system, is the variable that determines the two international outcomes assessed in the study.

From the two basic assumptions that the *international relations theory of war* has adopted, *anarchy* and *homeostasis*, one may conclude a very broad range of expectations concerning international political life. However, the distinction that the theory makes between the three different polarity models of the international system, all of which exist in an anarchic environment— multipolar, bipolar, or unipolar systems—allows the theory to present expectations that are much more exact than those of other realistic theories on the matter of the two international outcomes in each of the three different system models, and indicate different expectations in the values of each of these two international outcomes in the three different system models.

THE SYSTEMIC STATUS OF THE INTERNATIONAL RELATIONS THEORY OF WAR

In the *international relations theory of war*, the systemic outcome being assessed—stability of international systems—considers the international system to be a *dependent variable*. The intrasystemic outcome that is being assessed—the degree of territorial expansion of polar powers at the end of wars in which they will participate—treats the international system as an *independent variable*. Based on Wendt's argument that theory will be considered as systemic when it treats the international system as a dependent or independent variable,[96] the *international relations theory of war* belongs to the systemic paradigm in international relations theory.

Contemporary realists who argue that countries form a structure through the interaction between them also support the systemic paradigm.[97] The *international relations theory of war* considers the system of countries not only a system that reflects the individual countries and their properties but also a reality with properties and rules of its own. It argues that the international system as an aggregate is suitable for analyzing cognitive phenomena and that through the polarity of the system the behavior outcomes of the individual countries operating in it should be analyzed. The theory differs from other theories because it makes a distinction between the behavior of powers and the outcomes of their behavior. Some systemic realist theories argue that the behavior of powers—such as balancing, bandwagoning, buck-passing, or catching the buck—is the factor that affects international outcomes. According to the *international relations theory of war*, the individual manner of conduct of individual countries does not necessarily have an effect on the systemic international outcome or the intrasystemic international outcome, but to a great extent, the various systemic constraints imposed on countries in each of the three polarity models are the factors that influence the polar powers constituting them to act differently, and in a manner that the theory anticipates.

Great criticism has been voiced against systemic theories that deal with international politics.[98] They contend with forces at the international level and national level[99] and explain international politics according to the structure of the international system. Reductionist theories explain international politics according to the properties of the states or agents and the interaction between them. The relations between these two families of theories are competitive.[100]

Waltz's *Theory of International Politics* and Mearsheimer's *Theory of Great Power Politics* are individualist theories to a great extent. Waltz's theory attributes great importance to players and their balancing actions in determining international outcomes, whereas Mearsheimer's theory attributes great importance to players and the pattern of buck-passing in determining international outcomes. Another plea will be aimed at the assumption that the behavior of states is constant in both these theories. Waltz argues that countries will always aspire to maximize their security, whereas Mearsheimer argues that states will always aim to maximize their power. These constant assumptions of the two theories concerning the aspirations of the countries indicate that neither assumes that the system *structures* the behavior of the players.

The *international relations theory of war*, in contrast, belongs to the category of materialistic-holistic theories because it makes the following arguments. Firstly, the argument that the structure of the system, more than the internal properties of countries, is what influences the way in which countries behave. According to the theory, the same country will act differently under different polarity models. Here one may mention the clear difference in the way in which the United States behaved in the bipolar system of 1946–1991 and the unipolar system of 1992–2016. Secondly, the argument that the international system will *dictate* international outcomes of a certain type even when the behavior pattern is ostensibly to the contrary. According to the theory, balancing actions against a hyperpower in a unipolar world will be unsuccessful. Here the failed attempts of France, Germany, and Russia to balance the United States before the U.S. invasion of Iraq (2003) can be mentioned. Thirdly, the argument that the international system *structures* identities. According to the theory, each hyperpower in a unipolar world will be *motivated* by the system to expand. Here one may mention the change in the behavior pattern of the United States in the unipolar system: from a reserved power in the 1990s to an aggressive one after the 9/11 attacks in 2001.

THE INTERNATIONAL RELATIONS THEORY OF WAR AND OTHER KEY REALIST THEORIES

The *international relations theory of war* developed based on the argument by Thomas Kuhn that cumulative acquisition of innovations and gradual developments is preferable to destroying a previous paradigm when developing a new one.[101] The theory is based on the three key realist theories in the theoretical research of international relations: traditional realism,[102] neorealism, and offensive realism. Table 2.3 compares the four theories.

Comparing the *international relations theory of war* to the two main contemporary systemic realist theories in international relations theory, neorealism and offensive realism, emphasizes the difference between them. Firstly, both other theories argue that a unipolar system cannot exist,[103] unlike the *international relations theory of war*, which claims that a unipolar system is possible and occurred in 1992–2016. Therefore, one may argue against them that they neglect a third of the possible international systems. Secondly, both these theories are based on an analysis unit at the state level—balancing and bandwagoning according to neorealism; balancing and buck-passing according to offensive realism—to explain outcomes at the system level. Therefore, it may be determined that they indicated a bottom-up (inductive) direction of influence. Conversely, the *international relations theory of war* presents a systemic plea in which the direction of

Table 2.3

Traditional Realism, Neorealism, Offensive Realism, and the *International Relations Theory of War*

	Traditional Realism (Morgenthau)	Neorealism (Waltz)	Offensive Realism (Mearsheimer)	International Relations Theory of War (Israeli)
The inherent preference of the powers	**Revisionism,** that always exists to the same extent	**Status quo,** that always exists to the same extent	**Revisionism,** that always exists to the same extent	**Revisionism,** that always exists to the same extent
The degree of power that the powers are seeking	**How much they are able to achieve:** powers maximize relative power, and hegemony is their ultimate goal	**Not much more than what they have:** powers focus on preserving the balance of power	**How much they are able to achieve:** powers maximize relative power, and hegemony is their ultimate goal[1]	**How much they are able to achieve:** powers maximize relative power, and hegemony is their ultimate goal
What causes powers to compete for power	**Lust for power,** which is inherent to powers	**Structure of the system**	**Structure of the system**[2]	**Structure of the system,** allowing, increasing, or suppressing the *lust for power* inherent to the powers according to the system polarity model
The action strategies that the powers choose	******	Balancing and bandwagoning	Balancing and buck-passing	All possible action strategies that do not affect the international outcomes: *everything is permissible and the key outcomes are known*

	All the time.	Only under certain conditions.	All the time.	Only under certain conditions.
When the powers will act to expand	The only variable at the state level, the lust for power inherent to the powers, causes the powers to act to expand constantly	The sole variable at the system level, anarchy in the international system, causes the powers to act to maintain the status quo	The sole variable at the system level, anarchy in the international system, causes the powers to act to expand continuously	The only variable at the system level, polarity of the system, affects the inherent aspiration of the powers to expand: • Bipolarity will *suppress* expansion • Unipolarity will *allow* it • Multipolarity will *increase* it
Summary	*Traditional realism* is not a systemic theory, but a theory at the state level	*Defensive realism* does not present a satisfactory explanation for the periods in which powers do not act as status quo powers, according to the theory's expectation	*Offensive realism* does not present a satisfactory explanation for the periods in which powers do not act as revisionist powers, according to the theory's expectation	The *international relations theory of war* provides satisfactory explanations: A. For the different behavior—revisionism or status quo—of those powers, in different periods B. For the difference in international, systemic, and intrasystemic outcomes, in the different periods

1 Offensive realism disputes defensive realism concerning the degree of power that countries are seeking. For defensive realism, the international structure provides countries a limited degree of encouragement for increasing their power. Conversely, it pushes them to maintain the existing balance of power. The use of power, more than increasing it, is the main goal of countries, according to this theory. Offensive realism believes that status quo powers do not occur in international politics because the international system forms a very strong ambition for countries to achieve power by expansion at the expense of their adversaries and by acquiring advantages in cases in which the benefit exceeds the cost. The ultimate goal of countries, according to offensive realism, is being the hegemon of the system. Mearsheimer, *The Tragedy of Great Power Politics*, p. 21.

2 Both traditional realism and offensive realism argue that great powers demand power constantly. The main difference between these two theories is that the first argues that countries have an inherent offensive personality, whereas the latter argues that the international system encourages the great powers to maximize their relative power because that is the optimal way of maximizing their security. According to this approach, great powers behave aggressively not because they want to do so or have multiple inherent motivations to control, but because they must seek greater power if they want to maximize their survival odds.

Table 2.4

Neorealism, Offensive Realism, and the *International Relations Theory of War*

	Neorealism (Waltz)	Offensive Realism (Mearsheimer)	International Relations Theory of War (Israeli)
Possible International Systems	• Multipolar • Bipolar	• Balanced Multipolar and Unbalanced Multipolar • Bipolar	• Multipolar • Bipolar • Unipolar
Order Principles Controlling the International System	In an international system, there is a sole transhistorical order principle, *anarchy*, which dictates to the players to take two main courses of action: • *Balancing* • *Bandwagoning*	In an international system, there is a sole transhistorical order principle, *anarchy*, which dictates to the players to take two main courses of action: • *Buck-passing* in multipolar systems • *Balancing* in bipolar systems	In an international system, there are two transhistorical order principles: • *Anarchy*, in the sense of the absence of a common regime, leads the system to spur the players, primarily the polar powers constituting it, to tend always to *expansion* or formation of a hegemony for them to head • *Homeostasis*, in the sense of a property of the system that resists change, leads the system to *dictate* to players, primarily the polar powers constituting it, to tend always to *stagnation* and preserve the system in its existing state
Direction of Influence of the Analysis Units on the Outcomes in the System	**Bottom up (inductive).** Analysis units at the state level—*balancing* and *bandwagoning*—are what affect the outcomes at the system level	**Bottom up (inductive).** Analysis units at the state level—*balancing* and *buck-passing*—are what affect the outcomes at the system level	**Top down (deductive).** An analysis unit at the system level—*polarity of the system*—is what affects the two international outcomes: systemic and intrasystemic

influence is top down (deductive). Thirdly, both these theories are defined as systemic theories, but both base their *systemic* plea on a variable at the state level and differ from each other primarily in this variable: one argues that states tend to a status quo whereas the other argues that all states are tend to revisionism. Table 2.4 summarizes the differences between these three theories.

In addition to the theoretical flaws of the two main contemporary systemic realist theories, they have several empiric flaws. I shall state the key ones: neither theory is able to anticipate and explain the result or outcome of the behavior of polar powers in various international systems. They cannot explain the significant differences between the systemic international outcome and the intrasystemic international outcome that the *international relations theory of war* explains.

There are additional points for criticism. Firstly, Waltz's *Theory of International Politics* (also known as *the Balance of Power Theory*) states that any attempt by a polar power to disrupt the existing balance of power and rise to hegemon status will result in balancing actions by the other polar powers.[104] Therefore, it may be stated that the theory did anticipate the way in which the other powers acting in the current international system would act in response to the actions of the United States since it rose to hyperpower status in the unipolar world,[105] insofar as the other powers have consistently attempted to restrain its steps. However, the theory has failed to predict the results or outcomes of their behavior, for the United States has not been influenced by these attempts and has remained the sole polar power in the system. In the U.S. invasion of Iraq (2003), many countries in the system did act according to the predictions of the theory and acted to counterbalance the United States. However, the results or the outcomes of their action were not completely in contrast to the forecast of the theory. Their activity was purposeless and did not affect the international outcomes as defined in the current study: the United States' instigation of the war and its territorial expansion at its end.

Secondly, Mearsheimer's *Theory of Great Power Politics*, which argues that countries, primarily great powers, act to expand at all times, does not provide an explanation for outcomes that are inconsistent with this expectation, such as the two periods of peace in the 19th century and early 20th century, 1816–1848, 1871–1910, and the Cold War period, 1946–1991. The theory cannot explain why the United States did not act in a revisionist manner from the early 1990s after the collapse of the Soviet Union and the end of the Cold War until the terrorist attacks of September 11 either.[106]

Table 2.5 concentrates the key directions of the *international relations theory of war* that have been presented up to this point.

Table 2.5

The *International Relations Theory of War*

A. Basic assumptions of the theory:
   1. The theory's attitude to the international system:
      The international system is very important
   2. The theory's attitude to the players:
      The most important players acting in the system are the polar powers

B. The transhistorical order principles:
   A. The *anarchy* principle, in the sense of the absence of a common regime, leads the system to *spur* the players, primarily the polar powers constituting it, to tend always to expansion or formation of a hegemony for them to head
   B. The *homeostasis* principle, in the sense of a property of the system that resists change, leads the system to *dictate* to players, primarily to the polar powers constituting it, to tend always to stagnation and preserve the system in its existing state

C. The causal logic of the theory:
The independent variable, the polarity of the system → international outcomes—systemic and intrasystemic

---

	Multipolar Systems	**Bipolar Systems**	**Unipolar Systems**
The independent variable, or polarity of the system	**Three or more Great Powers:** • 1849–1870—22 years • 1910–1945—36 years	**Two Superpowers:** • 1816–1848—33 years • 1871–1909—39 years • 1946–1991—46 years	**Sole Hyperpower:** • 1992–2016—24 years
The systemic dependent variable, or stability of the system	**Low stability.** Many wars The system will *increase* the number of wars involving the great powers constituting it	**High stability.** Few wars The system will *reduce* the number of wars involving the two superpowers constituting it	**Medium stability.** Lies between the other two systems The system will *allow* the sole hyperpower constituting it to wage war against countries that will challenge its absolute supremacy in the system

---

(*continued*)

Table 2.5 (*Continued*)

The intra-systemic dependent variable, or degree of territorial expansion of the polar powers at the end of wars	1. No territorial expansion of the great powers: Multipolar systems will *dictate the absence of territorial expansion* of the great powers at the end of the *central wars* that they fight because any other outcome would position the victor as a potential hegemon in the system and may therefore impair the homeostasis, a result that the system resists	Maintaining the territorial status quo of the two superpowers: Bipolar systems will *dictate the preservation of territorial status quo* of the two superpowers at the end of the *minor wars* they fight, because any other outcome will lead to disruption of their supremacy in the system, which in turn may impair the homeostasis, a result that the system resists	Territorial expansion of the hyperpower: Unipolar systems will *dictate the territorial expansion* of the hyperpowers at the end of the *minor wars* they fight because any other outcome will lead to disruption of their supremacy in the system, which in turn may impair the homeostasis, a result that the system resists
	2. Territorial expansion of the great powers: Multipolar systems will *allow the territorial expansion* of the great powers at the end of the *major* and *minor wars* that they fight because such an outcome would not threaten the homeostasis of the system, a result that the system permits		

CHAPTER 3

Polarity of the System

In the period assessed in the study, 1816–2016, there were six instances of the three possible polarity models: two multipolar systems, 1849–1870 and 1910–1945; three bipolar systems, 1816–1848, 1871–1909, and 1946–1991; and one unipolar system, 1992–2016.[1]

Table 3.1 shows the summary of the system polarity models, 1816–2016, and a novel determination of the study—the definition of the international system in 1816–1945 as alternating between multipolar and bipolar. That deliberation confronts the current study with most other theoretical studies, which argue that the entire 19th century was multipolar.

Table 3.1
Summary of Polarity of the System, 1816–2016

	1816–1848 Bipolarity	1849–1870 Multipolarity	1871–1909 Bipolarity	1910–1945 Multipolarity	1946–1991 Bipolarity	1992–2016 Unipolarity
England/ Great Britain	*	*	*	*		
Russia/ Soviet Union	*	*		*	*	
Prussia/ Germany		*	*	*		
Austro-Hungary		*				
France		*		*		
Italy				*		
Japan				*		
United States				*	*	*
China						

The period assessed in the study, 1816–2016, is 200 years in total. In that period were three instances of the three possible polarity models: two instances of a *multipolar system* lasting a total of 58 years—1849–1870 (22 years) and 1910–1945 (36 years)—representing 29 percent of the entire length of the period; three instances of *multipolar systems* whose total length was 118 years—1816–1848 (33 years), 1871–1909 (39 years), and 1946–1991 (46 years)—which is 59 percent of the total duration of the period; and just one instance of *unipolar systems*, whose total length was 24 years, 1992–2016, representing 12 percent of the entire duration of the period.

Table 3.2 shows a comparison of the combined length of the three instances of the three possible polarity models in the period assessed in the study, 1816–2016.

Table 3.2

The Combined Length of the Six Instances of the Three Different Polarity Models, 1816–2016

	Multipolar Systems	Bipolar Systems	Unipolar Systems
The duration of each of the six instances of the different systems	1870–1849=22 1945–1910=36	1848–1816=33 1909–1871=39 1991–1946=46	2016–1992=24
The total duration of each of the three polarity models	58 years	118 years	24 years
The percentage of years of each of the three polarity models out of the tested period	58/200=29%	118/200=59%	24/200=12%

The book defines the different instances of the three possible polarity models in 1816–2016 in a different way from the one in which they are defined in most theoretical studies in international relations research. In the existing studies, a common division is into three periods.

1816–1945: Waltz argues that in this period, there was a multipolar system and there were always five or more powers.[2] Mearsheimer also argues that there was multipolarity in those years. However, he makes an original distinction between balanced multipolar systems, 1815–1902 and 1919–1938, and unbalanced multipolar systems, 1903–1918 and 1939–1945.[3] Schweller argues that there was a multipolar system between the two world wars, but unlike other researchers, he characterizes the system in that period as a tripolar system.[4]

1946–1991: researchers are nearly unanimous about this period having a bipolar system.[5]

1992–2016: concerning this period, four key approaches may be stated: (1) Mearsheimer states that once the Cold War ended and the Soviet Union dissolved in the late 1980s, the system became multipolar again;[6] (2) Huntington's definition of this international system is original and interesting and according to him it is uni-multipolar;[7] (3) Schweller, Walter Mead, and L. Silk argue that the world after the Cold War became a tripolar world;[8] and, (4) like me, Christopher Layne, Wohlforth,[9] and other researchers argue that it is a unipolar system.[10]

CHAPTER 4

How the Research Is Empirically Examined

There is an almost complete consensus concerning the argument that the ultimate test of theory in social science is its ability to explain events that occur in the real world. However, the question of whether theories can be empirically assessed is given two extreme answers. Michael Nicholson argues that theories can be theoretically assessed,[1] whereas Charles Taylor denies this and argues that phenomena can be explained logically.[2] Like other studies in theoretical international relations research,[3] the current study supports Nicholson's statements that theories can be empirically assessed.

The *international relations theory of war* makes an attempt to convert historical knowledge into an overall theory that will provide an explanation to the question of why the two international outcomes assessed in the study receive the values that the theory expects them to receive.[4] The theory helps in the development of useful knowledge for understanding two of the most important problems in international relations.[5] According to the study, the two international outcomes that it attempts to explain—the systemic outcome and intrasystemic outcome—are best explained at the system level rather than at the state level or individual level.

To ensure the validity of the conclusions that arise from the theory, I have maintained a number of principles and rules during its empiric examination:

1. The theory is examined by *observation* because in international relations research it is almost impossible to use experimentation.[6] As political science researchers, we cannot examine our hypotheses by initiating a war, for example.

2. The theory has been examined using two main approaches of *observation*—*quantitative analysis* and *qualitative analysis*—because neither method is preferable over the other.[7]
   - The *quantitative analysis* approach has been selected because at the time of empiric examination of historical events it is important to increase the number of test cases examined to avoid the main problem of causal deduction based on too few cases.[8]
   - *Qualitative analysis* and the test cases approach: according to this approach, test cases are assessed using reliance on historical records as a database not only for studying a single test case but also for equal research between a large number of test cases.[9]
3. The study does not present a detailed historical description of the test cases being assessed but rather focuses on the development of the causal explanations for the events being studied.[10]
4. The study is attempting to present an a priori forecast of these two outcomes in the current unipolar system of 1992–2016 and in other international systems that will be formed in the future,[11] and not just to explain a posteriori the two international outcomes that it assesses in international systems that have occurred in the past.
5. The study is based on the method of structured, focused comparison and uses historical knowledge for supporting the theory and explaining the complexity of the two phenomena that the theory is attempting to explain.[12]
6. The selection of test cases in the qualitative study was based on the similarity and difference methods:[13]
   - The *similarity method* was used for assessing test cases under the same international system models because the similar results of the two variables explained under those international system models prove that the pleas presented by the theory were correct. The three most significant wars in the different multipolar systems have been examined: the Crimean War in the multipolar system of the 19th century and the First and the Second World Wars in the multipolar system of the 20th century. In these three cases, the explanatory variable—the polarity of the system—is kept constant. The identical value of this variable provides the conditions for proving the argument of the study that multipolar systems encourage the great powers constituting them to fight more and larger wars than the two other polarity models.
   - The *difference model* was used for assessing five test cases in which polar powers fought Afghanistan: the First (1838–1842), Second (1878–1880), and Third (1919) Anglo-Afghan Wars; the Soviet-Afghan War (1979–1988); and the U.S.-Afghan War (2001). In these five cases, most key variables are held constant except for the explanatory variable, the polarity of the international systems, which varies between the five test cases. The difference in the explanatory variable helps prove the differences in the territorial outcomes of these five wars.

In the current chapter, I shall assess the *international relations theory of war* empirically through examining the two dependent variables that the theory assesses and based on the principles of the study described above. The check is done by empirically examining the two international outcomes that the theory is attempting to explain in 1816–2016. In the first part, the systemic international outcome, the stability of the three possible international system models is empirically assessed. In the second part, the intrasystemic international outcome, the degree of territorial expansion of polar powers at the end of wars that they have fought is assessed.

SYSTEMIC FACTORS AND STABILITY OF INTERNATIONAL SYSTEMS

Over the course of human history, some periods have been more stable than others. Comparing the following two periods reveals significant differences between European wars in terms of number of deaths: 1,858,000 in 1715–1792 compared with 635,000 in 1815–1914.[14] Similarly, a long-term examination of the system of European countries reveals that war periods were followed by periods of peace, and vice versa. For most of the 17th and 18th centuries, war in Europe was at low ebb. In the 19th century, there were longer periods of peace, but a number of wars and major crises still occurred during it. At the beginning of the century, the long, bloody Napoleonic Wars were fought. The Crimean War occurred in its middle, and in its last third were the Wars of the Union of Italy and Germany. Both World Wars, which occurred in the first half of the 20th century, continued that pattern. Security competition is therefore inherent to the international system, but war is not, because only in certain cases does security competition lead to war.

Because war is one of the most important and influential phenomena facing humankind, many theories deal with examining the causes that lead to the outbreak of wars. Some of these theories have pointed at human nature as the cause of conflict and war. Other theories have pointed at leaders, local politics, or the international system. Like the *international relations theory of war*, a number of other theories indicate the division of power as a factor that may explain conflicts in the international scene. Waltz argues bipolar systems will be stable compared with multipolar systems.[15] Mearsheimer states that bipolar systems will be the most stable, unbalanced multipolar systems will be the most war-inclined, and balanced multipolar systems will lie between them.[16] Unlike these theories, which offer an explanation for just two of the three possible system models, the *international relations theory of war* offers its assumptions concerning all three possible models—multipolar, bipolar, and unipolar systems.

As a structural theory, the *international relations theory of war* may assume that international anarchy is the main systemic factor that leads countries to fight each other, as the best way for countries to survive under international anarchy is to achieve greater capabilities than all other countries in the system. However, anarchy alone cannot explain why the security competition sometimes leads to war and sometimes does not, because the system is always under anarchy, whereas war does not always occur in the system. To explain this significant difference in the behavior of countries, the theory adds a systemic variable: the division of power between polar powers, or the polarity of the system. The theory states that power in an international system is usually divided in three main ways. Therefore, to assess the effect of the division of power on the feasibility of war, we must identify the polarity of the system at each point in time and determine whether the system is multipolar, bipolar, or unipolar. According to the book, for systemic theory, the key questions are how changes of the system affect the frequency of wars,[17] and how changes of the system influence the intensity of wars. The study implements the three existing structural models according to the *international relations theory of war* in evaluating the stability or belligerent tendency of each of these three systems and indicates that level of the international system as the key cause of the outbreak of wars involving polar powers. According to the study, each of the three possible polarity models will affect the stability of the system differently: bipolar systems will be the most stable, multipolar systems will be the most destabilized, and, unipolar systems will lie between them.

Confirmation of the argument that the polarity of the system is the factor affecting the stability of the system is provided by studies developed from broad databases and that have discussed the various aspects of wars.[18] The consequences of these studies are very important because only through empiric studies can we hope that patterns, trends, and possible causes of the outbreak and outcomes of wars may be identified.

The current subchapter assessed the degree of stability of the three possible system models by examining all instances of that polarity model in the period assessed in the study, 1816–2016: two instances of multipolar systems, 1849–1870 and 1910–1945; three instances of bipolar systems, 1816–1848, 1871–1909, and 1946–1991; and one instance of a unipolar system, 1992–2016. In the current subchapter, I present the causal explanation of my theory for the events. I ask to examine two key questions: firstly, how many years of war, the years in which the polar powers were involved in war, occurred in the three different polarity models; secondly, how many wars, of the three possible models of war—central, major, or minor wars—occurred in each of the three different polarity models.

We now turn to the two stages of the empiric assessment of the systemic dependent variable, stability of international systems. The *quantitative study* examines all interstate wars that involved polar powers under the six instances of the three polarity models in 1816–2016. The purpose of the assessment is to prove correlation between the assumptions of my theory concerning the stability of the three international systems and the number and intensity of wars under the different polarity models. Through the *qualitative study* a smaller number of important wars will be studied out of the various instances of the various international systems. The purpose of the study is to prove causality between the assumptions of my theory concerning the stability of the three international systems and the main test cases that occurred under the three different polarity models.

STABILITY OF INTERNATIONAL SYSTEMS— QUANTITATIVE RESEARCH

The quantitative study attempts to prove correlation between the study's assumption concerning the degree of stability of the three international system models and the empiric results under those systems: multipolar systems as the most destabilized ones; bipolar systems as the most stable; and, unipolar systems as stable ones that lie between the other two. The quantitative study is conducted by examining all wars in which the polar powers constituting the six instances of the three possible international system models fought in the period studied, 1816–2016.

SYSTEMIC FACTORS AND THE STABILITY OF MULTIPOLAR SYSTEMS

The Stability of the Multipolar System, 1849–1870

The multipolar system of 1849–1870 occurred according to the current study in Eurasia. It consisted of five polar powers: Great Britain, France, Russia, Prussia, and Austro-Hungary—the five great powers that constituted the system. In that period, 13 wars occurred between countries. These are the wars that the study deals with. Eight wars have not been included in the assessment—some because they were waged outside the Eurasian theater that represented, according to the current study, the international system in those years, and some because they did not include at least one of the five polar powers constituting the system.[19]

Five wars that were included in the study were fought in Eurasia and included at least one of the five great powers constituting the system:

1. Crimean War (#22), between Turkey, Italy, France, United Kingdom, and Russia (10/23/1853–3/1/1856)
2. Italian Unification War (#28), between Sardinia/Piedmont, Austro-Hungary, and France (4/29/1859–7/12/1859)
3. Second Schleswig-Holstein War (#46), between Prussia, Denmark, and Austria-Hungary (2/1/1864–4/25/1864; 6/25/1864–7/20/1864)

4. Seven Weeks' War (#55), between Italy, Hesse Grand Ducal, Wuert-temburg, Bavaria, Austria-Hungary, Prussia, Mecklenburg Schwerin, Hesse Electoral, Saxony, Baden, and Hanover (6/15/1866–7/26/1866)
5. Franco-Prussian War (#58), between Wuerttemburg, Baden, Prussia, Bavaria, and France (7/19/1870–2/26/1871)

Table 4.1 shows the degree of stability of the multipolar system that occurred in Eurasia in 1849–1870. This system did not cover the entire world but represents the international system of that time.

Table 4.1

Stability of the Multipolar System, 1849–1870

Central Wars	Great Wars	Small Wars	Duration (Days)	Deaths Total
	Crimean War (#22)		861	264,200
	Italian Unification War (#28)		75	22,500
	Second Schleswig-Holstein War (#46)		111	4,481
	Seven Weeks' War (#55)		42	44,100
	Franco-Prussian War (#58)		223	204,313

The Stability of the Multipolar System, 1910–1945

The multipolar system of 1910–1945 was formed in 1910 when the United States and Japan entered the great power global game; it ended in 1945 after the Second World War. That was the first system that ever represented an "international system." The system consisted of seven polar powers: the United States, Russia (later to be the Soviet Union), Germany, Great Britain, France, Japan, and Italy—the seven great powers that constituted the system.

In that period, 20 wars were fought between countries. This system is the first system that was not contained to Eurasia and encompassed the whole world. Therefore, the assessment includes all wars between countries that were fought worldwide and involved at least one of the seven polar pow-ers constituting the system. Seven wars were not included in the assess-ment because they did not involve at least one of the seven polar powers.[20]

Thirteen wars were included in the assessment because they involved at least one polar power of the seven great powers constituting the system:

1. Italian-Turkey War (#97) (9/29/1911–10/18/1912)
2. First World War (#106), between Yugoslavia, Russia, Bulgaria, United Kingdom, Japan, Portugal, Turkey, Belgium, Germany, Greece, Romania, Austria-Hungary, France, Italy, and the United States (7/29/1914–11/11/1918)

3. Russo-Polish War (#109) (2/14/1919–10/18/1920)
4. Franco-Turkish War (#116) (11/1/1919–10/20/1921)
5. Manchurian War (#118) (8/17/1929–12/3/1929)
6. Second Sino-Japanese War (#121), between China and Japan (12/19/1931–5/22/1933)
7. Conquest of Ethiopia (#127) (10/3/1935–5/9/1936)
8. Third Sino-Japanese War (#130) (7/7/1937–12/6/1941)
9. Changkufeng War (#133), between the Soviet Union and Japan (7/29/1938–8/11/1938)
10. Nomonhan War (#136), between the Soviet Union, Mongolia, and Japan (5/11/1939–9/16/1939)
11. Second World War (#139), between Hungary, Belgium, France, Yugoslavia, Finland, Norway, Canada, United States, United Kingdom, Netherland, Italy, Romania, Bulgaria, Greece, Brazil, Italy, Australia, New Zealand, the Soviet Union, Germany, Poland, France, Japan, Mongolia, China, South Africa, and Ethiopia (9/1/1939–8/14/1945)
12. Russo-Finnish War (#142) (11/30/1939–3/12/1940)
13. Franco-Thai War (#145) (12/1/1940–1/28/1941)

Table 4.2 shows the degree of stability of the multipolar system of 1910–1945.

Table 4.2

The Stability of the Multipolar System, 1910–1945

Central Wars	Great Wars	Small Wars	Duration (Days)	Deaths Total
		Italian-Turkish War (#97)	386	20,000
First World War (#106)			1,567	8,578,031
		Russo-Polish War (#109)	613	100,000
		Franco-Turkish War (#116)	720	40,000
		Manchurian War (#118)	109	3,200
		Second Sino-Japanese (#121)	521	60,000
		Conquest of Ethiopian (#127)	220	20,000

(continued)

Table 4.2   (*Continued*)

Central Wars	Great Wars	Small Wars	Duration (Days)	Deaths Total
		Third Sino-Japanese (#130)	1,614	1,000,000
	Changkufeng War (#133)		14	1,726
	Nomonhan War (#136)		129	28,000
Second World War (#139)			2,175	16,634,907
		Russo-Finnish War (#142)	104	151,798
		Franco-Thai War (#145)	58	1,400

SYSTEMIC FACTORS AND THE STABILITY OF BIPOLAR SYSTEMS

The Stability of the Bipolar System, 1816–1848

The bipolar system of 1816–1848 was formed once the Napoleonic Wars ended. It occurred in Eurasia and included two polar powers: Great Britain and Russia, as the two sole superpowers in the system.[21] In that period were seven wars between countries worldwide. Six wars were not included in the assessment, some because they were fought outside the Eurasian system, which represented, according to the current study, the international system in those years, and others because they did not involve at least one of the two superpowers constituting the system.[22]

Just one war that was included in the assessment was fought in part in Europe and in part in the Middle East. This war involved one of the two superpowers that operated in the system, Russia, and was therefore included in the assessment:

1. First Russo-Turkish War (#4) (4/26/1828–4/19/1829)

Table 4.3 shows the degree of stability of the bipolar system that occurred in Eurasia in 1816–1848.

Table 4.3

Stability of the Bipolar System, 1816–1848

Central Wars	Great Wars	Small Wars	Duration (Days)	Deaths Total
		First Russo-Turkish War (#4)	507	130,000

The Stability of the Bipolar System, 1871–1909

The bipolar system of 1871–1909 occurred in Eurasia. It consisted of two polar powers, Great Britain and Germany, as the only two superpowers in the system. The system was formed after the Franco-Prussian War (1870–1871), which led to Prussia's unification and transformation into Germany in 1871. The system reached its end when two extra-European powers, the United States and Japan, first entered the powers game in the international system in 1910 and upon the transformation of the system, for the first time, into a global system.[23] In this system, 16 wars were fought between countries around the world, none of which have been included in the study, some because they were fought outside the Eurasian system, which represented the international system in those years, and some because they did not involve at least one of the two superpowers constituting the system.[24]

Table 4.4 shows the degree of stability of the bipolar system that occurred in Eurasia in 1871–1909.

Table 4.4

Stability of the Bipolar System, 1871–1909

Central Wars	Great Wars	Small Wars	Duration (Days)	Deaths Total

The Stability of the Bipolar System, 1946–1991

The bipolar system of 1946–1991 occurred throughout the world. It included two polar powers, the United States and the Soviet Union, as the two superpowers that constituted the system. In that period, 23 wars were fought between the countries that the study deals with. Nineteen wars were not included in the study because they did not involve at least one of the two superpowers constituting the system.[25]

Four wars were included in the assessment because they did involve at least one polar power:

1. Korean War (#151), between China, Belgium, Canada, Columbia, United Kingdom, Netherland, Greece, France, Turkey, Philippines, Thailand, North Korea, Ethiopia, Australia, South Korea, and the United States (6/24/1950–7/27/1953)[26]
2. Soviet Invasion of Hungary (#156) (11/4/1956–11/14/1956)
3. Vietnam War (#163), between the United States, Cambodia, South Korea, Philippines, South Vietnam, Vietnam, Thailand, and Australia (2/7/1965–4/30/1975)[27]

4. Gulf War (#211), between Kuwait, the United States, Canada, United
   Kingdom, Italy, Morocco, Iraq, Egypt, Oman, France, United Arab
   Emirates, Qatar, Saudi Arabia, and Syria (8/2/1990–4/11/1991).[28]

Table 4.5 shows the degree of stability of the bipolar system that
occurred throughout the world in 1946–1991.

Table 4.5

Stability of the Bipolar System, 1946–1991

Central Wars	Great Wars	Small Wars	Duration (Days)	Deaths Total
		Korean War (#151)	1,127	910,084
		Soviet Invasion of Hungary (#156)	10	2,426
		Vietnam War (#163)	2,912	1,021,442
		Gulf War (#211)	86	41,466

SYSTEMIC FACTORS AND THE STABILITY OF
THE UNIPOLAR SYSTEM

The Stability of the Unipolar System, 1992–2016

The unipolar system of 1992–2016 occurred throughout the world and
involved one polar power, the United States, as a sole hyperpower constituting the system. In that period, just two wars were fought between
countries involving the sole polar power constituting the system:

1. Invasion of Afghanistan of 2001 (#225), between Canada, France,
   United Kingdom, the United States, Australia, and Afghanistan
   (10/7/2001–7/26/2003)[29]
2. Invasion of Iraq of 2003 (#227), between Australia, United Kingdom,
   the United States and Iraq (3/20/2003–6/28/2004)[30]

The end date of these two wars is disputed. The study assumes that the
Afghanistan War ended after the government of Afghanistan was formed,

and the Iraq War ended at the time of official handover of power to the Iraqi government.

Table 4.6 shows the degree of stability of the unipolar system that occurred worldwide in 1992–2016.

Table 4.6

Stability of the Unipolar System, 1992–2016

Central Wars	Great Wars	Small Wars	Duration (Days)	Deaths Total
		Invasion of Afghanistan of 2001 (#225)[1]	658	8,116
		Invasion of Iraq of 2003 (#227)[2]	467	30,976

1 The length of the U.S.-Afghan War and the number of coalition deaths in the war: October 7, 2001–December 31, 2001—86 days, 12 deaths; 2002—365 days, 68 deaths; January 1, 2003–July 26, 2003—207 days, 36 deaths. In total throughout the war: 658 days, 116 deaths.

2 The length of the U.S.-Iraq War and the number of coalition deaths in the war: March 20, 2003–December 31, 2003—287 days, 173 deaths; January 1, 2004–June 28, 2004—180 days, 803 deaths. In total throughout the war: 467 days, 976 deaths.

THE STABILITY OF INTERNATIONAL SYSTEMS— QUALITATIVE ASSESSMENT

The qualitative assessment attempts to prove causality between the study assumption concerning the differing stability of the three international system models and the empiric outcomes under those systems—multipolar systems as the most destabilized, bipolar systems as the most stable, and unipolar systems as lying between the other two. The qualitative assessment is done by examining a limited number of important wars that the polar powers constituting the six instances of the three possible international system models in 1816–2016 fought.

The issue of stability may be examined through the struggle or quest for hegemony by the great powers, which was expressed in two types of wars: major wars, involving one or more polar power in the system; and central wars, involving all of them. Therefore, the current subchapter examines all wars of this type fought in 1816–2016. To prove this argument, I have chosen to examine the factors that led to the outbreak of the three most significant wars fought in 1816–2016. These three wars were fought in two instances of multipolar systems: the Crimean War, which was a major war fought in the multipolar system of the 19th century, and the First and the

Second World Wars, both of which were central wars that were fought in the multipolar system of the 20th century.

STABILITY OF INTERNATIONAL SYSTEMS IN A MULTIPOLAR SYSTEM

Multipolar systems are the ones most inclined to war. The presence of three or more polar powers constituting the system increases the number of possible bipartite relations and the potential for development of conflicts that may deteriorate into the three types of wars that the polar powers would be involved in: central wars, major wars, or minor wars. In the current subchapter, the argument is that multipolar systems will dictate to the great powers constituting them to wage more central, major, or minor wars than the other two polarity models.

Wars as an Unintended Consequence or Systemic Dictate of the Players

It is sometimes argued that many wars stem from misconceptions, miscalculations, and silly mistakes. According to this view, wars are unintentional and a result of failure in crisis management.[31] This view focuses only on the interests of countries whereas a full explanation of the actions, including counteractions of countries, must relate both to the interests of countries and to the structure of the environment. Political leaders who prefer peace to war may end up in a war because the situation is structured in a manner that incentivizes rational players to act in a manner that leads them to undesirable outcomes. This dynamic is reflected well in the *prisoners' dilemma model*, in which the structure of the situation results in individual rational players waiving the advantages of cooperation and becoming trapped in crisis behavior.[32]

In the *prisoners' dilemma game* with two players in which each has the possibility to cooperate with his adversary or not (defecting), each of the players prefers the outcome of mutual cooperation (an output that is a result of the decision or strategies of the players) over mutual noncooperation. The best possible outcome for each of the players is *defecting* while his adversary is a *sucker* and continues to cooperate. The worst possible outcome is being a *sucker* by oneself. Therefore, irrespective of the player's view of the actions of the counterparty, for both of them, *defecting* would be better than *cooperation*. Following this, individual rational behavior of defecting leads to an outcome of mutual noncooperation, which is an irrational behavior because this is not the optimal outcome for either player, for whom mutual cooperation is better. That is the dilemma. Technically, in the *prisoners' dilemma game*, the crisis outcome is undesirable, but it is not unexpected and hence not inadvertent. Sensible leaders may be able to anticipate the structure module that will result in noncooperation that appears in *prisoners' dilemma games*, so that the outcome is not really unexpected. A simpler formula is the *security dilemma* in which actions taken by countries for increasing their own security (such as arms proliferation or alliances) lead their adversaries to feel threatened and react in manners that are perceived to be threatening.[33] The result is a *conflict spiral*, or an action-reaction process, involving higher levels of threat and response.[34] This dynamic may stem from completely rational reactions to a threatening situation and intensify because of misjudgment and emotional reactions.[35]

Crisis management researchers have not recognized that some crises are inherent in such a manner—in terms of preferences of players, alongside diplomatic, geographical, technological, and organizational crises that infringe on their freedom of action—which they prefer to escalate to war despite the wish of decision makers to avoid it.[36] These crises are factors that encourage rational players to take a series of actions that lead to war that they would rather avoid.[37]

I now discuss the three most significant wars fought in the study period, 1816–2016: the Crimean War, the First World War, and the Second World War. The theory states that these wars did not break out because of the failure of leaders in crisis management[38] but because of the structure of the international system at the time, or the polarity of the system, which like the *prisoners' dilemma game*, forced the individual rational players to be trapped in crisis behavior. These constraints are what caused, to a great extent, the outbreak of these three wars.

The Stability of the Multipolar System, 1849–1870

Despite the small number of wars fought in the multipolar system that occurred in Eurasia in the 19th century, 1849–1870,[39] one cannot ignore the Crimean War, which was the first war that involved the polar powers since the end of the Napoleonic Wars (1792–1815) at the beginning of that century.[40] There is no consensus on the reasons that led to the outbreak of the Crimean War. Even researchers who agreed that the war broke out because of the threat to the European balance of power do not agree on the question of whether the threat was made by France, Russia, or Britain.[41] According to the book, the culprit for the outbreak of the war was the multipolar model that prevailed at that time, which led to the transformation of a bilateral crisis, between Russia and France, into a multilateral crisis, which involved most of the polar powers that constituted the system at that time.

Crimean War

The Crimean War is a misnomer for a conflict that took place from the Arctic Ocean to the Pacific Ocean and affected almost every country in the

world. It was the most important and devastating conflict of the 100 years
from the end of the Napoleonic Wars (1815) to the outbreak of the First
World War (1914).[42]

The dispute that started the diplomatic snowball to the Crimean War
occurred more than six years before Britain and France declared war against
Russia in late March 1854. The dispute involved the Orthodox, Armenian,
and Catholic churches, concerning control over a number of sites holy to
Christianity in the Holy Land. In late 1847, there was a dispute among the
many Christian churches concerning the Church of the Nativity in Bethle-
hem. The Catholics did not possess the keys to the church's main entrance;
only the Orthodox and Armenians had that privilege. Therefore, Catholics
were limited to using a nearby chapel and had to enter the church through
a side door. The dispute intensified when a silver star with a Latin inscrip-
tion disappeared. The Catholics, who argued that the star had been sto-
len by Orthodox priests, attempted to use the "theft" to ask the broader
question of their rights and privileges. To that end, they sought support
from the French government. The argument culminated in a severe dispute between the various Christian churches in the Holy Land. Once the
intra-Christian conflict intensified, the Ottoman government had to move
forces in order to separate the antagonists who were fighting around the
holy site.[43] Only two years later, in 1849, did the French take practical
steps. France's support was accompanied by the support of other Catholic
powers: Portugal, Spain, Sardinia, Naples, and Belgium, but not Austria.
Russia, in contrast, stood by the Orthodox. Now the dispute involved two
major European powers, France and Russia, and each of them supported
the church associated with it: France supported the Catholics and Russia
the Orthodox. The Ottoman administration, contrastingly, preferred not
to intervene in the dispute. It abstained from associating itself with either
party as long as the crisis did not endanger its status.[44]

By 1852, the dispute concerning the holy sites had been waged for five
years. It seemed that there was no reason for it not to continue to unfold
for a few years longer. Nonetheless, within six months, Russia invaded
Ottoman Empire territory and less than a year later Russia and the Ottoman Empire were at war. In March 1854, France and Britain joined the war.
The dispute among the various churches helped the outbreak of the first
war involving the key European countries for 40 years.[45]

The Crimean War—Common Explanations for Its Outbreak. Researchers
tend to explain "major" events in terms of comparative causality. In contrast, for years, the predominant perception concerning the causes of the
Crimean War was that of an unintended war. Researchers usually explained
the outbreak of the Crimean War in terms of misunderstanding, misconceptions, overreactions, silly mistakes, and mismanagement of the crisis by
the political leaders who preferred peace over war, rather than as a conflict

of interests between countries. Such arguments have been promulgated by several researchers. Smith Anderson writes that the Crimean War was an outcome of a series of misjudgments, misunderstandings, and silly mistakes, pride and stubbornness, more than morbid wishes.[46] Gavin Henderson writes that the war was a result of diplomatic deterioration and lack of ruling skills among the great powers.[47] Richard Smoke argues that in the chain of actions and counteractions that led to the outbreak of the war, none of the decision makers in the major nations wanted the events to develop into a major European war. But they lost full control of the cycle of actions and counteractions.[48]

The argument that the Crimean War was unintentional is correct but only insofar as the political leaders of the great powers constructing the multipolar system did not want or anticipate a war. The current study rules out the argument that the war was a result of irrational behavior—such as misconceptions, silly errors, pride, or stubbornness—leading to mismanagement of crises and unintentional wars.[49]

The Crimean War—Systemic Causes of Its Outbreak. The religious dispute concerning the holy sites between the Christian churches in the Holy Land was not the direct cause of the outbreak of the Crimean War. The war broke out because France and Russia exploited the crisis in a manner that endangered the future of the Ottoman Empire and the disputed deteriorated in a manner that threatened vital strategic issues of the parties involved. The war could have easily been avoided but all the powers *chose*, at different times, to exacerbate the crisis. It must be asked why. Did all the powers choose to intensify the crisis because of errors and misunderstandings, or were they forced to do so because of systemic dictates? Systemic constraints are what forced the major European systems involved to instigate the war and the causes of the outbreak of the war must be sought in the broader European context.[50]

In the Crimean War, Britain fought in a pact with its traditional enemy, France, to help the *infidel* Islamic power, the Ottoman Empire, in its war against another European power, Russia. Although the diplomatic dispute started because of a religious one, it quickly became a struggle over power and influence in the Ottoman Empire, and this dispute significantly affected the strategic interests of each of the major European powers. The diplomacy that led to the war was clumsy, but the war broke out because Russia, France, and Britain believed that their vital interests were in danger.[51]

The revolutions of 1848 led to a number of important changes. The Tsar of Russia, Nikolai, was encouraged by the successful involvement of the Habsburg monarchy in the Hungarian revolution in 1848. He believed that Russia was a dominant land power in the system. In France, Louis Napoleon gained strength through a revolution, thus increasing the fear that he might attempt achieve the territorial arrangement of 1815, but that fear was not enough to lead the previous alliances that defeated Napoleon Bonaparte to pool their forces. Louis Napoleon feared both European radicalism and a direct challenge to the existing framework of agreements, and he sought ways of adding to his strength within his own country and without.[52]

From the beginning of the period of Louis Napoleon's rule, France's foreign policy was motivated by the expectation that the new Bonaparte would rewrite the international order in order to reestablish France as the dominant power in Europe. To achieve those goals, Louis Napoleon employed three key strategies. He attempted to improve his relations with France's former enemy, Great Britain, exploited national reasons to organize Europe under France's political and moral leadership, and acted to disrupt the international order that he established in the Vienna Congress after the Napoleonic Wars, which he considered the main obstacle to reestablishing France's supremacy in Europe. The French leader believed that Russia led the defense of the existing international order and that any action that would weaken Russia might reduce Tsar Nikolai's ability to support that international order. He believed that he would get the support of others, particularly that of Palmerston in Great Britain, who started to define Russia, more than France, as the key threat.[53]

The French leader identified the possibility of achieving these goals in the holy places in the Ottoman Empire. For hundreds of years, Christian churches and other important buildings in the holy sites were divided between Catholic and Orthodox churches. A number of agreements that received the consent of the Ottoman authorities over the years allowed a certain degree of freedom of religion for these two Christian sects. With nearly 13 million Orthodox believers throughout the Ottoman Empire, Russia was perceived as the external patron of the Orthodox.[54] A series of agreements between the Russian capital at that time, Saint Petersburg, and Porte, as the Turkish center of rule was called, which were based on the outcomes of a number of wars that were fought between these two countries, strengthened Russia's standing in the region. Besides these traditional areas of Russian influence, Louis Napoleon and his foreign minister, Drouyn de Lhuys, started to pressure the Turkish leader in Constantinople in 1850 to accept the Catholics' claims. The main demand was returning the right of the Latin Church over the holy sites in the Ottoman Empire.[55] These demands were based on both diplomatic and military threats.[56] For example, Louis Napoleon sent a French warship to Constantinople in clear violation of a previous Russo-Turkish agreement. Negotiations over the specific French demands continued until December 1852, when the sultan agreed to almost all of France's demands.[57]

In the revolutions of 1848, Great Britain remained relatively separated from the events on the continent, even though it provided symbolic support for countries that were attacked by radical forces.[58] For Britain, the Crimean War was the only European war in which London was involved in 1816–1914. In the decades that preceded the war, Britain relinquished Europe and focused on its empire. However, as a major European power, Britain could not ignore the events on the continent, and it was drawn into the land disputes in the Crimean War. Britain was not interested in fighting such a war because the size of the army that it could raise was about a quarter that of the French army, and its influence over strategy reflected those differences.[59]

The Crimean War—Its Consequences. A number of studies argue that the leaders of the countries could have solved the conflict without a war, as both the tsar and Porte had the possibility of reaching an agreement through contacts that led to the war, and Britain and France could both have abandoned Turkey to its fate in its war against Russia. But considering the interests of their countries, all the political leaders had an international incentive to fight a war that was greater than the incentive of negotiating an arrangement. However, the conclusion that many historians reached that the key cause of the war was silly errors or incompetence of political leaders was wrong.[60]

In the Crimean crisis, no leader wanted a war of great powers. Each of the leaders faced a series of significant choices that the system encouraged him to take, which eventually led to the outbreak of an unintentional war. Unlike the assumption that the war was caused by irrational concepts that were based on misconceptions of the key leaders, the players acted rationally for maximizing their own countries' interests. The multipolarity of the international system led to two significant influence models: (1) it reduced the options that the great powers had on the one hand; and on the other hand, (2) it forced the great powers to choose certain options that in many cases were in opposition to their aggregate interest.

The Crimean War was the first war of great powers after Napoleonic France was defeated in 1815. The war had many consequences. Firstly, it led to the end of the longest period of peace between the major European powers for 300 years; secondly, it formed the conditions that facilitated the unification of Italy and Germany; thirdly, it had a very significant effect on the future of the development of diplomacy and of European society. Although Austria maintained its neutrality during the war, its transition from supporting one side to supporting the other side annoyed the Western powers and also caused alienation on the part of Russia. Therefore, Austria remained without a great power as an ally in later struggles against the revolutionary forces in Italy and against Prussia's increasing power.[61]

The Crimean War also proved to London that Great Britain could not be a naval power only—the Royal Navy did help defend trade and the empire, but it could not contribute significantly in European conflicts. Britain quickly understood that if it wanted to have any real influence on the conduct of major land wars, such as the Crimean War, it had to raise a large army, whether it was interested in doing so or not. That was a painful lesson that was relearned in 1914.[62]

The Stability of the Multipolar System, 1910–1945

In the multipolar system of 1910–1945, there were numerous wars across the world between countries involving one of the seven polar powers or the great powers that constituted the system. Two of the wars, the First and the Second World Wars, stand out compared with the others. The two World Wars that were fought in the multipolar system support the book's argument concerning the dangers lying in a multipolar world.

The First World War

In international relations research, a number of explanations for the outbreak of the First World War have been discussed.[63] Some of them associate the outbreak of the war with the comprehensive arms race preceding it.[64] Other studies argue that in the decades preceding the war, a phenomenon called the "cult of the offensive" swept through Europe, which caused it to break out.[65] Additional studies argue that the war broke out to a certain degree because of the détente, a process of thawing of the Anglo-German relations that took place in 1914.[66] Three additional arguments may be presented that state the war broke out because of excessive, aggressive foreign policies and military policies: (A) a mutual incentive for preemptive attacks or rapid mobilization;[67] (B) a rigid organizational routine, particularly in Germany and Russia, which restricted the freedom of decision makers through demanding large-scale mobilization and, in the case of Germany, an early attack once the mobilization was accomplished;[68] and (C) a cycle of hostility that filled the relations between Germany and the other European powers that preceded the war. The supporters of this view argue that the British, French, and Russians reacted to the rise in the power of Germany, which appeared to be hostile, and that Germany's defensive reactions were understood to be offensive and therefore formed the atmosphere that was suitable for the outbreak of the crisis in June 1914.[69]

For years, the First World War was mentioned as an example of an unintentional war. It became the key source of many assumptions on the subject and serves as a common historical and strategic metaphor in the nuclear age.[70]

The main argument is while the *Triple Entente* countries preferred a peaceful solution for the June crisis, both Austro-Hungary and Germany wanted a war, as long as they believed that it could be limited to the

European continent. They sought a local war in the Balkans in which Austro-Hungary would almost certainly defeat Serbia and would therefore
avenge the assassination of Archduke Ferdinand and remove the constant
Slovak threat to the integrity of the Austro-Hungarian Empire. The central
powers aimed at risking Russia's involvement, believing that it would not
intervene, and the result was a war on the European continent in which
Germany and Austro-Hungary fought Russia, France, and Serbia. Austro-
Hungary, and particularly Germany, did not want a global war that would
be powered by British involvement in the war in the continent. Based on
these preferences and the assumption that Great Britain would remain
neutral in the first moves of war on the continent—which assumption was
not unreasonable given what was then known—Germany encouraged
Austro-Hungary to fight against Serbia.[71]

The paradox of the First World War is that although each of the leading
players preferred a certain arrangement over war, the result was a world
war. The explanation is that at each of the important decision nodes, the
political leaders were facing elections that could lead either to deterioration or nondeterioration of the crisis, and that in the international political
constraints that they faced they preferred the alternative of determination.
Each decision reduced the range of possibilities that followed it, and once
Britain made its intentions clear and Germany understood that Britain
would probably intervene in the war on the continent, the central powers
could no longer turn the wheel back. The great powers ended up with an
outcome that none of them wanted, but it was more of a result of a series
of basic rational decisions under a complicated series of international and
domestic conditions, than of crisis mismanagement.[72]

Systemic Causes of the Outbreak of the First World War. The sources of
the approach whereby systemic factors are what led to the outbreak of the
First World War are identifiable in a book from 1916, which stated that
the causes of the First World War did not lie in Germany or in any other
power. Rather, the main culprit lay in the European anarchy that formed a
strong ambition among countries to achieve superiority over other countries, based on both security and tyranny motives.[73]

The common view concerning the First World War, that it is a result
of the German aspiration for power, is exaggerated. Germany wanted a
local war rather than a total war involving the British. The war broke out
because the international forces shaped the priorities of the great powers and the strategic and political choices of their actions. In contrast, the
mismanagement of the crisis by the political leaders was only a second
cause of the outbreak of the war.[74] According to the *international relations
theory of war*, structuralism shapes the outcomes of the behavior of countries (i.e., the stability of the system or the tendency of the system to war).
Thus, the multipolarity that prevailed in the system from 1910 led the

main players to form alliances and counter alliances. Before the war, the polar powers were divided into two opposing blocks—Germany, Austro-Hungary, and the Ottoman Empire against France, Britain, and Russia—and therefore the conflicts were difficult to prevent because none of the polar powers was prepared to forfeit its allies.[75] Diplomacy was involved in instinctive interactions among the five great powers—Britain, France, Russia, Austro-Hungary, and Germany—and two small powers—Serbia and Belgium. Significant adverse relations appeared—namely, Germany against Britain, France, Russia, and Belgium, and Austro-Hungary against Serbia and Russia[76]—before the war agreements were signed between the great powers, such as the *Triple Alliance* between Germany, Austro-Hungary, and Italy, which was executed in 1882 and renewed in 1902, and the *Entente Cordiale* agreement between France and Britain of 1902.[77] Combined-alliance agreements increased the concern that an Austro-Serbian War might break out with Russia because of its support for Serbia, with Germany because of its support for Austro-Hungary, and with France owing to its support for Russia.[78]

A few years before the outbreak of the First World War, the bipolar system of 1871–1909—headed by the two superpowers that constituted it, Great Britain and (united) Germany—moved away in deference to a multipolar system, in which there were several players. Besides Great Britain, in the system from 1871, Germany, which wanted to compete with it over its international standing and status, was acting in the system. That aspiration was expressed by the declaration of the kaiser of Germany, Wilhelm II, in 1898, that "Germany is destined for important tasks outside the narrow boundaries of old Europe." Russia, which was also a rising power in the early 20th century, expanded and became a threat to Germany. The decline in the power of the Austro-Hungarian Empire, Germany's sole ally, increased Germany's fear of Russia, as expressed by its extreme reaction to the assassination of heir presumptive Archduke Franz Ferdinand. Germany, which feared an undesirable change in the balance of power in the case of a prolonged war, was convinced that a short, limited-scale war, which would end in victory, was possible. Therefore, when the advantages appeared clear, Germany gave Austro-Hungary free rein to crush Serbia. That step was later found to be a gross misjudgment.

For Germany's imperial leaders, the risk posed by giving a free hand made sense from the perspective of preserving the Austro-Hungarian Empire. The crumbling of the empire would have left Germany isolated and without allies. Unfortunately for Germany, the guarantee that it gave Austro-Hungary led to an unexpected response from France and Russia. These two powers joined forces to protect the Slavs. Britain relinquished its traditional *Splendid Isolation Policy* and joined France and Russia in a tripartite agreement resisting Germany and its allies. The immediate aim was to defend Belgium's neutrality. After some time, the war expanded across the ocean, and in 1917, the United States joined the war, in response to Germany's submarine warfare. A global war was fought for the first time.

That chain reaction and the speed of escalation that led to the First World War are consistent with the argument that many researchers have raised in the past that it was an unintentional war. The First World War might have been unintentional, but it was inevitable and not unexpected because of the multipolarity that prevailed at the time. In other words, the European leaders did not have absolute control over their own fate, and the systemic forces pushed them to act in manners that were in conflict with the narrow interests of their own countries. These phenomena, which stemmed directly from the multipolarity that prevailed in those years in the global system of countries, led the system to force the players to wage a central war that none of them wanted or clearly aimed for.

The First World War led to enormous destruction and loss of life—8.5 million dead.[79] At its end, three empires collapsed—the Austro-Hungarian, the Ottoman, and the Russian—and the independent countries of Poland, Czechoslovakia, and Hungary formed in their territories. In addition, the countries of Finland, Estonia, Latvia, and Lithuania were established.[80]

Despite its costs, the coalition that comprised Britain, France, Russia, and later the United States and Italy, was able to defeat the central powers that threatened the member states' dominance—Germany, Austro-Hungary, Turkey, and their allies. Moreover, the war prepared the ground for a determined effort to build a new global system that could have prevented another war. The war caused great revulsion to the war institutes and the realistic theory that justified the competition among the great powers and justified arms races, secret alliances, and balance of power politics. The high costs of the First World War led the decision makers who convened in Versailles Palace to reevaluate the realpolitik assumptions concerning the laws of statesmanship. Instead of that, they tried to remove the threat of another global war and of global dominance using a new plan that was based on liberalism and sought to form political and economic cooperation among the major powers.

Before the First World War, all the major European powers and Serbia preferred a negotiated peace over a global war. However, they found themselves involved in a global war that had enormous human and economic costs, solved little, and formed the scene for another global war two decades later.[81] This unintended consequence, another world war—the Second World War—stemmed primarily from the multipolarity that prevailed in the system in those years rather than the alternative explanations presented above.

The two decades following the First World War were the peak of liberal ideology. The liberal philosophy was reflected in a number of documents and arrangements. I shall mention the more prominent ones: the 14

Points Document of U.S. President Woodrow Wilson; the formation of the League of Nations; the Five-Power Naval Limitation Treaty, which was signed by Japan, Britain, France, Italy, and the United States in Washington in February 1922 and limited the construction of large ships; the Kellogg-Briand Pact of 1928, which legally restricted war as a tool of foreign policy; the Four Power Treaty, which called on Japan, France, Britain, and the United States not to attack each other's colonies; and the Nine Power Treaty, which imposed restrictions on the major powers against occupying additional territories in China. Despite these actions and arrangements, the liberal idealist concept failed and did not prevent new hostility among the major powers. Two decades later, another global war broke out, the Second World War, which I discuss extensively below.

The Second World War

The Second World War was of a global scale. It confronted a fascist coalition that was aspiring for global supremacy—*the axis powers* of Germany, Japan, and Italy—against a broad alliance of four great powers, which was unlikely given their competing ideologies—the Soviet Union's communism and the democratic capitalism of Britain, France, and the United States. The allies achieved success after six hard years of fighting whose cost was enormous and that led to the deaths of tens of millions of people around the world.

In international relations research, there is a prevailing belief that systemic constraints and pressures played an important function in the outbreak of the First World War, whereas systemic factors are not associated with the outbreak of the Second World War. Schweller argues that factors at the system level played an important function in the outbreak of the Second World War as well. Unlike the argument of a few researchers that the system in 1938 was multipolar,[82] Schweller argues that the system in that period was tripolar. He stated that the tripolar structure explains much of the allegiance models and foreign policy strategies of the great powers before and during the war.[83]

Some researchers have pointed at psychological forces that in their view led to the outbreak of the war. Van Evera argues that those forces included the dominance of military propaganda in civil discourse, which prepared the world for war, the enormous wave of ultranationalism that engulfed Europe, and the collapse of democratic regimes.[84]

A number of factors rekindled the German aspirations for hegemony. Domestically, German nationalism increased latent irredentism—an aspiration to annex homeland territories—and justified the expansion of Germany's borders to restore provinces that it had previously lost to other countries in wars and in order to absorb Germans who were living in Austria, Czechoslovakia, and Poland. The growth of fascism drove the renewed imperial effort. This set of beliefs glorified the "common will" of the nation and preached an extreme version of realism, known as "power politics" (in German, *Machtpolitik*), for justifying the forceful expansion of influence of Germany and the other axis powers that were its allies. Germany also rose up against the penalties that were imposed on it by the powers that won the First World War (France, Great Britain, Italy, Japan, and the United States). The Treaty of Versailles (1919) led to destruction of Germany's military forces; a loss of territories, such as the Alsace-Lorraine region, which Germany had annexed after the Franco-Prussian War (1870–1871); and to compensation payments that were imposed on it because of the damage caused by German militarism. The Austro-Hungarian empire was divided into separate political units. The Treaty of Versailles punished Germany, but the most significant and painful fact was that it prevented Germany from returning to the global system as a member of equal standing. It was denied membership in the League of Nations until 1926.

A few researchers argued that the Second World War was not possible without the leader of Nazi Germany and his plan to conquer the world by force. Based on the assertion of German supremacy as a master race and based on anti-Semitism and anticommunism that prevailed in Germany, Hitler chose to start a war to form an empire that in his view could solve once and for all the historical competition and instability of the great powers in Europe and destroy Germany's enemies.[85]

Systemic Analysis of the Outbreak of the Second World War. Before the Second World War, the conflicts were difficult to prevent because it was not clear which polar power or country would join an effort to prevent German power.[86] In addition, before the war, five polar powers acted in Europe—Britain, France, the Soviet Union, Germany, and Italy—and there were also seven small powers—Belgium, Poland, Czechoslovakia, Austria, Hungary, Romania, and Finland. These relations led to a number of conflicts: (1) Germany against Britain, France, the Soviet Union, Czechoslovakia, Poland, and Austria; (2) Czechoslovakia against Poland and Hungary; and (3) Romania against Hungary. The multitude of conflicts increased the chances of outbreak of wars. Many of the interests of the countries in each of these conflicts were mutual and increased the risk that each of the conflicts that became violent would catalyze a total war, which was what indeed happened in 1939. Before the war, Germany could join forces with other countries against a number of small countries and act so that other countries would join it. In 1939, Germany strengthened its power by joining forces with Poland and Hungary to divide Czechoslovakia and then join up with Russia against Poland. In 1938, Germany persecuted the Czech Republic until it surrendered in the Sudetenland and persecuted Austria until its total surrender. Through these successes, Germany broadened its power and became much stronger than its nearby neighbors. Therefore, it made deterrence much more effective.[87]

Multipolarity was the factor that led the winning powers of the First World War to allow Germany to rearm. Because of the multiple players that acted in the system, there was no single party—as is the case in unipolar systems, or two parties, as in the case in bipolar systems—to act to prevent Germany's offensive intentions. Multipolarity forced the players to act toward expansion, such as Germany's actions, and forced the other players not to risk any action to prevent Germany's offensive actions. The British aspiration for Anglo-American cooperation to maintain the world order collapsed after the United States adopted an isolationism policy and abstained from active international involvement. Britain and France employed conflicting strategies toward Germany that reflected their aspirations: France wanted to prevent Germany's return to the international system and revival, whereas Britain preferred to preserve the new balance of power by encouraging Germany's rearmament and recovery, to counteract the case of France or the Soviet Union acting to establish their control of Europe. Reconciliation with Germany's armament led to an appeasement policy toward it that manifested in placating Germany through concessions.

Hitler, who controlled Germany from the mid-1930s, declared that he would not expand Germany's territory by forceful means. He violated that promise in March 1938 when he forced Austria to unite with Germany (the Anschluss). Immediately afterward, he demanded the annexation of Sudetenland in Czechoslovakia, which was populated by Germans. The fear of further German expansion of influence led to the convening of the Munich Conference in September 1938, with the participation of Germany's leader, Hitler, the prime minister of Britain, Chamberlain, and leaders from France and Italy (Czechoslovakia was not invited). Because of the misbelief that appeasement would stop Germany's continued spread and would lead to peace, Chamberlain and the others acquiesced to Hitler's demands.

Not only did appeasement not satisfy Germany, but it also increased its appetite. Germany formed a new fascist coalition with Italy and Japan that was intended to engender a change in the status quo in the world, which was disappointed by Western liberalism and the Paris arrangement and suffered economically following the influences of the Great Depression of the 1930s, turning to militarism. The international climate that formed as a result of Germany's imperialist ambition of national expansion led Japanese nationalism to a policy of imperialism and colonialism. Japan's invasions of Manchuria in 1931 and China in 1937 followed Italy's involvement in Abyssinia in 1935 and in Albania in 1939.

After Germany occupied what was left of Czechoslovakia in March 1939, Britain and France formed an allegiance to defend the next expected victim—Poland. They also commenced negotiations with Moscow, hoping that they would be able to entice the Soviet Union to join the allegiance, but failed. Then, on August 23, 1939, the fascist Hitler and the communist Soviet dictator Josef Stalin amazed the world by signing a nonaggression pact in which they promised not to attack each other. Now, that Hitler was sure that Britain and France would not intervene, he invaded Poland. Britain and France, which honored their promise to defend Poland, declared war on Germany two days later. The Second World War had broken out.

The war quickly spread. Hitler turned his forces to the Balkans, North Africa, and westward, and German forces invaded Norway and crossed Denmark, Belgium, Luxembourg, and the Netherlands. The German army overwhelmed the Maginot Line.[88] In six weeks, France surrendered. The ominous German victory forced the British to evacuate an expeditionary force that consisted of some 340,000 troops and their equipment that were stranded on France's beaches. Paris itself fell in June 1940. At the same time, to make sure that the United States would not participate in the war, in September 1940 a tripartite agreement was signed between Japan, Germany, and Italy, which required each of the three axis countries to help the others if it were attacked by an unallied great power, such as the United States.

In the ensuing months, the German Luftwaffe bombarded Britain in an attempt to force it to surrender. Instead of invading Britain, Germany's forces launched a surprise attack on the Soviet Union, their former ally, in June 1941. On December 7, 1941, Japan launched a surprise attack on the United States at Pearl Harbor. Almost immediately, Germany also declared war on the United States. The Japanese attack on the United States, which was carried out without any provocation like the German challenged, put an end to American isolationism and allowed U.S. President Franklin Roosevelt to form a coalition with Britain and the Soviet Union against the fascists.

The chain of events that led to the outbreak of the Second World War and its expansion to the global world described above stemmed from the multipolarity in the distribution of global power that occurred in the world in the years preceding the war, which was characterized by three aspects: (1) *Atomization of the international system.* After the First World War, sovereign countries, which were divided into smaller components, became too many and of unequal power, particularly after 1919, when the number of great powers decreased and the number of countries formed on their ruins increased. Thus, in 1914, there were just 22 key countries in Europe, and in 1921 the number was nearly doubled; (2) *The absence of global leadership.* The decline of Great Britain as leader of the global economic system and the global economic crisis of the 1930s, combined with the reluctance of its heir, the United States, to lead the system, also catalyzed the war;[89] and (3) *The weakness of institutional barriers.* The failure of the League of Nations to respond collectively to aggressive actions underlined the weakness of the institutional barriers to preventing war. When Germany withdrew from the League of Nations in 1933 and Italy in 1937, war clouds hovered above, and the League of Nations did not have the ability to prevent its outbreak. In response to the Soviet invasion of neutral Finland in 1939, the League of Nations expelled the Soviet Union from its ranks. However, the burden of defense fell on the shoulders of the victims, as tens of thousands of Finns sacrificed their lives fighting the Soviet invasion,[90] while the rest of the world looked on without intervening.

The Multipolar System, 1910–1945—Summary and Consequences.   In May 1945, Germany was devastated. In August that year, the nuclear bombing of Japanese cities Hiroshima and Nagasaki by the United States led to the end of Japan's wars of occupation, America's occupation of Japan, which lasted for six years, and Washington forcing Japan to make social structural changes and adopt new values.

The victory of the allies against the axis powers redistributed power, reshaped borders around the world, and led to new geopolitical territory conditions. The Soviet Union annexed a territory of almost 600,000 square kilometers of the Baltic countries of Estonia, Latvia, and Lithuania and from Finland, Czechoslovakia, Poland, and Romania in response to the loss of territories in the Brest-Litovsk Agreement of 1918, after the First World War. Poland, which was a victim of Soviet expansion, was compensated by territories that were taken from Germany. Germany itself was divided into areas of control that later formed the basis for its division into two countries—East Germany and West Germany. Finally, pro-Soviet regimes formed in Eastern Europe. In the Far East, the Soviet Union took the four Kuril Islands from Japan—the western territories, as they were known by Tokyo—and Korea was divided into Soviet and American occupation zones by the 38th parallel, which division remains to this day.

The First World War, like the wars of great powers or central wars in the past, paved the way to change in global politics. The cooperation between the allies after the war in forming a new international organization for management of the postwar world order led to the formation of the UN organization. In view of the expectation of great powers being able to cooperate in managing the world, China was promised a seat in the UN's Security Council, with France and the three great powers—the United States, Great Britain, and the Soviet Union. The purpose of the Security Council was to ensure that all dominant countries would share the responsibility of keeping peace around the world.

A much more important phenomenon than postwar peace arrangements was the effect of the allies' victory over the systemic change that occurred. At the end of the war, one global system, the multipolar system of 1910–1945, ended, and a new global system, the bipolar system of 1945–1991, started. After the war, the United States and the Soviet Union remained the only two polar powers that were still strong and capable of forcing their will. Two of the defeated powers, Germany and Japan, lost their great power status because of their total defeat in the war. The other victorious great powers, particularly Great Britain and France, had exhausted themselves and also lost their polar power status in the system.

The multipolar system of 1849–1870 was relatively stable, and the wars fought during it and their lethality were relatively limited. The multipolar system of 1910–1945, in contrast, was one of the most unstable in human history, and the danger of multipolarity manifested in it prominently. In that period, two of the bloodiest wars in human history, the First and the Second World Wars, were fought, as well as a large number of major and minor wars.

Many parallels may be drawn between the Crimean War and the First World War. Both wars started as a local conflict between a great power and a small power—Russia and Turkey in 1853 and Austro-Hungary and Serbia in 1914—and both expanded to a major war in the case of the Crimean War and a central war in the case of the First World War in which other great powers were involved.

There is also similarity between the factors that led to the outbreak of both world wars. Each of them broke out for its own unique reasons, but in both cases, the leaders of countries acted rationally for maximizing their own countries' interests. However, the multipolarity of the international system led to two prominent phenomena. On the one hand, it reduced the range of possibilities that the countries had, and on the other hand, it forced them to choose certain options, which in many cases conflicted with their combined interests.

Before both world wars, German power could have withstood the resistance if other European countries had been able to balance it. In such a case, Germany might have been deterred and the wars averted. Despite that, the powers failed twice: before 1914 and before 1939.[91] This double failure, which led to the two bloodiest wars in human history, raises great doubts concerning the ability to explain their outbreak based on the manner of conduct of countries. In contrast, according to the current study, the cause of their outbreak lay in the multipolarity of the system before both cases. In both cases, the multipolarity formed conditions that led to miscalculations that in turn stimulated Germany's aggressiveness.

STABILITY OF INTERNATIONAL SYSTEMS
IN BIPOLAR SYSTEM

Bipolar systems are the most peaceful of the three possible international systems. The existence of just two superpowers constituting bipolar systems minimizes the number of existing bipartite conflicts and reduces the potential for the development of conflicts that may deteriorate into war. In these systems, there is only one relationship throughout which a war between powers may break out: a war between the two competing polar powers. The great powers that are not polar powers in the system are not in a position that allows them to defeat one of the two superpowers. Bipolar systems are rigid. The two polar powers will force the other great powers that are not polar powers to join forces with one of them, and almost no powers that are not aligned with one of the major blocks will remain. The transition from one side to the other is rare too. In addition, great powers have few possibilities of turning the polar powers against each other. This fact leads to the relatively great stability of these systems compared with the other polarity models.[92]

The current study bases its conclusions on three bipolar systems, 1816–1848, 1871–1909, and 1946–1991. The definition of the first two periods as bipolar contrasts this study with most theoretical studies in international relations regarding two main subjects. Firstly, the first two periods are assigned by most international relations theorists to the multipolar model that in their opinion prevailed from the time of the modern states system's formation in 1648 to the end of the Second World War in 1945. The other, the relative stability of these two periods, is attributed by many studies to the European Concert, while the current study attributes it to bipolarity.

The first debate was discussed in chapter 3 (the independent variable, the polarity of the system), in which the discussion of the various polarity models and the definition of these two outcomes as bipolar were presented. Following is the second debate, in which I rule out the alternative explanation in international relations research for the stability of these two periods.

The Stability of the Bipolar System, 1816–1848, 1871–1909

The two long periods of peace in 1816–1848 and 1871–1909 are attributed in the current study to the bipolarity that existed in the system. In theoretical international relations research, in contrast, a number of alternative explanations to this relative calm are commonly accepted. One explanation indicates the equal division of power between the great powers in Europe as a factor for peace and stability. Mearsheimer argues that throughout most of the 19th century until the 1920s, in 1815–1853 and 1891–1914, there was an equal distribution of powers between the European great powers and it was responsible for the peace and stability of the continent. In these two periods, there was no country with hegemonic aspirations in Europe. France, the strongest country in the early 19th century, lost its greatness to assume a position on par with its key rivals, whereas Germany started to appear as a potential hegemon only in the early 20th century.[93] According to the other explanation, the long difficult wars against revolutionary France in 1787–1815 formed an aspiration for peace and diplomatic arrangements, such as the European Concert, and European leaders' understanding the vitality of peace and expressing impressive multilateral support for keeping it.[94] These explanations explicitly rule out any systemic change in international politics in this period in three ways: (1) it is common to consider the arrangement of 1815 as a return of the balance of power that characterized the 18th century and a return to the classic political principles that prevailed in that century;[95] (2) most historians consider the change that occurred after 1815 to be a temporary state of stability and harmony of international politics that started to be destabilized in the 1820s, completely disappeared in 1830, and returned to normal political competition in 1848;[96] and (3) peace and stability are usually explained as being voluntary and a result of tendency more than structuralism, for example, as a result of statesmen choosing to engage in international politics more than actions that the system encouraged them to take or allowed them to take. The plea that the cause of peace in the 19th century was the good mood of European statesmen after 1815 is insufficient because previous European wars were almost always as vicious as those that occurred in 1792–1815, and the 30 Years' War was even worse.[97]

After the end of every major war in 1648, 1714, 1763–1783, 1801, 1807, and 1809, it was statesmen who devised the peace and wanted not only peace treaties but also durable peace arrangements. Therefore, the existence or absence of good will and peaceful intentions are simply insufficient to explain this phenomenon.[98] The spirit of the conservative Holy Alliance cannot explain the international stability of the 19th century either[99] because it never controlled Europe and did not survive the 1848 revolution, whereas the structural changes in the countries that were formed in 1815 did survive. The third explanation includes systemic arguments: (1) the international peace and stability of the 19th century stemmed primarily from a structural change that was reflected in key institutional arrangements and a practical deviation from the norms of the 18th century. The 1815 arrangement did not restore the balance of power of the 18th century, nor did it review the political practices of that century. (2) The European equilibrium that was formed in 1815 and survived the 19th century is completely different from what was known as the balance of power in the 18th century. (3) The systemic changed proved stabile and it existed until the last part of the century, except for the upheavals of 1848–1859 and the wars of 1854–1871.[100] And (4) the most prominent explanation attributed peace and stability in Europe to the existence of the European Concert.[101]

The European Concert occurred in 1815–1914. This was a common action system of the great powers, a policy for peaceful settlement of international problems that was based on cooperation between them[102] and that was performed through ad hoc conferences that were convened when international crises developed.[103] According to Mearsheimer, the Concert worked well in 1815–1823. After 1823, the Concert was able to serve as an effective coordinating instrument for the powers and continued to exist as an unsuccessful model until its final collapse when the Crimean War broke out in 1854.[104] Robert Jervis argues that the European Concert was held in 1815–1854 but was at its best only until 1822.[105] The appearance of the Concert was explained in a number of ways. Some argue that the formation of force-balancing systems or a concert depends on the preferences of the players.[106] At the system level, it is difficult to explain the appearance of the concert. Neorealist theory cannot explain any behavioral difference at the system or unit level before 1945, including the concert system, because its independent variable, the polarity of the system, remained constant throughout that period. Richard Elrod argues that the European Concert was a conscious and usually effective attempt made by European statesmen to maintain the peaceful relations between the sovereign states. According to him, the Concert had an important function in peace and stability in Europe between the Vienna Congress and the Crimean War. The Concert was a functional promising system of international relations that was markedly different from the power-balancing politics of the 18th century and the total wars of the first half of the 20th century.[107]

The two peaceful periods that occurred in the 19th century to the 1920s stemmed from the bipolarity that occurred in them. In 1815–1848 there was a bipolar system headed by Great Britain and Russia, two superpowers. The three alternative explanations that were shown above for the stability of the European system in the 19th century are ruled out, as is the argument that Great Britain served the purpose of suppressing conflicts that a unipolar country can play because even at the peak of its influence, after 1856, it was never a land power.[108]

The Stability of the Bipolar System, 1946–1991

International relations research assumes for the most part that the system in the Cold War period was bipolar and stable. The causes of the stability of this period are disputed. Some researchers assign it to bipolarity and some to the possession of nuclear weapons by the two superpowers that constituted the system, the United States and the Soviet Union. Now the book's argument of bipolarity being the cause of stability in this period will be established as being preferable to the alternative argument that the large arsenal of nuclear weapons that the two superpowers possessed was what caused the relative stability of the period.

The Long Peace in the Cold War Period and Its Causes

The peace of the Cold War strongly contrasted with the European politics of the first half of that century, in which two central wars, the First and the Second World Wars, along with a large number of major or minor wars were fought and several crises nearly led to war. About 50 million

Europeans were killed in the two world wars. Conversely, not more than 4,000 people were killed in the two European conflicts after 1945.[109]

The absence of a major war in Europe in the Cold War period led to its designation as the *long peace* period,[110] and it is attributed in the book to the bipolar system. In international relations research, three key additional alternative explanations are accepted for the relative quiet that prevailed in the global and European system in those years: (1) the supporters of *economic liberalism* argue that liberal economic order leads to peace. The theory will have difficulty explaining this phenomenon because the commerce between the Soviet Union and the West in that period was very limited; (2) the supporters of the *democratic peace theory* argue that democracies do not fight other democracies and are not peaceful when they confront authoritarian countries.[111] The theory would find it difficult to explain this phenomenon because the Soviet Union and its allies in Eastern Europe were not democratic countries in those 45 years; and (3) according to the idea of *obsolescence of war as an institute*,[112] the world has undergone Hollandization in the last few centuries.[113] Major wars became obsolete in the First World War, and the Second World War supported that concept. In 1945, it was obvious that a major war had become irrational and morally unacceptable, like past social institutions, such as dueling and slavery. Therefore, even without the appearance of nuclear weapons, political leaders in the Cold War period did not seriously encourage war and it became an anachronism. Therefore, war between modern Western nations became unacceptable.[114] This is probably the most comprehensive alternative explanation for the stability of the Cold War, but it is not completely convincing. The fact that the Second World War was fought sheds great doubt as to the validity of the theory, inasmuch as if any war could convince the Europeans to waive conventional wars, the First World War and its many victims would have done it.[115]

STABILITY OF INTERNATIONAL SYSTEMS IN UNIPOLAR SYSTEM

For neorealism, unipolarity is the least stable system because any large concentration of power threatens the other states operating in the system, makes them form a counterposition to the absolute power of the leading state, and leads them to take actions for restoring the balance.[116] At the other end is the *hegemonic stability theory*, under which unipolar systems are the most stable because any large concentration of power leads to peace.[117]

The *international relations theory of war* presents an opinion that opposes these two views. According to it, unipolar systems are on a continuum. They will be less stable than bipolar systems but more stable than multipolar ones because of the two systemic principles affecting the players in the system—*anarchy*, which spurs the powers to tend to hegemony, and *homeostasis*, which dictates to powers to operate to maintain the existing state of the system.

Hyperpowers in a unipolar world will not be able to escape their prominent status in the system, which requires them to prove their leadership constantly. If their leadership is weakened, they will be challenged by the second-level powers, which will try to exploit the opportunity to relegate them to second level and take their place. These two constraints, which were ostensibly supposed to lead to constant wars in the system, are mitigated by the power of the hyperpower. However, even if hyperpowers in unipolar systems behave with moderation, weak countries will fear their future behavior. This fear will lead to weak countries in the system to attempt to increase their power, or join forces with other countries through alliances, in order to restore the balance of the distribution of international power in the system.

The presence of one hyperpower that constitutes the system increases the number of possible bipartite relationships between it and second-level powers, and ostensibly increases the potential for the development of conflicts that may deteriorate into war. Whereas unipolar systems will spur hyperpowers to act to form hegemony headed by them in the face of *anarchy*, at the same time they will dictate acting to preserve the unipolarity owing to the other order principle, *homeostasis*. These two phenomena will lead to the relative stability of unipolar systems, their slow movement until their collapse, and a change in the polarity model to one of the two other possible models—a multipolar or bipolar system.

Unipolar systems will dictate to each hyperpower to tend always to expansion irrespective of its regime model—democratic or authoritarian.

The Stability of the Unipolar System, 1992–2016

The stability of the unipolar system has gained two extreme hypotheses. On the one hand, realism predicts instability.[118] Mearsheimer warned that "we shall miss the Cold War" all too soon, the onset of multipolarity leading to a strong chance of the outbreak of a major war in multipolar Europe.[119] On the other hand, Wohlforth argues that the current unipolarity is peaceful because the excess raw power of the United States means that no country will tend to perform any action that might cause the United States to resist it. At the same time, unipolarity minimizes security competition among the other great powers.[120]

According to the current study, Wohlforth's conclusion that unipolar systems are the most stable is wrong because it makes no distinction between unipolar systems and hegemonic systems. In hegemonic systems, there is a single power whose absolute superiority nullifies the threats of other countries to its status. In unipolar systems, there might be just one polar power, the sole hyperpower, which has very high power, but at the same time, there are other great powers acting in the system. Because unipolar systems are not hegemonic systems, the hyperpower will be constantly challenged by countries and great powers that will not accept it supremacy and will attempt to undermine it. This impulse will lead the hyperpower to wider military involvement than Wohlforth's forecast and this in turn will lead to partial destabilization of the system.

The Unipolar System and American Involvement

The American policy in the 1990s led it not to intervene excessively in events in the global scene. In this period, the United States might have understood that it was the sole polar power in a unipolar system. Conversely, it might have considered itself to be able to maintain its status as the leader of the system without "getting its hands dirty" in large-scale military involvements "far" from its own soil. Regardless of the reason for Washington's distance from military involvements in the 1990s, it may be shown that this system has not left it any possibility other than active involvement.

Persian Gulf Region.   The Gulf War (1991) ended in April 1991, the United States maintaining Iraq's territorial integrity and abstaining from occupying it after a ground invasion. However, after that war ended and until the Iraq War (2003) in which the United States conquered Iraq, Washington had to be involved five more times in crises in the region and use military power in them:

1. Iraq no-fly zone, a crisis that took place from August 18 to September 8, 1992, concerning the no-fly zone for Iraqi aircraft, which was forced by the United States (and Great Britain and France).[121]
2. Iraq troop deployment—Kuwait, a crisis that took place from October 7 to November 10, 1994, involving Kuwait, Saudi Arabia, the United States, and Iraq. The president of Iraq caused the crisis in order to pressure the United States and the international community to remove the sanctions imposed on his country.[122]
3. Desert Strike, from August 31 to September 14, 1996, involving the United States and Iraq in an international crisis, alongside significant involvement of Iran and Turkey. On August 31, 1996, approximately 40,000 Iraqi troops intervened in the Kurdish Civil War. The involvement was north of the 36th parallel, which was an area protected by the 1991 agreements. This motivated the United States to intervene in the crisis and led to a coalition of countries that forced constraints on Iraq's involvement by unilateral bombing of Iraqi military forces and air defense systems.[123]

4. UNSCOM I, between the United States and Iraq from November 13, 1997, to February 23, 1998. The crisis stemmed from the repeat obstacles that Iraq set before the operations of the United Nations forces (UNSCOM). The force operated in accordance with Resolution 687, which called Iraq to waive its weapons of mass destruction. The United States' response was decisive and included deploying many forces to the region.[124]

5. UNSCOM II Operation Desert Fox, held between the United States and Iraq from October 31 to December 20, 1998. The crisis resulted from Iraq violating the agreement that was achieved after the previous crisis concerning UN inspectors (UNSCOM I, ICB #422). During it, British and American forces attacked more than 90 Iraqi targets over a course of 72 hours.[125]

Thus, the United States' involvement in the Persian Gulf in the 1990s was comprehensive. On the one hand, in accordance with the *anarchy principle*, the unipolar system spurred the players in the system, in this case, Iraq, to apply positive feedback models (i.e. contest the supremacy of the sole hyperpower, the United States). On the other hand, according to the *homeostasis principle*, the system dictated to the United States to apply negative feedback models for restoring the system to a balance.

East Asia Region.   The status of the United States as the sole hyperpower in a unipolar system forced it to intervene in the 1990s in crises that occurred in East Asia too. North Korea Nuclear I, which involved North Korea, South Korea, and the United States (from March 1993 to October 21, 1994), threatened the United States' supremacy in the world order following the Cold War.[126]

Military Involvements of the United States

In the 1990s, the United States "disavowed" its many duties as the leader of the international system. It abstained from employing its power around the world and behaved in contravention of the expectation for the leading power of the system.

This pattern of behavior of the United States led the system to spur the other players in it to challenge its leadership and apply positive feedback models. Terrorist acts against the United States by Islamic organizations, such as Al Qaeda, are feedback models that the system spurred the players to take in order to contest the leadership of the sole hyperpower, the United States. Examples include attacks against the American forces in Somalia in 1993;[127] the attacks against the U.S. embassies in Nairobi, Kenya, and Dar es Salam in Tanzania on August 7, 1998; [128] the bombing of the destroyer USS Cole off Yemen on October 12, 2000, and an attempt to carry out a similar attack against the destroyer USS The Sullivans, which was docked at Eden Port for refueling;[129] and the terrorist attacks of September 11, 2001, in the heart of the United States, which were the most devastating of this type ever.[130]

Following a series of positive feedback actions taken by a number of terrorist organizations against the United States, primarily the September 11, 2001, terrorist attacks and the fear that they might destabilize the global balance, the system dictated to the United States to take significant positive feedback actions, which it took to maintain the homeostasis: (1) The U.S. invasion of Afghanistan, which was intended to uproot Al Qaeda from Afghanistan because of its responsibility for the terrorist attacks of September 11, 2001, described above;[131] and (2) the U.S. invasion of Iraq, which was a direct follow-on of the terrorist attacks of September 11, 2001. These events highlighted the need to prevent the proliferation of weapons of mass destruction, and primarily to prevent their transfer to Islamic terrorist organizations. Although there was no significant proof implicating Iraq in supporting Al Qaeda or the terrorist incidents of September 11, Iraq was perceived thereafter as a country posing a potential threat to the United States' national security.[132]

THE STABILITY OF INTERNATIONAL SYSTEMS— CONCLUSIONS

Table 4.7 shows the stability of the six instances of the three different models of polarity in 1816–2016 according to the *international relations theory of war*.

Table 4.8 shows the stability of the three different polarity models in 1816–2016 according to the *international relations theory of war*.

Based on the discussion held in the last chapter, Table 4.9 concentrates the arguments of the various realist theories concerning the degree of stability of the various polarity models compared with the *international relations theory of war*.

Systemic Factors and Territorial Outcomes of Wars

In the course of human history, certain periods have been characterized by the territorial expansion of the polar powers at the end of wars, whereas other periods have been characterized by their territorial nonexpansion. The comparison of the bipolar system of the Cold War period with the unipolar system thereafter, for example, shows significant differences in the territorial outcomes of polar wars. In the bipolar system, the Soviet Union's war in Afghanistan ended in maintaining of the territorial status quo, whereas the United States' war in Afghanistan in the unipolar system ended in territorial expansion of the polar power, the United States, despite Afghanistan's being located in the Soviet Union's backyard

Table 4.7

Causes of War by Periods, 1816–2016

Type of Polarity	Number of Wars			Length of the System in Years	Frequency of Wars		Average Length of wars	Severity of the Wars
The Six Instances of Polarity, 1816–2016	Central Wars	Major Wars	Minor Wars		War Years[1]	% of Years in which a War Was Fought[2]	Average Length in Days	Total Killed in Combat Only
Bipolarity, 1816–1848	0	0	1	33	1.4	4%	507	130,000
Multipolarity, 1849–1870	0	5	0	22	3.6	16%	1,312/5=262.5	539,594
Bipolarity, 1871–1909	0	0	0	39	0	0	0	0
Multipolarity, 1910–1945	2	2	9	36	22.5	62%	8,230/13=633	26,639,062
Bipolarity, 1946–1991	0	0	4	46	11.3	25%	4,135/4=1,033	1,975,418
Unipolarity, 1992–2016	2[3]			24	3.1	13%	1,125/2=562.5	39,092

1 The war years were calculated by dividing the total number of days by 365 (the length of one year). The bipolar system 1816–1853: a total of 507 days of war, or 1.4 years of war; the multipolar system of 1854–1870: a total of 1,312 days of war, or 3.6 years of war; the bipolar system of 1871–1909: a total of 0 days of war, or 0 years of war; the multipolar system of 1910–1945: a total of 8,210 days of war, or 22.5 years of war; the bipolar system of 1946–1991: a total of 4,148 days of war, or 11.4 years of war; the unipolar system of 1992–2016: a total of 1,125 days of war, or 3.1 years of war.

2 The percentage of years in which a war was fought was calculated by dividing the years of war by the length of the system in years. The bipolar system of 1816–1853: 1.4 years of war out of 38 years—4%; the multipolar system of 1854–1870: 3.6 years of war out of 17 years—21%; the bipolar system of 1871–1909: 0 years of war out of 39 years—0%; the multipolar system of 1910–1945: 22.5 years of war out of 36 years—62%; the bipolar system of 1946–1991: 11.4 years of war out of 46 years—25%; the unipolar system of 1992–2016: 3.1 years of war out of 24 years—13%.

3 In unipolar systems, every war involving the polar power, or the sole hyperpower constituting the system, may be included in the three categories of war: central war, major war, or minor war. Therefore, the three cells relating to the two wars in which the sole hyperpower, the United States, in the unipolar system of 1992–2016, were merged.

Table 4.8

Causes of War by Polarity Models, 1816–2016

Type of Polarity	Number of Wars				Frequency of Wars		Average Length of Wars	Severity of the Wars
The three Polarity Models, 1816–2016	Central Wars	Major Wars	Minor Wars	Length of the System in Years	War Years[1]	% of Years in which a War Was Fought	Average Length in Days[2]	Total Killed in Combat Only
Multipolarity, 1849–1870, 1910–1945	2	7	9	58	26.1	45%	9,542/18=530	27,178,565
Bipolarity, 1816–1848, 1871–1909, 1946–1991	0	0	5	118	12.8	10.8%	4,642/5=928	2,105,418
Unipolarity, 1992–2016	2[3]			24	3.1	13%	1,125/2=562.5	39,092

1 The total number of years in which there was a war in any of the three polarity models was calculated by dividing the total number of days of war in them by 365 (the length of one year). Multipolar systems: 1854–1870 and 1909–1945: a total of 9,522 days of war, or 26.1 years of war; bipolar systems: 1816–1853, 1871–1909, and 1946–1991: a total of 4,922 days of war, or 12.8 years of war; unipolar systems: 1992–2016: a total of 1,125 days of war, or 3.1 years of war.

2 The average length of the wars in days was calculated by dividing the total number of days of war by the number of wars fought in each of the three polarity models. Multipolar systems: 1854–1870 and 1909–1945: a total of 18 wars lasting 9,522 days of fighting—average length of 529 days per war; bipolar systems: 1816–1853, 1871–1909, and 1946–1991: a total of six wars lasting 4,655 days of fighting—average length of 931 days per war; unipolar systems: 1992–2016: a total of two wars lasting 1,125 days of fighting—average length of 562.5 days per war.

3 In unipolar systems, every war involving the polar power, or the sole hyperpower constituting the system, may be included in the three categories of war: central war, major war, or minor war. Therefore, the three cells relating to the two wars in which the sole hyperpower, the United States, in the unipolar system of 1992–2016, were merged.

and an enormous distance from the United States, which should have led to an opposite result. In the same manner, the United States' war against Iraq in the bipolar system (the Gulf War, 1991) ended with maintaining of the territorial status quo, whereas the United States' war against the same country about a decade later in the unipolar system (the Iraq War, 2003) ended in the territorial expansion of the polar power. The objective capabilities of polar powers to expand territorially at the end of wars in which they participate are well known, but the territorial outcomes of these wars are not constant, inasmuch as each of the three polarity models dictates different territorial outcomes.

The theoretical discussion of international relations research concerning territorial expansion at the end of the wars of the polar powers is limited. The *international relations theory of war* offers its assumptions concerning all three possible polarity models. Anarchy alone cannot explain why wars of polar powers sometimes end in territorial expansion and sometimes do not, because anarchy is constant whereas the patterns of the territorial outcomes vary. To explain this significant difference in the territorial outcomes of the wars of polar powers the theory adds a systemic variable: distribution of the power between the polar powers, or the polarity of the system. To examine the effect of the distribution of power over the territorial outcomes of wars, we must identify the polarity of the system at each point in time, and in other words, determine whether the system is multipolar, bipolar, or unipolar.

Confirmation of the argument that the polarity of the system is the factor that affects the territorial outcomes of wars of polar powers is possible through reliance on studies in which broad databases have been developed and various aspects of wars discussed. Only through empiric studies is it possible to identify possible patterns, trends, or causes that lead to the different territorial outcomes of the wars of polar powers.

Table 4.9

Stability of International Systems According to Various Realist Theories

	Multipolarity		Bipolarity	Unipolarity
Morgenthau	The most stable		Less stable than multipolar	******
Waltz	The most destabilized		The most stable	Nonexistent
Mearsheimer	**Balanced**	**Unbalanced**	The most stable	Nonexistent
	Partly destabilized	The most destabilized		
Wohlforth	******		******	The most stable
Israeli	The most destabilized		The most stable	Partly destabilized

In the current subchapter, the degree of territorial expansion of the polar powers at the end of the wars in which they participated is assessed by examining all instances of a given polarity model in the period assessed in the study, 1816–2016. In this subchapter I also present the causal explanation of my theory for the events.

We now turn to empiric assessment of the systemic dependent variable— the degree of territorial expansion of polar powers at the end of wars.

I should note that in a bilateral relationship in a war in which there are just two players, there may be two or more different territorial changes. In a war involving two polar powers, the expansion of one polar power and the contraction of the other polar power may occur. In a bilateral relationship involving more than two polar powers and an additional number of players that are not polar powers, the number of territorial changes that may occur is greater than the total number of players. One polar power may expand at the expense of the other parties involved, whereas other players may expand at the expense of one or more polar powers.

TERRITORIAL OUTCOMES OF WARS OF POLAR POWERS—QUANTITATIVE ASSESSMENT

The quantitative check that is done in the current subchapter attempts to prove the existence of correlation between the study assumption concerning territorial outcomes of the wars of polar powers in the three international model systems and the empiric results of those systems: bipolar systems as systems that encourage the preservation of the territorial status quo that preceded the outbreak of the war at the end of wars of polar powers; unipolar systems as systems that encourage territorial expansion of polar powers at the end of wars; and multipolar systems as systems that encourage nonexpansion (territorial contraction or status quo) at the end of central wars or as systems that allow for territorial expansion at the end of major or minor wars.

TERRITORIAL OUTCOMES IN MULTIPOLAR SYSTEMS

Territorial Outcomes in the Multipolar System, 1849–1870

The multipolar system of 1849–1870 occurred in Eurasia. During it, 13 wars were fought between countries worldwide. Five of them were fought in Europe and involved at least one of the five polar powers that constituted the system: Great Britain, France, Russia, Prussia, and Austro-Hungary.

Table 4.10 shows the territorial outcomes of the wars that involved the great powers that constituted the multipolar system that existed in Eurasia in 1849–1870.

Table 4.10

Territorial Expansion of Polar Powers, 1849–1870

War#[1]	Winning Side	Losing Side	Type of Territorial Exchanged[2]	Process of Territorial Change[3]						Type of Change[4]
				1 Conquest	2 Annexation	3 Cession	4 Secession	5 Unification	6 Mandated Territory	
Crimean (#22)	Turkey	Russia	1			12,264				Russia: −1
Crimean (#22)	Turkey	Russia	1			18,557				Russia: −1
Italian Unification (#28)	Sardinia/ Piedmont	Austria-Hungary	1			21,595				Austria-Hungary: −1
Second Schleswig-Holstein (#46)	Prussia	Denmark	1			1,046				Prussia:1
Second Schleswig-Holstein (#46)	Prussia	Denmark	1			9,194				Prussia:1
Second Schleswig-Holstein (#46)	Austria-Hungary	Denmark	1			8,534				Austria-Hungary:1
Seven Weeks (#55)*	Prussia	Hanover	1(Full)	38,474						Prussia:1
Seven Weeks (#55)*	Prussia	State 247	1(Full)		101					Prussia:1

Seven Weeks (#55)*	Prussia	State 254	1(Full)	4,709	Prussia:1
Seven Weeks (#55)*	Prussia	Hesse Electoral	1(Full)	9,586	Prussia:1
Seven Weeks (#55)	Prussia	Austria-Hungary	1	8,537	Prussia:1 Austria-Hungary: −1
Seven Weeks (#55)	Italy	Austria-Hungary	1	25,145	Italy:1 Austria-Hungary: −1
Franco-Prussian (#58)	Prussia	France	1	14,452	Prussia:1 France: −1
Franco-Prussian (#58)*	Prussia	Bavaria	1(Full)	76,073	Prussia:1
Franco-Prussian (#58)*	Prussia	Baden	1(Full)	15,311	Prussia:1
Franco-Prussian (#58)*	Prussia	Wuerttemburg	1(Full)	50,526	Prussia:1

1 The events marked with an asterisk (*) did not occur during the war stated but after it.

2 The type of change for the winning country: 0 for other territory; 1 for own territory. When the full territory was transferred, the reason is stated.

3 The degree of territorial change is stated in square kilometers.

4 The change model concerning the polar powers only: territorial expansion—1; territorial contraction——1; territorial status quo—0.

Table 4.11

Territorial Expansion of Polar Powers, 1910–1945 (first figure out of three)[1]

War#[2]	Winning Side	Losing Side	Type of Territorial Exchanged[3]	Process of Territorial Change[4]						Type of Change[5]
				1 Conquest	2 Annexation	3 Cession	4 Secession	5 Unification	6 Mandated Territory	
Italian-Turkish War (#97)	Italy	Turkey	0 (Full)	(Libya) 1,051,539						Italy:1
Italian-Turkish War (#97)	Italy	Turkey	0	(3353) 2,681						Italy:1
First World War (#106)	Belgium	Germany 1				1,000				Germany: −1
First World War (#106)	France	Germany 1				14,514				France:1 Germany: −1
First World War (#106)	Poland	Germany 1				420,000				Germany: −1
First World War (#106)	France	Germany 0 (Full)				(256) 1,945				France:1 Germany: −1
First World War (#106)	State 291	Germany 1 (Full)				(291) 2,056				Germany: −1
First World War (#106)	Italy	Austria 1				18,941				Italy:1

First World War (#106)	Italy	Austria	1 (Full)	(326) 96	Italy:1
First World War (#106)	France	Germany	0 (Full)	(Togo) 56,600	France:1 Germany: –1
First World War (#106)*	Britain	Germany	0 (Full)	(462) 32,634	Britain:1 Germany: –1
First World War (#106)*	France	Germany	0 (Full)	(Cameroon) 432,012	France:1 Germany: –1
First World War (#106)*	Britain	Germany	0 (Full)	(472) 80,290	Britain:1 Germany: –1

1 Due to the large amount of data, the presentation of data of the multipolar system of 1910–1945 was divided into three charts.

2 The events marked with an asterisk did not occur during the war stated but after it.

3 The type of change for the winning country: 0 for other territory; 1 for own territory. When the full territory was transferred, the reason is stated.

4 The degree of territorial change is stated in square kilometers.

5 The change model concerning the polar powers only: territorial expansion—1; territorial contraction— –1; territorial status quo—0.

Table 4.12

Territorial Expansion of Polar Powers, 1910–1945 (second figure out of three)

War#[1]	Winning Side	Losing Side	Type of Territorial Exchanged[2]	Process of Territorial Change[3]						Type of Change[4]
				1 Conquest	2 Annexation	3 Cession	4 Secession	5 Unification	6 Mandated Territory	
First World War (#106)	France	Germany	0			(480) 259,000				France: 1 Germany: −1
First World War (#106)	Portugal	Germany	0			(Mozambique) 1,040				Germany: −1
First World War (#106)*	South Africa	Germany	0 (Full)						(Namibia) 822,907	Germany: −1
First World War (#106)*	Australia	Germany	0 (Full)						(Nauru) 21	Germany: −1
First World War (#106)*	Denmark	Germany	1			3,800				Germany: −1
First World War (#106)*	Britain	Germany	0 (Full)						(Tanzania) 939,361	Britain: 1 Germany: −1
First World War (#106)*	Britain	Turkey	0 (Full)						(Iraq) 280,031	Britain:1
First World War (#106)*	France	Turkey	0 (Full)						(Syria) 184,920	France: 1
First World War (#106)*	Britain	Turkey	0 (Full)						(Jordan) 89,484	Britain: 1
First World War (#106)*	Britain	Turkey	0 (Full)						(Israel) 23,310	Britain: 1

War (number)	Winner	Opposing country	Type of change	Degree of territorial change (km²)	Change model (polar powers)
First World War (#106)*	Australia	Germany	0 (Full)	(912) 240,870	Germany: –1
First World War (#106)*	Japan	Germany	0 (Full)	(980) 2,476	Japan: 1 Germany: –1
First World War (#106)*	New Zealand	Germany	0 (Full)	(Samoa) 2,823	Germany: –1
Russo-Polish War (#109)	Poland	USSR	1	113,722	USSR: –1
Franco-Turkish War (#116)	Equality	Equality			0
Manchurian War (#118)	USSR	China			0
Second Sino-Japanese War (#121)	Japan	China	1 (Full)	(711) 1,302,292	Japan: 1
Conquest of Ethiopia War (#127)	Italy	Ethiopia	0 (Full)	906,499	Italy: 1
Third Sino-Japanese War (#130)	Japan	China	1	1,500,000	Japan: 1

1 The events marked with an asterisk did not occur during the war stated but after it.

2 The type of change for the winning country: 0 for other territory; 1 for own territory. When the full territory was transferred, the reason is stated.

3 The degree of territorial change is stated in square kilometers.

4 The change model concerning the polar powers only: territorial expansion—1; territorial contraction——1; territorial status quo—0.

Table 4.13

Territorial Expansion of Polar Powers, 1910–1945 (third figure out of three)

War#[1]	Winning Side	Losing Side	Type of Territorial Exchanged[2]	Process of Territorial Change[3]						Type of Change[4]
				1 Conquest	2 Annexation	3 Cession	4 Secession	5 Unification	6 Mandated Territory	
Changkufeng War (#133)	Japan	USSR								0
Nomonhan War (#136)	USSR, Mongolia	Japan								0
Second World War (#139)	Ethiopia	Italy	1 (Full)			906,499				Italy: −1
Second World War (#139)*	U.N.	Germany	Unknown (Full)	472,605						Germany: −1
Second World War (#139)	Poland	Germany	1			102,556				Germany: −1
Second World War (#139)	USSR	Germany	1			13,000				USSR: 1 Germany: −1
Second World War (#139)*	U.N.	Germany	Unknown (Full)			(Austria) 83,869				Germany: −1
Second World War (#139)	Czechoslovakia	Germany	1 (Full)			(Czechoslovakia) 127,860				Germany: −1
Second World War (#139)	Albania	Germany	1 (Full)			(Albania) 28,748				Germany: −1

Second World War (#139)	China	Japan	1	(China) 1,500,000	Japan: −1
Second World War (#139)	China	Japan	1 (Full)	(Taiwan) 35,763	Japan: −1
Second World War (#139)	U.N.	Japan	Unknown (Full)	(Korea) 220,891	Japan: −1
Second World War (#139)	U.N.	Japan	Unknown	(Japan) 371,205	Japan: −1
Second World War (#139)	USSR	Japan	1	(Japan) 41,063	USSR: 1 Japan: −1
Second World War (#139)	U.S.	Japan	0 (Full)	(741) 2,354	U.S.: 1 Japan: −1
Russo-Finnish War (#142)	USSR	Finland			0
Franco-Thai War (#145)	Thailand	France			0

1 The events marked with an asterisk did not occur during the war stated but after it.

2 The type of change for the winning country: 0 for other territory; 1 for own territory. When the full territory was transferred, the reason is stated.

3 The degree of territorial change is stated in square kilometers.

4 The change model concerning the polar powers only: territorial expansion—1; territorial contraction— −1; territorial status quo—0.

Territorial Outcomes in the Multipolar System, 1910–1945

In the multipolar system of 1910–1945, 20 wars were fought between countries around the world. This is the first system that was not confined to Europe and covered the whole world. Therefore, the assessment of all wars between countries that were fought worldwide and involved one of the seven polar powers constituting the system—the United States, Russia (later to be the Soviet Union), Germany, Britain, France, Japan, and Italy—were included.[133]

Thirteen wars included at least one polar power out of the seven great powers constituting the system and were therefore included in the assessment.

Tables 4.11, 4.12, and 4.13 show the territorial outcomes of the wars involving the great powers constituting the multipolar system that prevailed worldwide in 1910–1945.

TERRITORIAL OUTCOMES IN BIPOLAR SYSTEMS

Territorial Outcomes in the Bipolar System, 1816–1848

In the bipolar system of 1816–1848, seven wars were fought between countries.

Table 4.14 shows the territorial outcomes of the wars that involved the great powers constituting the bipolar system that prevailed in Eurasia in 1816–1848. This system did not include the whole world but represents the international system in that period.

Territorial Outcomes in the Bipolar System, 1871–1909

Under the bipolar system that prevailed in Eurasia in 1871–1909 and consisting of two polar powers, Great Britain and Germany as two super-powers, 16 wars were fought between countries around the world. None of the 16 wars were included in the assessment because they were fought outside of the European system that represented the international system in those years or they did not include at least one of the two polar powers constituting the system, Great Britain or Germany, the two superpowers.

Table 4.15 shows the territorial outcomes of the wars of the polar powers in the bipolar system that prevailed in Europe in 1871–1909. This system did not include the entire world but it represents the international system of that period.

Territorial Outcomes in the Bipolar System, 1946–1991

The bipolar system of 1946–1991 occurred throughout the world. It had two polar powers: the United States and the Soviet Union, the two

Table 4.14

Territorial Expansion of Polar Powers, 1816–1848

War#	Winning Side	Losing Side	Type of Territorial Ex-changed[1]	Process of Territorial Change[2]						Type of Change[3]
				1 Conquest	2 Annexation	3 Cession	4 Secession	5 Unification	6 Mandated Territory	
First Russo-Turkish (#4)	Russia	Ottoman Empire	1 (Middle East)			8,580				0

1 The type of change for the winning country: 0 for other territory; 1 for own territory. When the full territory was transferred, the reason is stated.

2 The degree of territorial change is stated in square kilometers.

3 The change model concerning the polar powers only: territorial expansion—1; territorial contraction— –1; territorial status quo—0.

Table 4.15

Territorial Expansion of Polar Powers, 1871–1909

War#	Winning Side	Losing Side	Type of Territorial Exchanged	Process of Territorial Change						Type of Change
				1 Conquest	2 Annexation	3 Cession	4 Secession	5 Unification	6 Mandated Territory	

superpowers that constituted the system. During it, 23 wars were fought between countries around the world.

Table 4.16 shows the territorial outcomes of the wars of the polar powers in the bipolar system that prevailed around the world in 1946–1991.

TERRITORIAL OUTCOMES IN UNIPOLAR SYSTEMS

Territorial Outcomes in the Unipolar System, 1992–2016

In the unipolar system of 1992–2016, two wars were fought between countries around the world in which the only polar power constituting the system—the United States as the sole hyperpower—was involved.

Table 4.17 shows the territorial outcomes of the wars in which the only hyperpower constituting the unipolar system of 1992–2016 was involved.

TERRITORIAL OUTCOMES OF WARS OF POLAR POWERS—QUALITATIVE ASSESSMENT

The qualitative assessment conducted in the current subchapter attempts to prove causality between the study assumption concerning the various territorial outcomes of wars of polar powers in the three international system models and the empiric outcomes in those systems: bipolar systems as systems that encourage the preservation of the territorial status quo preceding the war at the end of wars of polar powers; unipolar systems as systems that encourage territorial expansion of polar powers at the end of wars of the sole polar power; multipolar systems as systems that encourage nonexpansion (territorial contraction or status quo) at the end of central wars or as systems that allow for territorial expansion at the end of major or minor wars. The qualitative assessment is conducted by assessing a limited number of important wars in which the polar powers constituting the six instances of the three possible international system models in the period examined in the study, 1816–2016, participated.

I chose to examine the territorial outcomes of the wars involving polar powers using a qualitative assessment of five wars out of the three possible system models. The purpose of this procedure is to prove one of the arguments of the study that different international systems encourage different territorial outcomes at the end of the wars involving polar powers. This assessment was done based on the difference method and involved assessment of wars in which polar powers out of the three possible polarity methods fought against a small country, Afghanistan: the First Anglo-Afghan War (1838–1842), in the bipolar system of 1816–1848; the Second

Table 4.16

Territorial Expansion of Polar Powers, 1946–1991

War#	Winning Side	Losing Side	Type of Territorial Exchanged[1]	Process of Territorial Change						Type of Change[2]
				1 Conquest	2 Annexation	3 Cession	4 Secession	5 Unification	6 Mandated Territory	
Korea (#151)	Equality	Equality								0
Soviet Invasion of Hungary (#156)	USSR	Hungary								0
Vietnam (#163)	Vietnam	United States, Cambodia, South Korea, Philippines, South Vietnam, Thailand, Australia.								0
Gulf (#211)	Kuwait, United States, Canada, United Kingdom, Italy, Morocco, Egypt, Oman, France, United Arab Emirates, Qatar, Saudi Arabia, Syria	Iraq								0

1 The type of change for the winning country: 0 for other territory; 1 for own territory. When the full territory was transferred, the reason is stated.

2 The change model concerning the polar powers only: territorial expansion—1; territorial contraction— –1; territorial status quo—0.

Table 4.17

Territorial Expansion of Polar Powers, 1992–2016

War#	Winning Side	Losing Side	Type of Territorial Exchanged[1]	Process of Territorial Change						Type of Change[2]
				1 Conquest	2 Annexation	3 Cession	4 Secession	5 Unification	6 Mandated Territory	
Invasion of Afghanistan (#225)	Canada, France, United Kingdom, U.S., Australia	Afghanistan	1	*						U.S.: 1
Invasion of Iraq (#227)	Australia, United Kingdom, U.S.	Iraq	1	*						U.S.: 1

1 Type of change: the type of change for the winning country. 0 for other territory; 1 for own territory. When the full territory was transferred, the reason is stated.

2 The change model concerning the polar powers only: territorial expansion—1; territorial contraction—–1; territorial status quo—0.

Anglo-Afghan War (1878–1880), in the bipolar system of 1871–1909; the Third Anglo-Afghan War (1919), in the multipolar system of 1910–1945; the Soviet-Afghan War (1979–1988), in the bipolar system of 1946–1991; and, the U.S.-Afghan War (2001), in the unipolar system of 1992–2016. In all five cases, all variables are held constant except for the explanatory variable, the polarity of the international systems, which varies among the five test cases. The difference in the explanatory variable helps prove the differences among the territorial outcomes of these five wars.

TERRITORIAL OUTCOMES IN MULTIPOLAR SYSTEMS

All three possible models of wars may occur under multipolar systems—central wars, major wars, and minor wars. These systems will *dictate* two key territorial outcomes in accordance with the war model. *Multipolar systems* will *dictate* a single territorial outcome of the great powers constituting them at the end of all *central wars* in which they are involved—prevention of territorial expansion that will result in a *status quo* or *territorial contraction*—because any other result will promote the expanding power to the status of a potential hegemon in the system, which may lead to the collapse of the system, a result that the *homeostasis principle* dictates to players to act to prevent. In multipolar systems, great powers will also be *penalized* if they try to expand territorially at the end of central wars and will be *forced* to contract territorially at the end of these wars.

In the period assessed in the study, 1816–2016, there were two multipolar systems, 1849–1870 and 1910–1945. In that period there were two central wars, the First and the Second World Wars, and both were fought in the late multipolar system of 1910–1945. In the end, the great powers that aspired to expand territorially in the war had to contract territorially or preserve the territorial status quo that occurred before their outbreak. Germany was forced to contract territorially at the end of the two world wars, and Japan had to contract territorially at the end of the Second World War.

Territorial expansion is not a possibility at the end of *central wars* that will be fought in multipolar systems because it would lead to a rise in its total intensity and violate the equilibrium, endangering the homeostasis, which would dictate to the players to act to reduce it. In the period assessed in the study, 1816–2016, there were two multipolar systems, 1849–1870 and 1910–1945. In that period, many major and minor wars were fought. At the end of these wars, the system allowed for the territorial expansion of the great powers: in the multipolar system of the 19th century, the system allowed Prussia to expand territorially in its unification wars; in the multipolar system of the 20th century, the system allowed Italy to expand in its war against Ethiopia (1935–1936).

Territorial expansion of great powers at the end of major or minor wars in multipolar systems stems from the way in which multipolar systems affect the values of the two transhistorical order principles that constantly act in the international system. While the *anarchy principle* will spur the great powers to tend always to expansion through their enormous capabilities, this result will not conflict with the other order principle, *homeostasis*, inasmuch as an increase in the land force of great powers at the end of major or minor wars is unlikely to lead to the collapse of the system—a result that the *homeostasis principle* does not resist and therefore allows it to occur.

The Multipolar System, 1849–1870

Out of the five wars fought in the multipolar system in the European continent in 1849–1870, with the involvement of the five polar powers that constituted the system, three are noteworthy. These wars were of great importance and will also be examined qualitatively in the study: the Crimean War (1853–1856); the Seven Weeks' War (1866); and the Franco-Prussian War (1870–1871), which indicated the end of the multipolar system that the current subchapter discusses and the beginning of the bipolar system that was formed after it.

The Crimean War (1853–1856)

The Crimean War broke out in a system whose leadership was shared by two countries, Great Britain and Russia, while other countries had reasonable ability to achieve hegemony.[134] The war effectively destroyed everything that was left of the European hegemony and paved the way for the shocks of 1859–1871.[135] It was the first war between Europe's great powers for 39 years and become a European total war. Great Britain and Russia, global enemies and the strongest powers in Europe, fought each other. The war involved the most complicated, longest, and most dangerous question in European politics—the eastern question.[136]

After two years of tough fighting and diplomatic pressures, no country joined the war except for Sardinia/Piedmont. In the end, France convinced Britain, with Austria's assistance, to end the war and make peace before it wanted to. The war had a few other local and international consequences: humiliation and internal weakening of Russia, the lack of Britain's victory, and the significant influence of the system of European countries, particularly the long-term effect of unification of Germany.[137]

The Seven Weeks' War between Prussia and Austria (1866)

The Seven Weeks' War developed because each of the parties made demands concerning the dispute surrounding Elbe Duchies and no party was prepared to accept the demands of the other.[138] In 1864, Prussia and Austria fought as allies against Denmark in the Second Schleswig-Holstein

War. Following this conflict, these two German states promised to control the dispute concerning Schleswig-Holstein. Once the war was over, a destructive struggle started between Prussia and Austria over the control of the occupied territories. The Austro-Prussian conflict that developed and the shared victory over much weaker Denmark reached its evident end in late 1865 with the signing of the Gastein Convention. The convention was consistent with some of Prussia's aspirations while protecting and safeguarding Austrian prestige and control within the German confederation. However, after many months it was found that the agreement did not work. The first subject was about Bismarck's concern that the Austrian right to manage Holstein was akin to sovereignty over the territory. Such an outcome frustrated his immediate and long-term ambitions concerning the federation.

To rectify the situation from its own perspective, Prussia looked for authority over Holstein to a certain extent by violating the Gastein Convention. Austria considered expanding its control over Holstein, which also violated the Gastein Convention.[139] Prussia's main demand was status of honor within the leadership of Germany.

The Franco-Prussian War (1870–1871)

This war was fought between France and Prussia and its allies, which united after the war and became Germany.[140] Based on the argument that the system before the outbreak of the Franco-Prussian War was multipolar, Prussia in that period had not yet risen to potential hegemon status in the system, which it enjoyed in the decades after its victory in that war until the years preceding the outbreak of the First World War. Prussia's status at that time led Austria and France to pass the buck to each other.[141] Each of them believed that the other country could defeat Prussia unaided and they abstained from joining forces to prevent the Prussian victories against them—Prussia's victory against Austria in 1866 and against France in 1870. Prussia's resulting status led Great Britain and Russia to stand noncommittal. They effectively wanted a stronger Prussia—for Britain for counterbalancing France and Russia, for Russia for counterbalancing Austria and France.[142]

The Multipolar System, 1910–1945

This system was the first that covered the whole world. During it, 13 wars were fought involving at least one of the seven polar powers that constituted it: the United States, Russia (later to be the Soviet Union), Germany, Great Britain, France, Japan, and Italy. Two wars were of greater importance than the rest: World Wars One (1914–1918) and Two (1939–1945). The last war effectively indicated the end of the multipolar system and the beginning of the bipolar system that was formed after it.

The First World War (1914–1918)

On June 28, 1914, Serbian heir presumptive Archduke Franz Ferdinand and his wife, Sophie, were assassinated. In the month after their death, Austro-Hungary and Serbia were at war and the rest of Europe's countries quickly joined them.[143] The First World War broke out.

In that war, the system effectively forced the outcomes and prevented the rise of Germany to potential hegemon status. In the Germany unification wars in the second half of the 19th century, Germany did not have potential hegemon status in the system and the system did not force a series of constraints to suppress its expansion. In the First World War, Germany's victory would have raised it to the status of potential hegemon in the system—a result that the system resisted. Germany did not understand its status, and its instigation of the war led the system to apply a series of systemic pressures as soon as the war broke out in order to prevent its victory in the war and its ensuing expansion. Two key constraints that the system applied may be stated. Firstly, the German expectation that Russia would not intervene to protect its protégé Serbia was found to be wrong. Russia did intervene, thus transforming the small-scale war that Germany predicted and aimed for into a European total war, which Germany certainly did not want. Secondly, the German expectation that Great Britain would not intervene on the side of Belgium and France was also found to be wrong. Great Britain did intervene, and with the intervention of the United States three years later, the British intervention had a major influence resulting in Germany's complete loss. Great Britain could not reconcile with the collapse of the balance of power in Europe and the possibility of Germany rising to absolute hegemonic status in the continent. London feared that if France and Russia would be defeated by Germany, the European balance of power would collapse and Britain itself might face a threat and danger.[144]

The Second World War (1939–1945)

Like the First World War, at the end of the Second World War, the system also dictated the outcomes and prevented the rise of Germany to potential hegemon status in the system. The answer to the question of why Hitler lost after all his amazing early successes is the ultimate strategic error that he made by invading Russia. That is what changed his fate from enormous success to total destruction. Until Hitler's invasion of Russia, Germany was a great power in the system, but after the invasion, its status took an extreme change and Nazi Germany became a potential hegemon that posed a threat to the other players in the system. At that point, the systemic constraints started to act, and the system not only prevented Germany from winning the war but also dictated its loss and territorial contraction.

Bismarck and Hitler, two prominent German leaders, started their international career as careful, successful warmongers. Bismarck's three wars—against Denmark, Austria, and France—were all carefully considered and a complete success. Hitler's three early conquests—of Austria, Czechoslovakia, and Poland—were very similar in terms of discretion and success, but that is the only thing they had in common. In 1871, Bismarck achieved his rational Clausewitzian goals of uniting the German population and leading Germany to a period of prosperity. At the same time, he became a peaceful leader. Hitler's biography is the complete opposite. Unlike Bismarck, Hitler did not stop his actions after achieving, more or less, his rational Clausewitzian goals of forming hegemony in Central Europe using sufficient power and growing, stable prosperity, and by consolidating his achievements. Instead of doing so, like Napoleon, he continued from one splendid victory to another. The most basic psychological difference between the two leaders was that Bismarck had a sense of realistic limitation whereas Hitler did not.[145]

The diminishment of Germany's power, which manifested in the systemic constraint of not winning a war but losing and contracting territorially at its end, was accompanied by the American and Soviet military presence in the heart of Europe, which removed the threat of German aggression.[146]

TERRITORIAL OUTCOMES IN BIPOLAR SYSTEMS

This part assesses whether the territorial outcomes of the wars fought in the three bipolar systems, 1816–1848, 1871–1909, and 1946–1991, and which included the polar powers that constituted each of these bipolar systems, correspond with the *international relations theory of war* concerning the degree of territorial expansion of superpowers in bipolar systems at the end of the wars that they fought.

The subchapter attempts to prove that under bipolar systems, one principle result for a territorial outcome of polar powers at the end of wars that they have fought is possible: bipolar systems will dictate a territorial status quo of the two superpowers.

Under bipolar systems, starting a central or major war will result in the collapse of the system and the formation of another system in its place. In the period assessed, 1816–2016, there were three bipolar systems, 1816–1848, 1871–1909, and 1946–1991. During them, there was no central or major war in which the superpowers constituting the system fought each other; however, in bipolar systems minor wars may occur.

Bipolar systems will *dictate* a single territorial outcome of the two superpowers constituting them (i.e., *maintaining the territorial status quo* that prevailed before the outbreak of the war at the end of all minor wars in which they are involved). Any other result would promote the expanding power to potential hegemon in the system and might lead to the collapse of the system.

In all three bipolar systems in 1816–2016, in all the minor wars in which the polar powers constituting the system were involved, the bipolar system dictated to the two superpowers to maintain the territorial status quo preceding the wars. In the two bipolar systems that prevailed in Eurasia in the 19th century until the beginning of the 20th century, 1816–1848 and 1871–1909, Great Britain had to maintain the status quo preceding its two wars against Afghanistan. In the bipolar system that occurred in the second half of the 20th century, 1946–1991, the two superpowers constituting the system, the United States and the Soviet Union, had to preserve the territorial status quo that existed before *all* the wars in which they were involved—the wars of the United States against Korea, Vietnam, and Iraq (1991), and the Soviet invasion of Hungary and war against Afghanistan.

The preservation of the territorial status quo preceding the war at the end of the wars involving superpowers in bipolar systems stems from the way in which bipolar systems affect the values of the two transhistorical order principles that always work in the international system. The two other territorial outcomes, territorial contraction or territorial expansion, are not a possibility at the end of minor wars that are fought in bipolar systems. Territorial contraction of superpowers in bipolar systems at the end of wars that they fight may impair the homeostasis, inasmuch as a decrease in the land power of the superpower that loses territory must lead to a decrease in its total power. Following this, the equilibrium will be violated and the homeostatic in danger. Territorial expansion of superpowers in bipolar systems at the end of wars in which they will participate may impair the homeostasis, for a rise in the land power of the superpower that acquires new territory must lead to an increase in its total power. Following this, the equilibrium will be violated and the homeostasis will be at risk.

The Bipolar System, 1946–1991

The U.S.-Korea War (1950–1953)

The outbreak of the Korean War led the bipolar system that prevailed at the time to apply a series of systemic constraints to deny the United States territorial expansion, maintain the status quo preceding the war, and effectively restore it thereafter.[147] A number of significant events faithfully represent this argument. The term *limited war* that was introduced following the Korean War was coined because the United States abstained from engaging in maximal military activity, failed to vanquish its adversary, and negotiated an armistice agreement as a compromise. It is not clear whether the communist concession stemmed from the insinuation that the United States might use nuclear weapons or was because of the weakening of the stiff Soviet line that resulted from Stalin's death. It is quite clear that neither party was prepared to pay the price to unite the country and each of the sides was determined to prevent the other side from doing so.[148] Once the war broke out with direct involvement of the United States—one of the two polar powers constituting the system—parties at the system level started to act in order to restore the former state, maintain the territorial status quo preceding the war, and prevent the strengthening of one of the two strong players in the system and its rise to potential hegemon status in the system.

The Korean War could be defined as a victory, a loss, or a draw. Some researchers have categorized the Korean War as a tie,[149] whereas others have defined South Korea as the victor. However, the main test for measuring war according to the current theory is the degree of territorial expansion of the polar power in that war. According to this test, the United States did not expand at the end of that war and the territorial status quo was maintained in a tangible, prominent, and even defiant manner. One cannot ignore that the war started when the border between North Korea and South Korea was the 38th parallel and ended at the same 38th parallel.[150]

The U.S.-Vietnam War (1968–1975)

The traditional way in which the U.S. military operated in the war against Vietnam included using American advantages in power and mobility to isolate the enemy's armies.[151] The United States implemented the lesson that it had learned from the Korean War of not threatening the existence of Chinese buffer states, which in that war was North Vietnam, and in that war the U.S. military was prohibited from using those advantages against North Vietnam. Following this, the restrictions against transferring the land war into North Vietnam made this war an unwinnable one. The great failure, or even catastrophe, of the Vietnam War would not have occurred had the United States better understood the importance of the regional influence areas and the balance of power.[152]

The results of the Vietnam War serve as an important lesson concerning the relations between events in military terms and political ones. In military terms, Vietnam did not defeat the United States but the United States, which was at that time one of the two superpowers dominating the international system, lost politically. Such a phenomenon was not known in classic strategy in which it is inconceivable for a power to be defeated and expelled from territory by a smaller local force. The United States had enormous military superiority over Vietnam whether this superiority was exploited or not. It was found that practically the unequivocal military superiority that it enjoyed relative to Vietnam is relevant to the results of the war, which were determined by other factors outside the military scene, which also forced a superpower to act in contravention to the way in which it saw the occurrences and unilaterally withdraw its military forces from that small country.[153]

Harry Summers, who served as an American colonel in the Vietnam War, argues that the United States won the war tactically but lost strategically.[154] Like earlier and later militarists, Summers bases his work on Clausewitz's book, which emphasized the importance of balancing out "the trinity of war": civilians, government, and military.[155] Based on this distinction, Summers points out two factors that led to the American failure: the environment—the relations between the U.S. military and the American people, the importance of American public support for the military actions, and the institutional responsibility that Congress had in giving that support legitimacy—and the failure of the U.S. military strategy.[156] Unlike Summers, the theory cited here claims that the reason that the United States failed to win the war was systemic.

The Gulf War (1991)

The Gulf War marked the transition from the bipolar system to the unipolar system that was formed after it.[157] Upon its conclusion, the United States expanded its foothold in the Persian Gulf region, an area of great strategic importance.

The great importance of that region is supported by the fact that the United States spent $60 billion a year to ensure the free flow of oil from the Gulf States worth $30 billion—oil that would also have flowed without its protection.[158] The U.S. involvement in the war and the expansion of its presence in the region, along with the Soviet Union's withdrawal from its protégé countries, led to the significant systemic change: the transition from the bipolar system to the unipolar system.

TERRITORIAL OUTCOMES IN UNIPOLAR SYSTEMS

In the current subchapter, I assess whether the territorial outcomes of the wars in which the United States participated as a sole hyperpower correspond with the hypothesis of the *international relations theory of war* concerning the degree of territorial expansion of polar powers at the end of wars in which they have participated. The current subchapter shows that in unipolar systems one main result may occur: territorial expansion of the sole hyperpower because any other result would undermine its stability as the sole hyperpower in the system and might lead to collapse of the system—a result that the homeostasis principle dictates to the players to act to prevent.

In the only unipolar system that has occurred since 1816, in 1992–2016, all the minor wars in which the United States was involved as the sole hyperpower ended with that territorial result. In other words, the unipolar system dictated to the sole hyperpower, the United States, to expand territorially at their end: the U.S. invasion of Afghanistan (2001) and the U.S. invasion of Iraq (2003).

Constant territorial expansion of hyperpowers in unipolar systems at the end of minor wars in which they participate stems from the manner of influence that these systems have over the values of the two transhistorical order principles that constantly act in the international system—*anarchy* and *homeostasis*. Any preservation or decrease in the land force of the hyperpower at the end of wars in which it participates may lead to a collapse of the system—a result that the *homeostasis principle dictates* to the players to act to prevent. Therefore, in unipolar systems, the two transhistorical order principles will force the sole hyperpowers constituting them to expand territorially. The two other territorial outcomes are not possible at the end of minor wars that are fought in unipolar systems. *Territorial contraction* may infringe on the homeostasis, inasmuch as a decrease in the land power of the hyperpower that loses territory must lead to weakening in its total power. As a result, the equilibrium will be impaired and the homeostasis will be in danger. A *territorial status quo* may infringe on the homeostasis as the failure of the hyperpower that does not expand territorially to gain land power effectively undermines the homeostasis principle, under which individual hyperpowers in unipolar systems are supposed to behave according to their status as the leading powers of the system—in other words, to uproot those that rise up against them.

TERRITORIAL OUTCOMES AT THE END OF THE POLAR POWERS' WARS AGAINST AFGHANISTAN

In the period assessed in the study, 1816–2016, five wars were fought involving one of the polar powers constituting the various systems against Afghanistan—a small country in the system. These five wars were fought in all three polarity models existing and assessed in the study: the First Anglo-Afghan War (1838–1842), in the bipolar system of 1816–1848; the Second Anglo-Afghan War (1878–1880), in the bipolar system of 1871–1909; the Third Anglo-Afghan War (1919), in the multipolar system of 1910–1945; the Soviet-Afghan War (1979–1988), in the bipolar system of 1946–1991; and the U.S.-Afghan War (2001), in the unipolar system of 1992–2016.

The five test cases are suitable for examining the theory because they clearly correspond with the requirements that Alexander George presented for conducting the method of structured, focused comparison.[159] In each of these cases, the polar powers—Great Britain (in three wars), the Soviet Union, and the United States—fought against the same country, Afghanistan. In each of the periods in which these five wars were fought, the region was of high geostrategic importance for the other polar powers that constituted the system at that time.

The assessment of these wars attempts to prove at a high level of certainty that the explanation of their results lies in the system level rather than at lower levels.

"THE GREAT GAME" IN CENTRAL ASIA AND THE IMPORTANCE OF AFGHANISTAN

The central Asia region was and is of great importance to the global powers: in the 19th century, the region was perceived by Great Britain as an important buffer zone vital for prevention of Russian aggression and ensuring continued British dominance in India. Toward the end of this century, the region became a key source of raw materials, particularly oil, and as such, it was no longer perceived as a buffer zone but as having intrinsic value by itself.[160] The Great Game in Asia, the struggle of forces between the great powers in central Asia, was separated from Europe despite it being connected to the continent. This was an Anglo-Russian competition over the entire region, from the Bosporus Straits to India, including Turkey, Egypt, and other Arab territories, and also Persia and the Persian Gulf, Afghanistan, central Asia, and northwest India. The scale of the competition expanded and included commerce, military relations, and high diplomacy, and it also presented a clear model or constant subject. However, in 1833–1841, Persia and Afghanistan formed their central positions. Although a number of British officials in India started to warn of the Russian threat back at the beginning of the 19th century, the idea started to be common in Britain only after Turkey was defeated by Russia in 1829.[161]

The rise of Russia along with the weakness of Persia posed a number of possible dangers for Britain, from the least possible and immediate— additional Russian expansion in Persia and central Asia—to the worse scenarios—that Persia, encouraged by Russia, might expand its own territorial aspirations eastward toward Herat in Afghanistan, or that Persia, which would dissolve because of domestic conflicts and economic bankruptcy, would fall in Russia's hands. Through cooperation with Russia, Britain was able to prevent both dangers. However, Persia and Afghanistan remained a cause of concern for it.[162]

Something similar happened to Britain in India itself in which London contended mainly with the question on how to maintain its supremacy over a large area, at low costs, or with no costs at all, and without any foreign or domestic challenge. While the East Indian Company then controlled vast territories directly, most of India remained under the direct control of local princes. Britain's key problem in India was not maintaining the security of maritime transport lines with Britain but maintaining domestic calm. The northwestern border had to serve not only as a protective wall but as a ring wall. The strategy that the British preferred reflected their position toward Turkey in the 1830s that broad protective measures had to be maintained for India by replacing the Russian influence in Persia with British influence. Two missions in Persia, in 1835–1836 and 1836–1837, in search for a commerce agreement and renewal of a political agreement, ended in success. The obstacles appeared to be less important when a Persian expedition against Turkmen tribes in northern Afghanistan failed. This convinced British Minister John McNeill that Persia was not a threat. But McNeill's optimism was challenged when the dispute between Persia and Afghanistan concerning the city Herat arose again in 1837. McNeill could not broker the crisis, and Persia, under the encouragement of Simonich, the Russian minister for Persia, conquered Herat. This move pushed Britain to its alternative strategy: turning Afghanistan into a safe buffer state for India against Persia and Russia.[163]

This strategy was not new. Britain had already tried, unsuccessfully, to turn Afghanistan into a strong supporting country by supporting a certain candidate for the Afghan throne in 1809–1810 and 1833–1834. Afghanistan was part of two broad, interrelated plans that were intended to protect the security of northwestern India. One was possible British territorial expansion and political and economic penetration of the nearby regions Sindh and Panjab. The other was building of a balance of power in northeast India (Afghanistan, Sindh, and Panjab) in particular and southwest Asia in general. The British thought of a system of stable independent countries with recognized nonviolated borders with British general supremacy. While that position was generally defensive, there were British government figures who started to think of its expansion to British control of Afghanistan to prevent Russia from penetrating central Asia and to represent British assets and influence in the region.[164]

Afghanistan is the gateway to India. Within it lies the only quick route for transferring military forces and starting a war despite the difficult topography of northwest Asia—the Hindu-Kush region reaches a height of 20,000 feet. The city Herat is on the way from the plains of northern Iran to the cities Kabul and Kandahar and from there to India. Because of its central location at the crossroads of central Asia, Afghanistan played an important role in Asia's long military history. In 327 BCE, Alexander the Great passed through it on his way from western India. Five hundred years later, Genghis Khan arrived from the east and ordered one of his people to conquer Herat as a prelude to conquering Persia.[165]

THE FIRST ANGLO-AFGHAN WAR (1838–1842)

In the 19th century, the great imperial adversity between Russia and Great Britain covering territory from the Balkans to Afghanistan occurred.[166]

In that century, Afghanistan was transformed into a key "playing field" in the *Great Game* in central Asia. Great Britain started to control India in the 18th century. In 1779, its sovereignty over the eastern subcontinent was recognized in the Paris Agreement. In the first quarter of the 19th century, while Britain was consolidating its power in India, the Russian tsar expanded the territory under his control eastward by conquering central Asian kingdoms and the northern parts of Persia (the Caspian Sea provinces and the cities Darband and Baku). The constant advantages of Russia caused displeasure in Great Britain concerning the security of its empire in India. Afghanistan's strategic location as the "gateway to India" made it a focus point for British diplomacy and military strategy for decades. The British invasions of Afghan territory in that century occurred in the First and Second Anglo-Afghan Wars.[167]

The British decision to intervene directly in fights between the Afghan tribes and politics of the Afghan dynasty, as it developed in India and Britain, was a response to the way in which the Russo-Persian threat from the city Herat was perceived by London. This led Lord Auckland, the governor general of India, to relinquish unwillingly his previous reliance on economic penetration into Afghanistan in favor of a plan that was raised by his military secretary, William Hay MacNaughten, who suggested replacing the khan bearing the crown in Kabul, Dost Muhammad, with a claimer of the throne with British support, Shah Shuja, but without any extensive British action. The sheikhs of Panjab were supposed to provide the necessary military ability alongside political support from the amir of Sindh.[168]

The same change in approach occurred in London. British Foreign Secretary Palmerston, who feared a confrontation with Russia concerning Persia, in which Russia's position was strong and Britain's weak, rejected any action to guard Herat. However, in mid-1838, Palmerston decided in end to part from Persia and adopt Auckland's plan for intervention in Afghanistan, where he believed that Britain's status was strong and Russia's weak. The action would not only stop Persia and protect Herat, he thought, but would also restrain Russia and strengthen Britain in central Asia, in the Ottoman Empire, in Europe, and even in America. With the enthusiastic support of the president of the Board of Control of India Hobhouse, Palmerston obtained the consent of the cabinet in early October. Immediately afterward, he confronted Russian Foreign Minister Nesselrode with testimonies of the Russian plots in Persia and Afghanistan. Nesselrode expressed his true astonishment, pressured Persia to withdraw and apologize to Britain, and pleaded to Britain to cooperate with Russia in Asia for achieving an agreement on borders and on influence regions. Palmerston refused. Despite the Russian concession and the Persian withdrawal from Herat, which included an unwilling apology, the British plan advanced and its goals remained clearly anti-Russian, as before. Because a Russo-British confrontation or war concerning Asia was supposed to break out sooner or later, at that time it was just a matter of when and where.[169] Great Britain launched the first Anglo-Afghan War (1838–1842) in 1838.

Why Did Britain Invade Afghanistan?

The source of the British involvement in Afghanistan may be assigned to the Russian expansion into northwestern Persia in the 1820s. Ahmad Shah Qajar, the leader of Persia, was encouraged by the Russians to accept compensation for his losses in the country's northwest by occupying Herat, which at that time was controlled by Kamran, the grandson of Timur Shah Sadduzai. In 1837, the Russians backed the Persian army in attacking and besieging Herat. The siege of the city led to total resistance against the Persians. While the Persians were busy besieging the city, a Russian delegation arrived in Kabul to form commercial relations with the Afghan ruler Amir Dost Mohammad Khan. Great Britain interpreted the Persian attack on Herat and the dispatch of the Russian delegation to Kabul as a prelude to a Russian invasion of India through Afghanistan.[170]

The Invasion

The British responded by conquering Kharak, the Persian island in the Persian Gulf, forcing the Persians to concede their claims to Herat. Afterward, the British tried to expand their control northward to prevent broader Russian maneuvers. The best way of preventing the Russian influence in Afghanistan was in their opinion installing a leader in Kabul who would be committed to British interests. In 1838, Lord Auckland, the British governor general of India, started to negotiate with Shah Shujah, the ousted leader of Afghanistan (1804–1809), who was then in exile in India, and with the ruler of Panjab, Maharaja Ranjit Singh, for cooperation in a military move against the leader of Afghanistan at the time, Amir Dost Muhammad Khan. In 1838, the three parties signed the agreement that promised Shah Shujah the throne in Afghanistan on the condition that he would consent to the permanent presence of British forces in Kabul. Parts of Afghanistan, including areas that were later intended as the northwestern border of the province of British India, were promised to Maharaja Ranjit Singh. In 1839, the combined forces, known as the Hindus Army, departed toward Kabul, and on August 7, they reinstated Shah Shujah to the Afghan throne with very little resistance, forcing Amir Dost Mohammad Khan, Afghanistan's acting leader, to move to Bukhara.[171]

The Systemic Pressures for the British Pullout from Afghanistan

Initially, the British invasion of Afghanistan did not encounter any strong resistance,[172] and the First Anglo-Afghan war enjoyed slight successes and

involved very few losses. As early as the autumn of 1839, Dost Mohammad was replaced, Shah Shujah was crowned in Kabul, and the British
controlled the country by agreement and in practice, in addition to the
prestige that they had achieved in the surrounding area. However, the
foundations of British supremacy were unstable. The attempt to control
the entire country from the distant north in Kabul was learned to be an
error. In 1841, it was obvious to the British that the adventure had failed.
The preservation of Afghanistan as a buffer state was not worth the cost.
Nonetheless, unlike their military advisers, they could not expedite the
withdrawal out of concern regarding the overall influence that such an
action could have over British prestige. Because occupation was no longer a vital option either, the only thing left to do was wait.[173] Brittan's
aspiration to strengthen its foothold in Afghanistan symbolized, alongside
additional things, the beginning of a more effective British policy toward
Russia. The realization of this option would not have helped it control Russia's
policy in Europe and ensure that Britain would not depend on Russian
help there. That aspiration also countered Russia's action toward Khiva in
central Asia, which started in 1839, for punishing the Uzbeks for having
taken slaves in raids on Russian caravans.[174]

The British Withdrawal from Afghanistan

The situation remained quiet until 1841, when William MacNaughten,
the British representative in Kabul, was appointed as supervisor of events
and it was learned that the king had been acting as a puppet. The resistance to the British occupation started in Kabul in late 1841 and quickly
expanded to the provinces.[175] It quickly expanded to form a national
uprising of tribal leaders against the British and Shah Shujah. A temporary agreement that was achieved allowed the British to withdraw from
Kabul, but the trust was breached and the garrison in Kabul massacred it
on its way to retreat in January 1842. The British reestablished their prestige through a successful, albeit cruel massacre, and afterward completed
the withdrawal, leaving on the throne again Dost Mohammad, who in
turn surprisingly united Afghanistan.[176] In December 1842, 4,500 British
troops left Kabul en route to Jalalabad.[177]

The First Anglo-Afghan War and Its Consequences

Both Sindh and Panjab suffered from the consequences of the British
defeat in the First Anglo-Afghan War. Motifs of prestige and military strategy led Britain to a series of wars, and these reached their peak in the occupation of Sindh (1843) and Panjab (1849). Later, the British defeat in the
first Anglo-Afghan War led to a strategy that was intended to defend the
British Empire in India against extensive Russian expansion. That strategy

developed into an offensive plan for British expansion in Afghanistan and central Asia. The British Empire's major failure in Afghanistan led it to great expansion in India itself and significant improvement in Britain's relations with Russia concerning central Asia, based on a quiet Anglo-Russian cooperation agreement for peace in Europe, leaving regions of influence on the other side of Asia alone—a sensible policy that Russia offered and the government in India always wanted.[178]

THE SECOND ANGLO-AFGHAN WAR (1878–1880)

Why Did Britain Invade Afghanistan?

The second British invasion of Afghanistan stemmed from the constant progress of Tsarist Russia in central Asia in the 1860s and 1870s.[179] The Russo-Turkish War in the Balkans (1877–1878) is particularly noteworthy.[180] When Benjamin Disraeli rose to power in Britain, the British policy toward Afghanistan was redefined. The policy of "supremacy without activity" was relinquished in favor of what was known as "advancing policy": moving forward into Afghan territory, achieving dominance, and forming a buffer state for defending India. At the same time, the British conquered Sindh (1842) and Panjab (1849) and positioned themselves closer to the Afghan border.[181]

The Invasion

In 1878, a Russian diplomatic delegation arrived uninvited to the royal court of Amir Sher Ali Khan (1867–1879), the son and successor of Amir Dost Mohammad Khan. Furious at the Russian presence in Kabul, Lord Lytton, the assistant to the king of India, demanded that the Amir receive a corresponding British delegation. Amir Sher Ali Khan's reluctance to comply immediately with the demand gave the British a reason to invade Afghanistan. In November 1878, British forces attacked Kandahar, Kurram, and Kabul. When they reached the capital, Amir Sher Ali Khan moved northward hoping to get help from the Russians, leaving his weak son Mohammad Yaqub Khan behind. Because of lack of will and ability to resist, Mohammad Yaqub Khan signed the Treaty of Gandamak in May 1874, which forced the new amir to receive a permanent British delegation in Kabul and transferred Kurram Valley and the Kandahar Passage to British India.[182]

The Systemic Pressures for the British Pullout from Afghanistan

A change in the Russian attitude toward Afghanistan provided a good reason for the major British withdrawal. On April 14, 1869, Lord Clarendon, the British foreign secretary, received a positive promise from Russian

Foreign Minister Prince Gortschakoff that the Russian ruler considered Afghanistan to be a region outside Russia's region of influence, and Russian offices would no longer be permitted to visit Afghanistan.[183]

SUMMARY OF THE FIRST (1838–1842) AND SECOND (1878–1880) ANGLO-AFGHAN WARS

In the 19th century, the competition between the two imperial powers, Tsarist Russia in the north and British India in the south, turned Afghanistan into a battlefield between the two powers and something that was later known as "the Great Game of Asia."[184]

The current study indicates systemic factors, primarily the polarity of the system, as factors that led to the displacement of the British from Afghanistan in the First and Second Anglo-Afghan Wars. According to another explanation, all parts of Afghan society and all ethnic groups were involved in the armed Afghan resistance to the British invaders. According to this explanation, it is important to recognize the important role of clerics (*ulama*) in these two wars, not only as participants and those who motivated the masses, but also as the individuals who led and directed the war efforts. While the resistance to the foreign occupiers united the divided Afghan forces by resisting the British, the religious leaders stood at the front of the resistance as the defenders of Islam. The call for jihad became the most effective incentive for defending the territorial integrity and traditional culture of Afghanistan. As leaders of the jihad, the religious leaders gained considerable political power.[185]

THE THIRD ANGLO-AFGHAN WAR (1919)

Why Did Britain Invade Afghanistan?

The land route from Europe to India and the Indian Ocean is guarded by a natural land fortress, Afghanistan. Along this route, Germany had many strategic interests in both First and Second World Wars. Therefore, it is unsurprising that Afghanistan was a significant component in German geographic and strategic thinking. The German plans to conquer central Asia started back in the First World War. A German expeditionary force, were it to advance toward Afghanistan, could have allowed the German high command, after the collapse of Russian resistance in 1917, to exploit the advantages in the east without restricting them in other theaters. A German force effectively made its way to Kabul, Afghanistan, in 1916. Its goal was to incite the Afghan Muslim majority to join the war and to form a diversion in the British backyard, on the northwestern border of the Indian province. However, the German plans of action in central Asia were prepared but never implemented. They were also part of Hitler's plans in the Second World War.[186]

Britain conquered India from the sea and held onto it owing to the superiority of its navy. Therefore, Afghanistan served in British military policy as an obstacle between British and Russian interests in central Asia, more than as a land passage. From the 1840s, Britain, and later Russia's tsars, was involved in military actions against the Afghans. These wars were fought as broad wars. Both Britain and Russia failed, despite significant local successes, to conquer and hold onto major parts of Afghan territory. The British forces reconquered Kabul and Kandahar. The Afghan armies were no match to the European armies in open battles, but the tribesmen proved themselves as experts in guerilla warfare in the mountains and inflicted severe losses on the European invaders. A war in the Afghan mountains posed difficulties for movement and resupply, and the European armies had not yet found suitable answers for them. As a result, the Afghans were able to maintain a great degree of political independence.[187]

The Invasion

The complexity of war in Afghanistan was evident in the Third Anglo-Afghan War (1919). In that war, both sides employed large forces: nearly 340,000 British troops fought against 200,000 Afghan regulars and guerillas. The British troops were equipped with state-of-the-art weaponry that was developed in the First World War, such as strong explosives, armored vehicles, wireless communications, and aircraft.[188]

The Systemic Pressures for the British Pullout from Afghanistan

The Afghan attack on India was a delayed consequence of a plot that the German delegation that visited Kabul in the First World War started, as it was the Afghans who started the hostile actions. In February 1919, the pro-British Amir Habibullah Khan was murdered. After a short uprising, he was replaced by Amir Amanullah Khan, who owed his throne to anti-British leaders of the Afghan army. Considering the British preoccupation with the unrest in India and probably with Soviet support too, Amanullah put his forces on alert on April 25. At the same time, an outpour of anti-British propaganda flowed from Kabul toward the British forces on the northwestern border of the province. The agents of Amanullah in Peshawar disseminated, using fast trucks, leaflets that declared that the Germans had resumed the war and India and Egypt were rising up against Britain. Owing to the unique timing of the Afghan attack, which paradoxically was carried out at the peak of Britain's victories in Europe, the British authorities were surprised. In contrast, the Anglo-Indian forces were deployed more quickly than the Afghans expected and counterbalanced, with some degree of success, the initiative that was intended to harm them.[189]

THE SOVIET-AFGHAN WAR (1979–1988)

The Soviet invasion of Afghanistan started in 1979. It ended in 1988 after a treaty signed between the parties in Geneva following long negotiations held in Geneva, Kabul, Moscow, and at the UN headquarters in New York. In the end, the enormous Soviet army withdrew after having bled in Afghanistan for years, like the withdrawal of another polar power, Great Britain, from that country at the end of three previous wars: the First and Second Anglo-Afghan Wars in the 19th century and the Third Anglo-Afghan War in the early 20th century. According to the current study, the Soviet Union did not learn the lessons of those past three wars in which the ability of polar powers to expand territorially is not dependent only on their own capabilities but also on constraints on the part of significant systemic forces.

Why Did the Soviet Union Invade Afghanistan?

The Soviet Union intervened in the civil war in Afghanistan because of ideological factors and invaded the country because it believed that the communist rule was not allowed to fall, particularly owing to its close ties with the Soviet Union. Fixated on their self-expansion doctrine, the Soviets deployed elite units to Afghanistan equipped with modern weaponry and aircraft and built a big base in Shindand in the country's northwest, which had nothing to do with the country's domestic security. Moreover, their actions were perceived to a great extent as having strategic goals—building a large airbase—so they alarmed the West and thawed the détente relations, the process of thawing of relations between the two blocs. The cost of the war to the Soviets was high: 15,000 troops killed, more than 1,000 aircraft, thousands of trucks, artillery pieces, and tanks, and about $96 billion (in historical terms).[190]

The Systemic Constraints That Were Employed in the War

The Soviet invasion of Afghanistan led the bipolar system that existed at that time to apply a series of systemic constraints to bring the invasion to an end, to maintain the territorial status quo preceding the war, and effectively to restore the former situation. A number of significant events demonstrate this: the threat that China felt owing to the Soviet invasion of Afghanistan led it to cooperate with the United States in order to contain the Soviet military adventure;[191] the Soviet involvement in Afghanistan hurt Soviet foreign policy in a number of regions of influence, primarily in the Persian Gulf. It pushed Pakistan, China, and the United States to closer strategic cooperation;[192] the invasion strengthened the United States' strategic relations with Egypt and with key countries in the Gulf;[193] the invasion reduced the Soviet Union's political relations with key Gulf states;[194] the invasion focused Soviet energy on Afghanistan, which otherwise could have challenged American security in the Gulf region.[195] The freedom of action given to the United States because of the Soviet Union's commitment to Afghanistan allowed it to expand its influence around the world, and it was what eventually forced the Soviet Union to abstain from continuing that adventure.

In addition to the systemic constraints that were applied to the Soviet Union for maintaining the territorial status quo that was held before the outbreak of the war, the American military and economic aid extended to the rebels should also be focused on. After the Second World War, the United States was already concerned by the Soviet influence in Afghanistan and made sure to protect its investments in neighboring Pakistan, particularly the U-2 base in Peshawar, the capital of the northwestern border province.[196] Immediately after the Soviet invasion of Afghanistan on December 27, 1979, U.S. President Jimmy Carter reacted by sending arms to the Afghan rebels. However, the partnership between the parties was limited.[197] A few days after the invasion, President Carter signed an executive document approving the transfer of arms to the rebel forces (mujahedeen) to harass the Soviet forces in the country. The first shipment landed in Pakistan on January 10, 1980, 14 days after the Soviet invasion. Carter constantly increased the aid and President Ronald Reagan expanded it. In the mid-1980s, the successes of the rebel forces, combined with more aggressive Soviet tactics, led to significant expansion of the American involvement.[198] The turning point of the war came in 1985. For the first time, the Soviet withdrawal from Afghanistan had become likely. In Washington, the aim changed from "making the Soviets pay the price" to "making them withdraw." National Security Resolution No. 166 of March 1985 authorized the United States to supply arms to the rebel forces for forcing the Soviets out of Afghanistan. The U.S. involvement increased, and in 1986 the first significant non-Soviet weapon was introduced to the theater—Stinger surface-to-air missiles. This action removed the fig leaf of America's denial of involvement in the war. The use of the missiles, which started in September 1986, had an immediate effect, particularly on Soviet helicopters, which were an important component of intensifying the Soviet actions against the rebels. The American aid to the Afghan program stood at about $300 million during those years,[199] and in the whole period the aid totaled at about $2 billion.[200] In the period after the Soviet withdrawal from Afghanistan, the Americans reduced their aid to the rebel forces.

THE U.S.-AFGHAN WAR (2001)

Why Did the United States Invade Afghanistan?

At 8:45 a.m., U.S. local time, on September 11, 2001, a hijacked American airliner crashed into the northern tower of the World Trade Center in New York. Eighteen minutes later, another hijacked jet crashed into the southern tower. An hour after the first attack, a third hijacked airliner crashed into the Pentagon in Washington and caused part of the building to collapse. At 10:05 a.m., the northern tower of the World Trade Center collapsed, and at 10:28 a.m., the southern tower collapsed. At 10:10 a.m., a fourth hijacked airliner crashed in Pennsylvania, north of Pittsburgh.[201] An analogy was immediately made to the Japanese attack on Pearl Harbor, and the U.S. administration was on a way to make a complete change in U.S. foreign policy and concerning the threats that Washington was facing.[202]

This was not the first attack on American objectives. In 1998, the U.S. embassy in East Africa was attacked, and 224 people were killed, including 12 Americans, and about 5,000 injured. On October 12, 2000, the USS Cole destroyer was attacked, resulting in 17 sailors being killed. Aircraft hijacking attempts were not new either. In 1995, an attempt to hijack simultaneously nine American aircraft over the Pacific Ocean was thwarted. The World Trade Center itself was a target of a terrorist attack in 1993—six people were killed and more than 100 injured.[203] What made the terrorist attacks of September 11 special compared with previous attacks was the combination of the scale of civilian losses and the fact that the attacks occurred in the West itself, and in the United States in particular, and the comprehensive media coverage of the events.[204]

The events of September 11 were shocking because they destroyed the war model that had been formed by the system in the 1990s. In the preceding decade, war was a phenomenon that occurred a safe distance away. However, on September 11, the attacks were on home soil, against the capital of the United States, Washington, and against one of its most famous and visited cities, New York. The U.S. president declared to Congress on September 20 that the American nation had discovered that it was not immune to attack.[205] The attacks were described not only as attacks on the United States but also as attacks on the "free world" and on the "civilized world."[206]

The Invasion

The Afghanistan (2001) and Iraq (2003) Wars were to a great extent a result of the vicious terrorist attacks on September 11, 2001. These events had a significant effect on American public opinion, on the media, on the two main political parties, and, of course, on the official foreign policy makers.[207] The American military response to the terrorist attacks started on October 7, 2001. The aims of the U.S.-Afghan War were unclear. Two different options were raised. One was punishing the Taliban regime for giving shelter to and cooperating with Al Qaeda and forcing the regime to bring the culprits to justice. The other was collapsing the Taliban regime and opening the way to an alternative regime that would allow direct American access to Al Qaeda people who had hidden in Afghanistan. The failure of the Taliban regime to cooperate with the American demands led the United States to seek how to remove it, both as a punitive action and for deterring other countries that had sheltered terrorists.[208]

The Systemic Pressures for the United States' Departure from Afghanistan

The entry of the United States to central Asia complicated the region's geostrategic dynamics. If there was ever a "great game" in central Asia in the period after the collapse of the Soviet Union, it was after the outbreak of the U.S.-Afghan War (2001).[209]

In the 1990s, the United States accepted Moscow's view of central Asia being its "backyard." The region was too far for American strategic involvement and it was not worth endangering its relations with Russia. Central Asia held an enormous concentration of highly valuable natural resources, so Washington was determined to bring the economy of central Asia, particularly the oil and gas industries, to the international market in order to reduce global dependence on these resources from the Persian Gulf. However, these goals were advanced through private businesses and international organizations with very limited involvement of the U.S. administration.[210]

The September 2001 terrorist attacks challenged the assumption that central Asia was too far away geographically and therefore posed no threat to American security. "The international war on terrorism," combined with its many targets, was recognition that it was no long possible to consider geography a constant factor in security calculations. Following the terrorist attacks, the central Asia region was perceived to be a significant threat to U.S. national security, owing to which it became a primary source of great tension with Moscow. Russia did not remain alone in the attempt to prevent the expansion of U.S. presence in central Asia. China, Russia's neighbor and traditional adversary, was also worried by the long-term presence of American forces near it.[211]

The Prolonged American Presence in Afghanistan

Despite the pressures applied on the United States to withdraw from Afghanistan, primarily by the two neighboring key great powers, Russia and China, the outcome was completely different—American forces remained in Afghanistan and American involvement in the region deepened. In addition, one cannot ignore the fact that the outcome of the war was different from the outcome of all the previous four wars in which polar powers invaded that country—the First, Second, and Third Anglo-Afghan Wars, and the Soviet-Afghan War—at the end of which the powers had to withdraw from Afghanistan. According to the current study, the cause of that outcome was systemic. I now turn to support this argument.

The arrival of U.S. forces in central Asia was the result of a significant change in American thinking concerning the region and its importance to U.S. national security,[212] following the terrorist attack on September 11, 2001, on U.S. soil. The scale of the change in U.S. policy could be compared to a certain extent to the influence of the Japanese attack on Pearl Harbor on December 7, 1941, which led the United States to join the Second World War, as both of them were catalysts for significant changes in U.S. foreign policy.[213]

The terrorist events significantly affected U.S. foreign policy. It became assertive and aggressive, militaristic and unilateral, and had idealist rhetoric. It also asked to disseminate American values and used moral crusade parlance and freedom and human rights rhetoric. The U.S. foreign policy started to support preemptive strikes and actions too.[214]

Globally speaking, the fact that the United States was a sole hyperpower in a unipolar system spared it from the systemic constraints that were applied on the polar powers in the previous four polar powers wars against Afghanistan, which effectively led to their withdrawal from Afghanistan. The United States had very close ties with Great Britain, despite the significant ideological differences between the regimes of U.S. President George W. Bush and British Prime Minister Tony Blair. However, one cannot ignore the fact that the relations between Europe and the United States greatly weakened.[215] The UN's position regarding the United States weakened greatly following the collapse of the Soviet Union in the early 1990s. Afterward, the United States was influenced less by the largest and most significant international organization in the global scene. The United States' significant military superiority over all other countries was clear and absolute at that time. That fact prevented the other powers operating in the system from applying military constraints against the United States by threatening to use military force, which occurred in some of the previous cases.

Thus, it is shown that the U.S. invasion of Afghanistan and retention of its forces in that country, unlike the previous four cases in which the polar powers that invaded Afghanistan had to withdraw from it, stems from the uniqueness of the current case. This is the only case out of the five wars of the polar powers against Afghanistan in which the polar power, the United States, as a sole hyperpower in the unipolar system, enjoyed full freedom of action. In addition, the United States did not face any extrinsic systemic dictate that held it back in that country or elsewhere. This led it to take, in effect, an independent foreign policy that did not depend on any extrinsic pressures.

The Consequences of the U.S.-Afghan War

The outcomes of the U.S.-Afghan War can be summarized in quantities terms: the killing of 3,000–4,000 Taliban combatants.[216] Conspicuously, only about 25 percent of them were members of the organization. The rest were foreign volunteers who had been brought into Afghanistan to fight under Al Qaeda's leadership. Until January 15, 2002, nearly 7,000 Taliban and foreign combatants were captured, and fewer than 500 of them were transferred to American custody.[217] Most leaders of the Taliban regime survived and were not apprehended. Many of them fled to Pakistan. From about three dozen Taliban leaders on the Pentagon's "wanted list," more than a dozen were killed or injured or fled.[218] At least eight of the 20 senior Taliban leaders and their assistants were killed.[219] Eleven training camps and other infrastructures of Al Qaeda were destroyed.

I shall translate these achievements into qualitative terms. The Taliban was removed from power in Afghanistan, was split as a political force, and fell into disrepute as an ideological movement. Despite that, many members of the Taliban regime became integrated in Afghan politics— some of them in provincial functions and others as members and leaders of various political frameworks. The infrastructures and operations of Al Qaeda in Afghanistan were destroyed and its ability to operate globally was significantly reduced—although maybe only temporarily.[220]

In addition to the direct consequences of the war for the Taliban regime and Al Qaeda, the United States might hope that the action in Afghanistan will serve other, broader goals. The fate of the Taliban regime should cause a number of violent countries to be more careful in their relations with independent terrorist organizations, which like Al Qaeda, may consider the United States as a target. The speed, scale, and intensity of the American reaction to the September 11 terrorist attacks certainly dashed any expectation that the attack would lead to a reduction in American military actions around the world. The expansion in U.S. foreign military commitment that followed the attack was part of the campaign against terrorism. The war improved with certainty the United States' standing in central Asia in general and in Afghanistan in particular. It also strengthened the status of the United States in Pakistan—the regime of the president of Pakistan at the time, Pervez Musharraf, remained closely dependent on American support. In addition, the war formed a new basis for cooperation with India.[221]

SUMMARY OF THE FIVE WARS OF POLAR POWERS AGAINST AFGHANISTAN

The various values of the independent variable, the polarity of the system, in all five test cases allowed me to check whether the variable affected the dependent intrasystemic variable that is being assessed in the study—the degree of territorial expansion of polar powers at the end of the wars being studied. Analysis of the empiric results of these five test cases showed that the territorial outcomes of the test cases indeed correspond with the study hypotheses.

Maintaining the territorial status quo in bipolar systems. All three wars that occurred under the various three instances of bipolarity ended with maintaining the territorial status quo that occurred before the outbreak of the war: the First Anglo-Afghan War (1838–1842), which was fought in the bipolar system of 1816–1848; the Second Anglo-Afghan War (1878–1880), which was fought in the bipolar system of 1871–1909; and, the Soviet-Afghan War (1979–1988), which was fought in the bipolar system of 1946–1991.

The territorial expansion of the hyperpower in unipolar system. In the test case that occurred under the single instance of unipolarity, the war ended with the territorial expansion of the hyperpower, the United States, at the end of the war: the U.S.-Afghan War (2001), which was fought under the unipolar system of 1992–2016.

Territorial nonexpansion of great powers in multipolar systems. In the test case that occurred under the instance of multipolarity, the war ended with the territorial nonexpansion of the polar power Great Britain at the end of the war: the Third Anglo-Afghan War (1919), which was fought in the multipolar system of 1910–1945.

The territorial outcomes of these five test cases correspond with the study hypotheses. In the unipolar system, the polar power the United States expanded territorially as the sole hyperpower in the system at the end of the war. In the bipolar systems, the territorial status quo that occurred before the war was maintained in all three wars (the First and Second Anglo-Afghan Wars and the Soviet-Afghan War). In the Third Anglo-Afghan war too, which was fought in the multipolar system, the territorial status quo preceding the war was maintained.

TERRITORIAL OUTCOMES OF THE WARS OF POLAR POWERS—INTERIM SUMMARY

Table 4.18 shows the degree of territorial expansion of the polar powers under the six instances of the three different polarity models, 1816–2016, according to the *international relations theory of war.*

Table 4.19 summarizes the degree of territorial expansion of the polar powers under the three different polarity models, 1816–2016, according to the *international relations theory of war.*

Table 4.20 concentrates the degree of territorial expansion of the polar powers at the end of the wars they participated in under the three possible polarity models. The table shows the degree to which the results correspond with the forecast of the *international relations theory of war.*

Table 4.21 shows the main wars in which the polar powers were involved under the six instances of the three possible polarity models and their territorial outcomes.

Table 4.18

Territorial Expansion of Polar Powers at the End of Wars by
Periods, 1816–2016

Type of Polarity	Number of Wars	The Territorial Result at the End of the War		
		Territorial Expansion	Territorial Contraction	Territorial Status Quo
Bipolarity, 1816–1848	1	0	0	1
Multipolarity, 1849–1870	5	13	6	0
Bipolarity, 1871–1909	0	0	0	0
Multipolarity, 1910–1945	13	23	32	6
Bipolarity, 1946–1991	4	0	0	4
Unipolarity, 1992–2016	2	2	0	0

Table 4.19

Territorial Expansion of Polar Powers at the End of Wars by
Polarity, 1816–2016

Type of Polarity	Number of Wars	The Territorial Result at the End of the War		
		Territorial Expansion	Territorial Contraction	Territorial Status Quo
Bipolarity, 1816–1848, 1871–1909, 1946–1991	5	0	0	5
Multipolarity, 1849–1870, 1910–1945	18	36	38	6
Unipolarity, 1992–2016	2	2	0	0

Table 4.20

Summary of Territorial Expansion of Polar Powers at the End of Wars, 1816–2016

Type of Polarity	Number of Wars	Total of Three Types of Territorial Expansion	The Territorial Result at the End of the War					
			Territorial Expansion		Territorial Contraction		Territorial Status Quo	
			Number	% of Total of Changes	Number	% of Total of Changes	Number	% of Total of Changes
Bipolarity, 1816–1848, 1871–1909, 1946–1991	5	5	0	0	0	0	5	100%
Multipolarity, 1849–1870, 1910–1945	18	80	36	45%	38	48%	6	7%
Unipolarity, 1992–2016	2	2	2	100%	0	0	0	0

Table 4.21

Key Test Cases, Under the Three Possible Polarity Models

Multipolar Systems	Bipolar Systems	Unipolar Systems
Germany Unification Wars: • **Second Schleswig-Holstein War (1864)** • **Seven Weeks' War (1866)** • **Franco-Prussian (1870–1871)** The multipolar system *allowed* one of the major powers constituting the system, Prussia, to *expand territorially* at the end of these three wars because that expansion did not position it as a potential hegemon of the system • **First and Second World War** The multipolar system *prevented* one of the major powers constituting the system, Germany, to *expand territorially* at the end of these two wars because such an expansion would have positioned it as a potential hegemon of the system; the system also *penalized* Germany for its attempt to become a hegemon in the system and *forced it to contract territorially* at the end of the wars	• **Korean War (1950–1953)** • **Vietnam War (1965–1973)** • **Gulf War (1991)** The bipolar system *led* one of the two superpowers, the United States, to *maintain the territorial status quo* preceding the outbreak of the wars • **Soviet Invasion of Hungary (1956)** • **Soviet-Afghan War (1979–1988)** The bipolar system *led* one of the two superpowers, the Soviet Union, to *maintain the territorial status quo* preceding the outbreak of the wars	• **US Invasion of Afghanistan (2001)** • **US Invasion of Iraq (2003)** The unipolar system *dictated* to the sole hyperpower, the United States, to *expand territorially* at the end of the wars

CHAPTER 5

The Distribution of Power and International Outcomes: Conclusions

By examining the range of theories in international relations, a number of key assumptions have been identified that are often used for explaining the systemic international outcome that the *international relations theory of war* attempts to explain: the degree of stability of the three models of possible international systems. None of the alternative theories in the international relations field presents a satisfactory explanation for the fact that the period covered by the study, 1816–2016, is alternatingly stable and destabilized. In addition to this, the theoretical research in the international relations field barely deals with the intrasystemic international outcome that is explained using the *international relations theory of war*—the degree of territorial expansion of the polar powers at the end of the wars in which they participate.

Most studies from the realistic paradigm in the international relations field indicate that the international system encourages the players to act in one of two key ways: in a revisionist manner, according to offensive realism, or for preserving the status quo, according to neorealism and the defensive branch of realism.

After reviewing all the wars between countries that involved the polar powers of 1816–2016, the two outcomes were compared between the various instances of the same polarity models and between the various instances of the three polarity models. The last, summary chapter will deal with two subjects: firstly, the summary of the empiric check of the two variables that the theory examines for presenting its conclusions, and secondly, analysis of the international system from the end of the Cold War to the present.

INTERNATIONAL OUTCOMES: ANALYSIS AND EVALUATION

INDEX OF STABILITY OF INTERNATIONAL SYSTEMS

The conclusions concerning the stability of the possible international system models correspond with the study assumptions. The two instances of multipolarity in 1849–1870 and 1910–1945 proved to be the least stable of the systems. The three instances of bipolarity, 1816–1848, 1871–1909, and 1946–1991, were discovered to be the most stable. The single instance of unipolarity, 1992–2016, has proved to be somewhere in the middle—more stable than multipolarity but less stable than bipolarity. Table 5.1 summarizes the data.

In the two multipolar systems that were studied, which lasted for 58 years in total, 1849–1870 and 1910–1945, a total of 18 wars involving polar powers were fought—two central wars, seven major wars, and nine minor wars. The number of war years at that time was 26.1, 45 percent of the entire period; the average length in days of the wars was 530 days each; and the total number of deaths in these wars was 27,178,565.

In the three bipolar systems that were studied, which lasted for 118 years in total, 1816–1848, 1871–1909, and 1945–1991, five wars involving polar powers were fought. There were no central wars or major wars, and there were a total of five minor wars. The total number of war years in that period was 12.8, 10.8 percent of the entire period; the average length in days of the wars was 928 days per war; and the total number of deaths in these wars was 2,1051,418.

In the only unipolar system that has been studied, which existed for 24 years in total, 1992–2016, two wars involving the polar power were fought. These wars cannot be cataloged as central, major, or minor wars because these systems are composed of a single polar power. The total number of war years in this period was 3.1, 13 percent of the entire period; the average length of the wars in days is 562.5 days per war; and the total number of deaths in the wars was 39,092.

As the preceding table shows, the most important index for examining the stability of international systems—the total number of years in which there was a war in each of the three systems—proves the starting point of the theory that multipolar systems will be the least stable. The two sentences of the multipolar systems had 45 percent of the war years out of the total number of years in the systems. Bipolar systems will be the most stable—the three instances of bipolar systems contained 10.8 percent of the war years out of the total number of years in which the systems existed. Unipolar systems will be in the middle—they will be more stable than multipolar systems and less stable than bipolar systems. The only instance of unipolar systems had 13 percent of the war years out of the total number of years existing in the systems.

Table 5.1

Causes of War by Polarity Models, 1816–2016

Type of Polarity	Number of Wars			Length of the System in Years	Frequency of Wars		Average Length of Wars	Severity of the Wars
The Three Polarity Models, 1816–2016	Central Wars	Major Wars	Minor Wars		War Years[1]	% of Year in which a War was Fought	Average Length in Days[2]	Total Killed in Combat Only
Multipolarity, 1849–1870, 1910–1945	2	7	9	58	26.1	45%	530	27,178,565
Bipolarity, 1816–1848, 1871–1909, 1946–1991	0	0	5	118	12.8	10.8%	928	2,105,418
Unipolarity, 1992–2016	2[3]			24	3.1	13%	562.5	39,092

1 The total number of years in which there was a war in any of the three polarity models was calculated by dividing the total number of days of war in them by 365 (the length of one year). Multipolar systems: 1854–1870 and 1909–1945: a total of 9,522 days of war, or 26.1 years of war; bipolar systems: 1816–1853, 1871–1909, and 1945–1991: a total of 4,922 days of war, or 12.8 years of war; unipolar systems: 1992–2016: a total of 1,125 days of war, or 3.1 years of war.

2 The average length of the wars in days was calculated by dividing the total number of days of war by the number of wars fought in each of the three polarity models. Multipolar systems: 1854–1870 and 1909–1945: a total of 18 wars lasting 9,522 days of fighting—average length of 529 days per war; bipolar systems: 1816–1853, 1871–1909, and 1946–1991: a total of six wars lasting 4,655 days of fighting—average length of 931 days per war; unipolar systems: 1992–2016: a total of two wars lasting 1,125 days of fighting—average length of 562.5 days per war.

3 In unipolar systems, every war involving the polar power, or the sole hyperpower constituting the system, may be included in the three categories of war: central war, major war, and minor war. Therefore, the three cells relating to the two wars in which the sole hyperpower, the United States in the unipolar system of 1992–2016, were merged.

ESTIMATION OF TERRITORIAL OUTCOMES OF WARS OF POLAR POWERS

The conclusions concerning the degree of territorial expansion of polar powers at the end of wars between countries in which they participate correspond with the study assumption. In the three instances of bipolarity, in 1816–1848, 1871–1909, and 1946–1991, all wars between the countries involving the polar powers, or the two superpowers constituting each of the three instances, ended in maintaining the territorial status quo that preceded the war. In the single instance of unipolarity, 1992–2016, all wars between countries in which the polar power, or the sole hyperpower constituting that instance, ended in the hyperpower's territorial expansion. In the two instances of multipolarity, 1849–1870 and 1910–1945, when the territorial outcome of expansion of the polar power could not position the expanding power as a potential hegemon in the system, the system allowed the polar power to expand at the end of the war—such as the territorial expansion of Prussia in the Germany unification wars. When a territorial outcome of expansion of the polar power could have positioned the expanding power as a potential hegemon in the system, the system prevented the expansion of the polar power at the end of the war (i.e., the system dictated a status quo or territorial contraction of the polar power at the end of the war—such as the territorial contraction of Germany in the First and the Second World Wars and of Japan at the end of the Second World War).

Table 5.2 concentrates the degree of territorial expansion of the polar powers at the end of the wars between countries in which they participated under the three different polarity models and shows the degree of correlation between the results and the forecast of the *international relations theory of war*.

Under the two multipolar systems that were examined, lasting 58 years in total, 1849–1870 and 1910–1945, a total of 18 wars involving the polar powers constituting them were fought—two central wars, seven major wars, and nine small wars. In total, there were 80 types of territorial expansion in those years—36 of them, 45 percent of the total number of changes, ended in territorial expansion of the polar power; 38 of them, 48 percent of all changes, ended in territorial contraction of the polar power; and six of them, 7 percent of all changes, ended in preservation of the territorial status quo preceding the war. As the study anticipated, about half of the territorial expansion types ended in territorial expansion and about half ended in territorial contraction.

Under the three instances of the bipolar systems that were studied, which lasted 118 years in total, 1816–1848, 1871–1909, and 1946–1991, there were a total of five wars involving the polar powers constituting them.

Table 5.2

Summary of Territorial Expansion of Polar Powers at the End of Wars, 1816–2016

Type of Polarity	Number of Wars	Total of Three Types of Territorial Expansion	The Territorial Result at the End of the War					
			Territorial Expansion		Territorial Contraction		Territorial Status Quo	
			Number	% of Total of Changes	Number	% of Total of Changes	Number	% of Total of Changes
Bipolarity, 1816–1848, 1871–1909, 1946–1991	5	5	0	0	0	0	5	100%
Multipolarity, 1849–1870, 1910–1945	18	80	36	45%	38	48%	6	7%
Unipolarity, 1992–2016	2	2	2	100%	0	0	0	0

All five wars were minor wars, and no central or major wars were fought during those years. In total, there were five types of territorial expansion. As the study anticipates, all five, 100 percent of all changes, ended in maintaining of the territorial status quo preceding the war.

Under the single unipolar system that was assessed, which has lasted for 24 years in total to date, 1992–2016, there have been two wars involving the hyperpower. These wars cannot be cataloged as central, major, or minor wars, because unipolar systems have a single polar power. In total, two types of territorial expansion occurred. As the study anticipated, both cases—100 percent of all changes—ended in the territorial expansion of the polar power.

The preceding table strongly supports the arguments of the study concerning the three possible polarity models. *Bipolar systems* will *dictate* to the polar powers constituting them to maintain the territorial status quo preceding the outbreak of the wars in which they have participated. *Unipolar systems* will *dictate* to the polar powers constituting them to expand territorially at the end of the wars in which they have participated in. *Multipolar systems* on the one hand will *dictate* to the polar powers constituting them not to expand territorially, to maintain the territorial status quo, or to contract territorially if their expansion may position them as a potential hegemon in the system (an outcome that homeostasis opposes), and on the other hand will *allow* for their territorial expansion at the end of wars in which they have participated when these results do not position them as a potential hegemon in the system (an outcome that homeostasis allows).

A NEW WORLD ORDER?[1]

The end of the Cold War and the collapse of the Soviet Union in the early 1990s led to an optimistic period in international relations. It would seem that American philosopher Francis Fukuyama's *End of History* is materializing and that human history, which was previously characterized by struggles between ideologies and different regime forms, has indeed reached its end.[2] From this point on, the advocates of this approach argue, we shall be living in a world in which liberal democracy will debut worldwide without facing any other ideological challenges.

After the 21st century and the third millennium commenced, the 9/11 attacks in 2001 shattered those optimistic forecasts. All at once, it seemed that the opposing *Clash of Civilizations Theory* of American political science professor Samuel Huntington, which holds a pessimistic view of the struggle between peoples and civilizations, was more suitable for the analysis of the global scene.[3]

Thus, before the dust from the collapsing World Trade Center settled, the U.S. foreign policy sharply changed its conduct and started to act based on neoconservatism principles. This view of the use of U.S. military and economic power for imposing liberal democratic regimes upholding human rights as a means of disseminating world peace was finally realized by President George W. Bush in two wars that the United States waged far from its homeland—in Afghanistan in 2001 and in Iraq in 2003.

The Afghanistan and Iraq Wars had significant regional consequences. Firstly, they shattered the balance of power in the Persian Gulf, leading to the rise of the status of Iran, for which it was a windfall. It was Washington that eliminated the ideological threat against the ayatollahs' regime from the east by the Taliban regime in Afghanistan, and it later removed the military threat posed against Teheran from the west by Saddam Hussein's regime in Iraq. Thus, through elimination of the power of its former adversaries and without acquiring new military power, Iran soared to a strong, threatening regional status, resulting in an increase in the historical hostility between Sunni and Shia.

Another influence of no lesser effect was the democratic *bang* that President George W. Bush wished to instigate throughout the Middle East, which eventually worked, but only after he finished his term of office and had unintended consequences.

The voting of Barack Obama into power as president in January 2009 gave new spirit to seekers of peace and freedom worldwide. The Cairo address that Obama gave in June that year talked of the need to spread democracy and human rights in the Arab and Muslim world. The "Arab Spring," which broke out about a year later, expressed the ambitions of many residents of the region to replace oppressive regimes with more open and liberal political systems.

The political about-turn of President Obama and his abstention from military involvement in the Middle East led a great degree to the deterioration of the Arab Spring into a serious regional crisis, which instead of leading to the welcome change of "spreading democracy and human rights" had many adverse consequences. Obama relinquished Egyptian ally President Hosni Mubarak, resulting in Egypt entering a chaotic period that included two coups. U.S. and Western operations in Libya eventually led to the downfall of the President Muammar Gaddafi regime and the breakdown of the state. Following the civil war, Syria became a failed state with no effective government in which many radical forces—such as the Islamic State, armed rebel groups, and Hezbollah—fought alongside regional and global powers, including Turkey, Iran, the United States, and primarily Russia.

However, the war in Syria has also caused one of the worst humanitarian crises of modern times, leading to the deaths of about half a million people. Obama's leading from behind policy,[4] which did not change even after Syrian President Bashar al-Assad used chemical weapons, contributed greatly to the influx of refugees that is sweeping over European countries. The ironical result may be interpreted as a kind of unintentional formation of "historical justice" because Europe, which had left the Middle East at the end of the Second World War after decades of financially plundering the region and its residents, now has to accept the descendants of its former subjects.

The 9/11 attacks led to a broadening of U.S. influence in the Middle East, disrupted the regional balance of power, and caused the Arab Spring to break out. However, the consequences of the terrorist attack were not confined to the Middle East. It would seem that the attempt to spread liberal democracy in the Arab-Muslim world has not only been unsuccessful, but to a great extent it may also be identified as one of the factors that have resulted in decaying of these values in the Western world itself.

What should be called "Western Winter" that is developing in the mostly rich, free, and democratic Northern Hemisphere, is characterized by a comprehensive liberal movement that is transforming into a right-wing fascist direction and a left-wing anti-global direction. The plight that Western liberal democracy is facing is disrupting the existing order, as demonstrated by the rise of right-wing powers and xenophobic parties in Europe and Brexit, the United Kingdom's secession from the European Union. The echoes of this bang also crossed the ocean toward the United States and manifested in a hateful struggle between opposing factions in the 2016 U.S. presidential election campaign.

To complete the picture, two other important changes in the international scene should be mentioned. The first is the rise in the importance of nonstate entities in the international scene. These include terrorist organizations such as Al Qaeda, which perpetrated the 9/11 attacks, with its manifold consequences, and the Islamic State and the pre-biblical state model that it established, as well as individuals such as Julian Assange, the founder of the Wikileaks Web site that released information that strained relations between the United States and many of its friends, and Edward Snowden, the leaker of the secret surveillance plans of the U.S. National Security Agency, which influenced processes in U.S. foreign policy and the politics of the United States itself.

The second significant change is the transition from traditional, slow, and regulated media to new, rapid, and universally accessible media. The Arab Spring events in the Middle East region proved that social networks are capable of mobilizing large crowds to rise up and demonstrate and even overthrow regimes. The abortive coup attempts in Turkey also demonstrated that regimes may use social media to retain their power. For example, President Recep Tayyip Erdoğan utilized the masses to defend his regime by real-time video broadcasting.

Going back to the Middle East reveals that the region, which has been managed in the last 100 years based on the Sykes-Picot Agreement and the principles of the European nation-states that developed after the signing of the Treaty of Westphalia in 1648, also includes many areas that are lacking in governability—Syria, Iraq, Libya, and Sinai—and that the forced-state mechanisms have been replaced with prestate or nonstate mechanisms that involve control by gangs and wielding horrific terrorism against civilians.

In the previous century, three universal wars led to systemic changes—the First and the Second World Wars and the Cold War. Although the current century is only in its infancy, it will probably be identified with the 9/11 attacks, which had a limited degree of destruction and death toll, but the events and changes occurring in their wake have made the world a different place and to a great extent a much more dangerous one.[5]

APPENDIX A

The Greatest Powers According to the Cow Project

Entry and Exit Dates for States to Be Designated as Major Powers, COW, 1816–2016[1]

State	Start Date	End Date
USA (United States) 2	13/8/1898	31/12/2016
UKG (United Kingdom) 200	1/1/1816	31/12/2016
FRN (France) 220	1/1/1816 15/8/1945	22/6/1940 31/12/2016
GMY (Prussia/Germany) 255	1/1/1816 1/1/1925 11/12/1991	11/11/1918 7/5/1945 31/12/2016
AUH (Austria-Hungary) 300	1/1/1816	3/11/1918
ITA (Italy) 325	1/1/1860	2/9/1943
USR (Russia / Soviet Union) 365	1/1/1816 1/1/1922	5/12/1917 31/12/2016
CHN (China) 710	1/1/1950	31/12/2016
JPN (Japan) 740	1/4/1895 11/12/1991	14/8/1945 31/12/2016

1 COW, Major Powers

APPENDIX B

Interstate War, 1816–2007, According to the Cow Project

Interstate War, 1816–2007 (Table 1/3)[1]

War #	War Name	War Start 1	War End 1	War Start 2	War End 2	Duration (Days)	Deaths Total	Where Fought
#1	Franco-Spanish	7/4/1823	13/11/1823			221	1,000	Europe
#4	First Russo-Turkish	26/4/1828	14/9/1829			507	130,000	Europe, Middle East
#7	Mexican-American	25/4/1846	14/9/1847				19,283	W. Hemisphere
#10	Austro-Sardinian	24/3/1848	9/8/1848	12/3/1849	30/3/1849		7,527	Europe
#13	First Schleswig-Holstein	10/4/1848	26/8/1848	25/3/1849	10/7/1849	247	6,000	Europe
#16	Roman Republic	8/5/1849	2/7/1849			56	2,600	Europe
#19	La Plata	19/7/1851	3/2/1852			200	1,300	W. Hemisphere
#22	Crimean	23/10/1853	1/3/1856			861	264,200	Europe
#25	Anglo-Persian	25/10/1856	5/4/1857				2,000	Middle East
#28	Italian Unification	29/4/1859	12/7/1859			75	22,500	Europe
#31	First Spanish-Moroccan	22/10/1859	25/3/1860			156	10,000	Middle East
#34	Italian-Roman	11/9/1860	29/9/1860			19	1,000	Europe
#37	Neapolitan	15/10/1860	13/2/1861				1,000	Europe
#40	Franco-Mexican	16/4/1862	5/2/1867			1,757	20,000	W. Hemisphere
#43	Ecuadorian-Columbian	22/11/1863	6/12/1863			15	1,000	W. Hemisphere

#	War							Region
#46	Second Schleswig-Holstein	1/2/1864	25/4/1864	25/6/1864	20/7/1864	111	4,481	Europe
#49	Lopez	12/11/1864	1/3/1870			1,936	310,000	W. Hemisphere
#52	Naval War	25/9/1865	9/5/1866				1,000	W. Hemisphere
#55	Seven Weeks	15/6/1866	26/7/1866			42	44,100	Europe
#58	Franco-Prussian	19/7/1870	26/2/1871			223	204,313	Europe
#60	First Central American	27/3/1876	25/4/1876			30	4,000	W. Hemisphere
#61	Second Russo-Turkish	24/4/1877	31/1/1878				285,000	Europe, Middle East
#64	War of the Pacific	14/2/1879	11/12/1883			1,762	13,868	W. Hemisphere
#65	Conquest of Egyptian	11/7/1882	15/9/1882			67	10,079	Middle East
#67	Sino-French	15/6/1884	9/6/1885				12,100	Asia
#70	Second Central American	28/3/1885	15/4/1885			19	1,000	W. Hemisphere
#72	Franco-Thai	13/7/1893	3/8/1893			22	1000	Asia
#73	First Sino-Japanese	25/7/1894	30/3/1895				15,000	Asia
#76	Greco-Turkish	15/2/1897	19/5/1897			94	2,000	Europe
#79	Spanish-American	22/4/1898	12/8/1898			113	3,685	W. Hemisphere
#82	Boxer Rebellion	17/6/1900	14/8/1900			59	3,003	Asia

(continued)

Interstate War, 1816–2001 (Table 2/3) (*Continued*)

War #	War Name	War Start 1	War End 1	War Start 2	War End 2	Duration (Days)	Deaths Total	Where Fought
#83	Sino-Russian	17/7/1990	10/10/1900				4,000	Asia
#85	Russo-Japanese	8/2/1904	15/9/1905			586	151,831	Asia
#88	Third Central American	27/5/1906	20/7/1906			55	1,000	W. Hemisphere
#91	Fourth Central American	19/2/1907	23/4/1907			64	1,000	W. Hemisphere
#94	Second Spanish-Moroccan	7/7/1909	23/3/1910			260	10,000	Middle East
#97	Italian-Turkish	29/9/1911	18/10/1912			386	20,000	Middle East
#100	First Balkan	17/10/1912	19/4/1913			185	82,000	Europe, Middle East
#103	Second Balkan	30/6/1913	30/7/1913			31	60,500	Europe
#106	World War I	29/7/1914	11/11/1918			1,567	8,578,031	Europe, Africa, Middle East, Asia
#107	Estonian War of Liberation	22/11/1918	3/1/1920				11,750	Europe
#108	Latvian War of Liberation	2/12/1918	3/1/1920				13,246	Europe
#109	Russo-Polish	14/2/1919	18/10/1920			613	100,000	Europe
#112	Hungarian Adversaries	16/4/1919	4/8/1919			111	11,000	Europe
#115	Second Greco-Turkish	5/5/1919	11/10/1922			1,256	50,000	Europe, Middle East

#	War						Region
#116	Franco-Turkish	1/11/1919	20/10/1921		720	40,000	Middle East
#117	Lithuanian-Polish	15/7/1920	1/12/1920		140	1,000	Europe
#118	Manchurian	17/8/1929	3/12/1929		109	3,200	Asia
#121	Second Sino-Japanese	19/12/1931	22/5/1933		521	60,000	Asia
#124	Chaco	15/6/1932	12/6/1935		1,093	92,661	W. Hemisphere
#125	Saudi-Yemeni	20/3/1934	13/5/1934		55	2,100	Middle East
#127	Conquest of Ethiopian	3/10/1935	9/5/1936		220	20,000	Africa
#130	Third Sino-Japanese	7/7/1937	6/12/1941		1,614	1,000,000	Asia
#133	Changkufeng	29/7/1938	11/8/1938		14	1,726	Asia
#136	Nomonhan	11/5/1939	16/9/1939		129	28,000	Asia
#139	World War II	1/9/1939	14/8/1945		2,175	16,634,907	Europe, Africa, Middle East, Asia, Oceana
#142	Russo-Finnish	30/11/1939	12/3/1940		104	151,798	Europe
#145	Franco-Thai	1/12/1940	28/1/1941		58	1,400	Asia
#147	First Kashmir	26/10/1947	1/1/1949			3,500	Asia
#148	Arab-Israeli	15/5/1948	18/7/1948	15/10/1948 1/7/1949	150	8,000	Middle East
#151	Korean	24/6/1950	27/7/1953		1130	910,084	Asia
#153	Off-shore Islands	3/9/1954	23/4/1955			2,370	Asia
#155	Sinai	29/10/1956	6/11/1956		9	3,221	Middle East
#156	Soviet Invasion of Hungary	4/11/1956	14/11/1956		10	2,426	Europe
#158	Ifni War	21/11/1957	10/4/1958			1,122	Africa

(continued)

Interstate War, 1816–2001 (Table 3/3) (Continued)

War #	War Name	War Start 1	War End 1	War Start 2	War End 2	War End 1	Duration (Days)	Deaths Total	Where Fought
#159	Taiwan Straits	23/8/1958	23/11/1958			23/11/1958		1,800	Asia
#160	War in Assam	20/10/1962	22/11/1962			22/11/1962	34	1853	Asia
#163	Vietnam	7/2/1965	30/4/1975			30/4/1975	3,735	1,021,442	Asia
#166	Second Kashmir	5/8/1965	23/9/1965			23/9/1965	50	7,061	Asia
#169	Six Day	5/6/1967	10/6/1967			10/6/1967	6	19,600	Middle East
#170	Second Laotian	13/1/1968	17/4/1973			17/4/1973		11,625	Asia
#172	War of Attrition	6/3/1969	7/8/1970			7/8/1970	520	5,368	Middle East
#175	Football	14/7/1969	18/7/1969			18/7/1969	5	1,900	W. Hemisphere
#176	War of Communist Coalition	23/3/1970	2/7/1971			2/7/1971		6,525	Asia
#178	Bangladesh	3/12/1971	17/12/1971			17/12/1971	15	11,223	Asia
#181	Yom Kippur	6/10/1973	24/10/1973			24/10/1973	19	14,439	Middle East
#184	Turco-Cypriot	20/7/1974	29/7/1974	14/8/1974	16/8/1974	29/7/1974	13	1,500	Europe
#186	War over Angola	23/10/1975	12/2/1976			12/2/1976		2,700	Africa
#187	Second Ogaden	23/7/1977	9/3/1978			9/3/1978		10,500	Africa
#189	Vietnamese-Cambodian Border	1/8/1977	14/3/1978			14/3/1978	226	6,000	Africa
#190	Ugandan-Tanzanian	28/10/1978	11/4/1979			11/4/1979	166	3,000	Africa

#	War						Region
#193	Sino-Vietnamese Punitive	17/2/1979	16/3/1979	16/3/1979	28	21,000	Asia
#199	Iran-Iraq	22/9/1980	20/8/1988	20/8/1988	2,890	1,250,000	Middle East
#202	Falklands	25/3/1982	15/6/1982	15/6/1982	83	1,001	W. Hemisphere
#205	War over Lebanon	21/4/1982	15/9/1982	15/9/1982	148	1655	Middle East
#207	War Over the Aouzou Strip	15/11/1986	11/9/1987	11/9/1987		8,000	Africa
#208	Sino-Vietnamese	5/1/1987	6/2/1987	6/2/1987	33	4,000	Asia
#211	Gulf War	2/8/1990	11/4/1991	11/4/1991	253	41,466	Middle East
#215	War of Bosnian Independence	7/4/1992	13/5/1992	13/5/1992		5,240	Europe
#216	Azeri-Armenian	6/2/1993	12/5/1994	12/5/1994		14,000	
#217	Cenepa Valley	9/1/1995	27/2/1995	27/2/1995		1,500	W. Hemisphere
#219	Badme Border	6/5/1998	12/12/2000	12/12/2000		120,000	Africa
#221	War of Kosovo	24/3/1999	10/6/1999	10/6/1999		5,000	Europe
#223	Kargil	8/5/1999	17/7/1999	17/7/1999		1,172	Asia
#225	Invasion of Afghanistan of 2001	7/10/2001 (COW: 7/10/2001)	26/7/2003 (COW: 22/12/2001)	26/7/2003 (COW: 22/12/2001)	658 (COW: 77)	8,116 (COW: 4,000)	Middle East
#227	Invasion of Iraq of 2003	20/3/2003 (COW: 19/3/2003)	28/6/2004 (COW: 2/5/2003)	28/6/2004 (COW: 2/5/2003)	467 (COW: 45)	30,976 (COW: 7,173)	Middle East

1 COW, Interstate Wars

Notes

INTRODUCTION

1. Emile Durkheim took society to reflect not the mere summation of individuals and their characteristics, but "a specific reality which has its own characteristics." Emile Durkheim, *The Rules of Sociological Method* (New York: Free Press, 1982), pp. 102, 103, 116; Emile Durkheim, *The Division of Labor in Society*, translated by George Simpson (New York: Free Press, 1964).

2. It should be noted that not all scholars regard the institution of war as a source of evil and some even support its existence. Samuel Huntington, for example, worships wars and views them as a primary motive in advancing humanity. The American War of Independence created the American state, the Civil War created the American nation, the wars in France and Spain strengthened their nations, the First World War promoted the concept of equal citizenship, and the Second World War ended discrimination against blacks. He claimed that the worst thing that happened to the United States was the disintegration of the Soviet evil kingdom, while the best thing that happened was the terrorist attacks of September 11, which brought back the sense of external threat and brought about the renewal of American patriotism and the declaration of war against global terrorism. Samuel P. Huntington, *Who Are We? The Challenges to America's National Identity* (New York: Simon & Schuster, 2004). Bradley Thayer presents a less sharp argument. According to him, wars are rarely a good thing, but from time to time they produce good things. Wars, he says, have caused significant social changes in Western societies, increased political rights, increased literacy and educational opportunities, and led to a number of important technological developments—from the invention of radar to the invention of antibiotics. Equally important, he says, is the fact that wars create opportunities for victors to improve their interests in international politics. Bradley A. Thayer, "The *Pax Americana* and the Middle East: U.S. Grand Strategic Interests in the Region after September 11," *Mideast Security and Policy Studies*, No. 56 (December 2003), pp. 1–56.

3. Thucydides, *The History of Peloponnesian War* (Franklin Center, PA: Franklin Library, 1978).

4. Kenneth N. Waltz, "The Emerging Structure of International Politics," *International Security*, Vol. 18, No. 2 (Fall 1993), pp. 44–79, at pp. 44, 50.

5. Bruce Bueno De Mesquita, *The War Trap* (New Haven, CT: Yale University Press, 1981), pp. 1–2.

6. Hegemony was widely used, but only rarely was it defined accurately. Jack Levy has compiled several definitions of the term. Wallerstein argues that hegemony is defined as the ability of one superpower to impose its laws and desires on the system by its dominance over the output of agricultural production, trade, and finance in the world market. Immanuel Wallerstein, *The Politics of the World-Economy: The States, The Movements, and the Civilizations* (Cambridge: Cambridge University Press, 1984), pp. 38–40. Nicole Bousquet argues that hegemonic power must include a status of political leadership in addition to being paramount in production, commerce, and finance. Nicole Bousquet, "From Hegemony to Competition: Cycles of the Core?" in Terence K. Hopkins and Immanuel Wallerstein, eds., *Processes of the World System* (Beverly Hills, CA: Sage Publications, 1980), chapter 2, pp. 46–100, at p. 49. Robert Keohane defines hegemony as superior to material resources. Robert O. Keohane, *After Hegemony: Cooperation and Discord in the World Political Economy* (Princeton, NJ: Princeton University Press, 1984), p. 32. Robert Keohane and Joseph Nye argue that a hegemonic system is one system in which one state is strong enough to maintain the vital laws governing relations between states and that they have the will to do so. Robert O. Keohane and Joseph S. Nye, *Power and Interdependence: World Politics in Transition* (Boston: Little Brown, 1977), p. 44. Raymond Aron argues that under hegemony the states of autonomy or the ability to make their decisions freely are denied. Raymond Aron, *Peace and War: A Theory of International Relations*, translated from the French by Richard Howard and Annette Baker Fox, Abridged by Remy Inglis Hall (Garden City, NY: Anchor Press, 1973), p. 62. All in: Jack S. Levy, "Theories of General War," *World Politics*, Vol. 37, No. 3 (April 1985), pp. 344–374, at pp. 348–349, fn. 20. Immanuel Wallerstein claims that hegemony is rare and short and is identified with the periods of Holland, Great Britain, and American dominance after the two world wars. He claims that the short Dutch hegemony in the 17th century was limited in relation to the later hegemony of Britain and the United States because it was the weakest militarily of its time, compared with other countries that were operating at that time in the system. Immanuel Wallerstein, *Historical Capitalism* (London: Verso, 1983), pp. 58–59; Immanuel Wallerstein, *The Modern World System II: Mercantilism and the Consolidation of the European World Economy, 1600–1750* (New York: Academic Press, 1980), p. 38. Albert Bergeson, on the other hand, argues that Dutch dominance in world production in the 17th century did not suffice for hegemony, and therefore leaves the dominance of Britain in the 19th century and of the United States in the 20th century as the only two periods of true hegemony. Albert Bergeson, "Cycles of War in the Reproduction of the World Economy," paper presented at the Annual Meeting of the International Studies Association, Atlanta, GA, March 27–31, 1984, at p. 10. The hegemonic powers were first and foremost maritime powers but they became land powers to confront land-based challengers that tried to convert the world economy into a world empire. This leads to a world war, the result of which is the rebuilding of the global system, in favor of the hegemonic power. Leadership

costs, accelerating the decline in productivity of the agricultural industry, hegemonic decline, and erosion in the network of alliances of the bishop. Two superpowers usually arise as claims to the crown and the victor becomes the one who can successfully obtain the support of the incoming bishop. The hegemonic powers do not have to fight all wars but they must prepare for the climate of world war. Outputs of hegemonic struggle are determined primarily by economic factors rather than by military elements. All in Levy, "Theories of General War," pp. 349–350, fns. 21–22.

7. Numerous researchers argue that the current single-polar system will not be maintained over time and will become multipolar as very soon. Charles Krauthammer, "The Unipolar Moment," *Foreign Affairs*, Vol. 70, No. 1 (1990–1991), pp. 23–33; Christopher Layne, "The Unipolar Illusion: Why New Great Powers Will Rise," *International Security*, Vol. 17, No. 4 (Spring 1993), pp. 5–51, at p. 7; Michael Manstanduno, "Preserving the Unipolar Moment: Realist Theories and U.S. Grand Strategy after the Cold War," *International Security*, Vol. 21, No. 4 (Spring 1997), pp. 49–88; Glenn H. Snyder, *Alliance Politics* (Ithaca, NY: Cornell University Press, 1997), p. 18; Charles A. Kupchan, "Rethinking Europe," *The National Interest*, Vol. 56 (Summer 1999), pp. 73–79; Charles A. Kupchan, "After Pax Americana: Benign Power, Regional Integration, and the Sources of Stable Multipolarity," *International Security*, Vol. 23, No. 2 (Fall 1998), pp. 40–79; Kenneth N. Waltz, "Evaluating Theories," *American Political Science Review*, Vol. 91, No. 4 (December 1997), pp. 913–917, at p. 914.

8. Bruce W. Jentleson and Christopher A. Whytock, "Who 'Won' Libya? The Force-Diplomacy Debate and Its Implications for Theory and Policy," *International Security*, Vol. 30, No. 3 (Winter 2005/06), pp. 47–86.

9. William C. Wohlforth, "Realism and the End of the Cold War," *International Security*, Vol. 19, No. 3 (Winter 1994/95), pp. 91–129.

10. Paul M. Kennedy, *The Rise and Fall of the Great Powers: Economic Change and Military Conflict from 1500 to 2000* (New York: Random House, 1987).

11. Christopher Layne discusses this subject particularly in the context of unipolar systems. Layne, "The Unipolar Illusion"; John Ikenberry asks why no balancing forces against the United States formed after the end of the Cold War. John G. Ikenberry, ed., *America Unrivaled: The Future of the Balance of Power* (Ithaca, NY: Cornell University Press, 2002); Peter Turchin presents a mathematical formula for solving one of the major historical questions: the reasons for the rise and fall of great civilizations. Peter Turchin, *Historical Dynamics: Why States Rise and Fall* (Princeton, NJ: Princeton University Press, 2003). Also see Peter Turchin, *War and Peace and War: The Life Cycles of Imperial Nations* (New York: Penguin Group, 2007); and Peter Turchin, *War and Peace and War: The Rise and Fall of Empires* (New York: A Plum Book, 2007).

12. One of the main expectations of international relations theory is that it will be able to forecast the occurrence of significant events in the international scene. The end of the Cold War, for example, was not the first major event that surprised international relations researchers and will probably not be the last, but without doubt it is one of the most significant events that none of the main theories in the field, including the realistic theory, anticipated. William C. Wohlforth, "Reality Check: Revising Theories of International Politics in Response to the End of the Cold War," *World Politics*, Vol. 50, No. 4 (July 1998), pp. 650–680, at p. 651.

13. Eric J. Labs, "Beyond Victory: Offensive Realism and the Expansion of War Aims," *Security Studies*, Vol. 6, No. 4 (December 1997), pp. 1–49; Randall L. Schweller, "Neorealism's Status-Quo Bias: What Security Dilemma?" *Security Studies*, Vol. 5, No. 3 (Spring 1996), pp. 90–121; Jeffrey W. Taliaferro, "Security Seeking under Anarchy: Defensive Realism Revisited," *International Security*, Vol. 25, No. 3 (Winter 2000/01), pp. 128–161.

14. Jack L. Snyder, *Myths of Empire: Domestic Politics and International Ambition* (Ithaca, NY: Cornell University Press, 1991), pp. 11–12; Kenneth N. Waltz, *Theory of International Politics* (Reading, MA: Addison-Wesley, 1979); Stephen M. Walt, *The Origins of Alliances* (Ithaca, NY: Cornell University Press, 1987); Stephen Van Evera, "Offense, Defense, and the Causes of War," *International Security*, Vol. 22, No. 4 (Spring 1998), pp. 5–43; Benjamin Miller, *When Opponents Cooperate: Great Power Conflict and Collaboration in World Politics* (Ann Arbor: The University of Michigan Press, 2002); John J. Mearsheimer, "Back to the Future: Instability in Europe After the Cold War," *International Security*, Vol. 15, No. 1 (Summer 1990), pp. 5–56; John J. Mearsheimer, "The False Promise of International Institutions," *International Security*, Vol. 19, No. 3 (Winter 1994/95), pp. 5–49; John J. Mearsheimer, *The Tragedy of Great Power Politics* (New York: W. W. Norton & Company, 2001); Randall L. Schweller, "Bandwagoning for Profit: Bringing the Revisionist State Back In," *International Security*, Vol. 19, No. 1 (Summer 1994), pp. 72–107; Labs, "Beyond Victory"; Fareed Zakaria, *From Wealth to Power: The Unusual Origins of America's World Role* (Princeton, NJ: Princeton University Press, 1998).

15. Gideon Rose, "Neoclassical Realism and Theories of Foreign Policy," *World Politics*, Vol. 51, No. 1 (October 1998), pp. 144–172, at p. 144; Colin Elman, "Horses for Courses: Why *Not* Neorealist Theories of Foreign Policy?" *Security Studies*, Vol. 6, No. 1 (Autumn 1996), pp. 7–53, at p. 12; Colin Elman, "Cause, Effect, and Consistency: A Response to Kenneth Waltz," *Security Studies*, Vol. 6, No. 1 (Autumn 1996), pp. 58–61; Kenneth N. Waltz, "International Politics Is Not Foreign Policy," *Security Studies*, Vol. 6, No. 1 (Autumn 1996), pp. 54–57; Labs, "Beyond Victory," p. 5; Rose, "Neoclassical Realism and Theories of Foreign Policy"; Taliaferro, "Security Seeking under Anarchy," p. 35.

16. Morton A. Kaplan, "Some Problems of International Systems Research," in *International Political Communities: An Anthology* (Garden City, NY: Doubleday and Company, 1966), pp. 469–501; Waltz, *Theory of International Politics*; Waltz, "Evaluating Theories," pp. 915–916; Mearsheimer, *The Tragedy of Great Power Politics*, p. 270; William C. Wohlforth, "The Stability of a Unipolar World," *International Security*, Vol. 24, No. 1 (Summer 1999), pp. 5–41, at pp. 9–22.

17. Quincy Wright, *A Study of War* (Chicago: The University of Chicago Press, 1942), Appendix 20, Table 43; Krauthammer, "The Unipolar Moment"; Layne, "The Unipolar Illusion"; Manstanduno, "Preserving the Unipolar Moment"; Snyder, *Alliance Politics*; Kupchan, "After Pax Americana"; Waltz, "Evaluating Theories"; Wohlforth, "The Stability of a Unipolar World," p. 8 fn. 11, and pp. 28–37.

18. Waltz, "The Emerging Structure of International Politics"; Waltz, *Theory of International Politics*; Waltz, "Evaluating Theories"; Wohlforth, "The Stability of a Unipolar World."

19. Kaplan, "Some Problems of International Systems Research"; Waltz, *Theory of International Politics*.

20. Second Schleswig-Holstein War (#46), Seven Weeks' War (#55), and the Franco-Prussian War (#58). Katharine A. Lerman, "Bismarckian Germany and the Structure of the German Empire," in Mary Fulbrook, ed., *German History since 1800* (London: Arnold, 1997), chapter 8, pp. 147–167, at p. 147. Kennedy, for example, claims that after 1870, Germany, backed by its high industrial power and led by Bismarck, dominated the European great powers. According to him, diplomats in those years claimed that all roads led to Berlin. Kennedy, *The Rise and Fall of the Great Powers*, pp. 149, 160–162, 171, 185–188.

21. Sun Tzu, *The Art of War*, translated by Ralph Sawyer (New York: Basic Books, 1994); Thucydides, *The Peloponnesian War* (New York: Penguin, 1978).

22. Dale C. Copeland, *The Origins of Major War* (Ithaca, NY and London: Cornell University Press, 2000), p. 1.

23. Leslie H. Gelb, "Vietnam: The System Worked," *Foreign Policy*, No. 3 (Summer 1971), pp. 140–167; Leslie H. Gelb and Richard K. Betts, *The Irony of Vietnam: The System Worked* (Washington, DC: The Brookings Institution, 1979).

24. Waltz, *Theory of International Politics*.

25. Mearsheimer, *The Tragedy of Great Power Politics*.

26. According to *Hegemonic Stability Theory*, peace will prevail when one country establishes supremacy, for a hegemonic country will not have the need to fight whereas other countries will lack the ability to do so. A. F. K. Organski, *World Politics* (New York: Knopf, 1968); Robert Gilpin, *War and Change in World Politics* (Cambridge: Cambridge University Press, 1981).

27. Wohlforth, "The Stability of a Unipolar World."

28. For general criticism on neorealism and especially on Waltz, see Robert O. Keohane, ed., *Neorealism and Its Critics* (New York: Columbia University Press, 1986); John G. Ruggie, "Continuity and Transformation in the World Polity: Toward a Neorealist Synthesis," *World Politics*, Vol. 35, No. 2 (January 1983), pp. 261–285; Alexander Wendt, "The Agent-Structure Problem in International Relations Theory," *International Organization*, Vol. 41, No. 3 (Summer 1987), pp. 335–370.

CHAPTER 1

1. Waltz supports this plea. According to him, international relations theory is written in terms of the major powers of the period, and theories relating to self-help systems are written in terms of the main parts constituting the system. According to him, it would be ridiculous to build international relations theory based on Malaysia or Costa Rica; the fate of all countries constituting the system is affected primarily by the actions and interaction between the major powers and not those of the small powers. Therefore, a general theory of international politics must be based on the major powers. Waltz, *Theory of International Politics*, pp. 72–73.

2. The COW Typology of War: Defining and Categorizing Wars.

3. Wohlforth, "The Stability of a Unipolar World," p. 8 fn. 11.

4. Kenneth N. Waltz, "The Stability of a Bipolar World," *Daedalus*, Vol. 93, No. 3 (Summer 1964), pp. 881–909.

5. Waltz, *Theory of International Politics*, pp. 161–162.

6. According to Waltz, the anarchic structure of the system is what has presented its change. In a hierarchic world, the appearance of a potential dominant force, such as a leading election candidate, may motivate attempts to balance it. However, if its success potential exceeds a certain point, it is likely that it will enjoy bandwagoning of additional players that will ensure its victory. In an anarchic world, in contrast, the appearance of a potential dominant force, such as a great power that has the ability to become a hegemon in the system, may also experience enrolling players, but only upon it reaching the point at which its success will appear possible. After this, the attempts to balance it will increase. Waltz, *Theory of International Politics*, pp. 123–128.

7. Alexander Wendt, "Anarchy Is What States Make of It: The Social Construction of Power Politics," *International Organization*, Vol. 46, No. 2 (Spring 1992), pp. 391–425.

8. Samuel Huntington presented an argument to the contrary. He states that the unipolar system will quickly reach its end because political leaders and intellectual leaders in most countries strongly object to it and prefer the appearance of a multipolar world in its place. Samuel P. Huntington, "The Lonely Superpower," *Foreign Affairs*, Vol. 78, No. 2 (March 1999), pp. 35–49, at p. 42.

9. It is important to note that Jack Levy has ruled out this approach. He states that because realism does not explain war well, it is difficult to say how war will act as an agent of change within the realistic theory. Levy, "Theories of General War," p. 345.

10. Stephen G. Brooks and William C. Wohlforth, "Power, Globalization, and the End of the Cold War: Reevaluating a Landmark Case for Ideas," *International Security*, Vol. 25, No. 3 (Winter 2000–2001), pp. 5–53; Randall L. Schweller and William C. Wohlforth, "Power Test: Evaluating Realism in Response to the End of the Cold War," *Security Studies*, Vol. 9, No. 3 (Spring 2000), pp. 60–107; Wohlforth, "Realism and the End of the Cold War."

11. Ofer Israeli, "The Unipolar Trap," *American Diplomacy* (April 2013), pp. 1–8; Niall Ferguson, *Colossus: The Price of America's Empire* (New York: Penguin Press, 2004).

12. Harrison R. Wagner, "The Theory of Games and the Balance of Power," *World Politics*, Vol. 38, No. 4 (July 1986), pp. 546–576, at pp. 546–547.

13. Randall L. Schweller, "Tripolarity and the Second World War," *International Studies Quarterly*, Vol. 37, No. 1 (March 1993), pp. 73–103, at p. 77.

14. Waltz, *Theory of International Politics*, p. 135.

15. Waltz, *Theory of International Politics*, p. 202.

16. Mearsheimer, "Back to the Future," p. 7 fn. 6.

17. Jack S. Levy, "Contending Theories of International Conflict: A Levels-of-Analysis Approach," in Chester A. Crocker and Fen O. Hampson, eds., *Managing Global Chaos: Sources of and Responses to International Conflict* (Washington, DC: United States Institute of Peace, 1996), pp. 3–24, at p. 6.

18. The decision to include these four components stems from the fact that combining them provides a wider spectrum of stability indices relative to tests that were shown in other studies and were based on one index only. Two additional main sources used the four components on which the current study is based for checking the stability of the system: Jack S. Levy, *War in the Modern Great Power*

System, 1495–1975 (Lexington: University Press of Kentucky, 1983); Mearsheimer, *The Tragedy of Great Power Politics*.

19. Zakaria, *From Wealth to Power*, p. 5.

20. James Kurth, "America's Grand Strategy: A Pattern of History," *The National Interest*, Vol. 43 (Spring 1996), pp. 3–19.

21. Ross H. Munro, "The Asian Interior: China's Waxing Spheres of Influence," *Orbis*, Vol. 38, No. 4 (Fall 1994), pp. 585–605.

22. Leszek Buszynski, "Russia and the CIS in 2003: Regional Reconstruction," *Asian Survey*, Vol. 44, No. 1 (January–February 2004), pp. 158–167.

23. This discussion is drawn from Ofer Israeli, "The Necessary Russian Involvement within the Disintegrated Middle East," *Maariv*, August 2, 2015 [Hebrew]; and Ofer Israeli, "An Israeli Perspective on the Russian Chess Game in Syria." Unpublished: Prepared for "The Russian Foreign Policy in the Middle East," University of Haifa, June 8, 2015 [Hebrew].

24. Kurth, "America's Grand Strategy."

25. Ismail Sharif, "Growing Discontent with Globalization," *World Affairs*, Vol. 7, No. 3 (July–September 2003), pp. 14–27.

26. Territorial Change, 1816–2008 (v4.01).

27. David B. Rivkin Jr. and Darin R. Bartram, "Military Occupation: Legally Ensuring a Lasting Peace," *The Washington Quarterly*, Vol. 26, No. 3 (Summer 2003), pp. 87–103; Eric Carlton, *Occupation: The Policies and Practice of Military Conquerors* (New York: Routledge, 1992); Minxin Pei and Sara Kasper, *Lessons from the Past: The American Record of Nation Building* (Washington, DC: Carnegie Endowment for International Peace, 2003).

28. In certain occupations, such as the occupation of Istanbul after the First World War, just one area was occupied. David M. Edelstein, "Occupational Hazards: Why Military Occupations Succeed or Fail," *International Security*, Vol. 29, No. 1 (Summer 2004), pp. 49–91, at p. 52 fn. 9.

29. Peter Liberman, *Does Conquest Pay? The Exploitation of Occupied Industrial Societies* (Princeton, NJ: Princeton University Press, 1996).

30. Mark Dow, "Occupying and Obscuring Haiti," *New Politics*, Vol. 5, No. 2 (Winter 1995), pp. 12–26.

31. Edelstein, "Occupational Hazards."

32. The unification, Anschluss, of Germany and Austria in 1938, in which Austria became part of the German Reich, is an example of annexation. The unification was in violation of the Versailles Treaty that ended the First World War and led to Austria's becoming a province of the German Third Reich, in 1938–1945. Evan Burr Bukey, *Hitler's Hometown: Linz, Austria, 1908–1945* (Bloomington: Indiana University Press, 1986); F. Parkinson, ed., *Conquering the Past: Austrian Nazism Yesterday and Today* (Detroit: Wayne State University Press, 1989); Bruce F. Pauley, *Hitler and the Forgotten Nazis: A History of Austrian National Socialism* (Chapel Hill: University of North Carolina Press, 1981); Kurt Schuschnigg, *The Brutal Takeover: The Austrian Ex-Chancellor's Account of the Anschluss of Austria by Hitler* (London: Weidenfeld and Nicolson, 1971).

33. Two prominent cases of acquisition of territories that were not in wartime in which the United States purchased territories for money may be mentioned. On April 30, 1803, the United States purchased the territory of Louisiana from France,

which consisted of more than 2 million square kilometers, for approximately $15 million; on April 19, 1867, the United States purchased Alaska from Russia for $7.2 million.

CHAPTER 2

1. Ecclesiastes 1:9.

2. Reuben Ablowitz, "The Theory of Emergence," *Philosophy of Science*, Vol. 6, No. 1 (January 1939), pp. 1–16, at p. 1.

3. To paraphrase the expression *large history*, which David Landes coined, an expression that relates to studies that review long periods over history (Paul M. Kennedy, "Mission Impossible?" *New York Review of Books*, Vol. LI, No. 10 (June 10, 2004), 16–19, at p. 19b), the current study develops a *large theory*. This is because the *international relations theory of war* is attempting to provide tools for understanding and analyzing international processes and outcomes over a long period, 1816–2016.

4. Robert O. Keohane, "Institutionalist Theory and the Realist Challenge after the Cold War," in David A. Baldwin, ed., *Neorealism and Neoliberalism: The Contemporary Debate* (New York: Columbia University Press, 1993), chapter 11, pp. 269–300.

5. Anarchy, its importance, meaning, and consequences for international politics, were first discussed by Lowes G. Dickinson, *The European Anarchy* (New York: The Macmillan Company, 1916).

6. Hedley Bull, *The Anarchical Society: A Study of Order in World Politics* (New York: Columbia University Press, 2002); Robert Jervis, "Cooperation under the Security Dilemma," *World Politics*, Vol. 30, No. 2 (January 1978), pp. 167–214; Keohane, *After Hegemony*; Mearsheimer, *The Tragedy of Great Power Politics*; Helen Milner, "The Assumption of Anarchy in International Relations Theory: A Critique," *Review of International Studies*, Vol. 17, No. 1 (January 1991), pp. 67–85; Waltz, *Theory of International Politics*; "Cooperation under Anarchy" special Volume of *World Politics*, Vol. 38, No. 1 (October 1985), edited by Oye.

7. Bull, *The Anarchical Society*, pp. 24–25.

8. Waltz, *Theory of International Politics*.

9. Robert W. Tucker, *The Inequality of Nations* (New York: Basic Books, 1977), p. 3.

10. Bull, *The Anarchical Society*, p. 42.

11. Mearsheimer, *The Tragedy of Great Power Politics*, p. 3; Milner, "The Assumption of Anarchy in International Relations Theory," pp. 69–70.

12. Robert Powell, "Anarchy in International Relations Theory: The Neorealist-Neoliberal Debate," *International Organization*, Vol. 48, No. 2 (Spring 1994), pp. 313–344, at pp. 330–331.

13. Waltz, *Theory of International Politics*; Mearsheimer, *The Tragedy of Great Power Politics*; Martin Wight, *Power Politics* (London: Harmondsworth, 1978); Frederick S. Dunn, "The Scope of International Relations," *World Politics*, Vol. 1, No. 1 (October 1948), pp. 142–146.

14. Waltz, *Theory of International Politics*, pp. 103–104.

15. Wight, *Power Politics*, p. 102.

16. Kenneth A. Oye, "Explaining Cooperation under Anarchy: Hypotheses and Strategies," *World Politics*, Vol. 38, No. 1 (October 1985), pp. 1–24, at pp. 1–2.

17. For the constructivism theory of international relations, see Nicholas G. Onuf, *World of Our Making: Rules and Rule in Social Theory and International Relations* (Columbia: University of South Carolina Press, 1989); Emanuel Adler, "Seizing the Middle Ground: Constructivism in World Politics," *European Journal of International Relations*, Vol. 3, No. 3 (September 1997), pp. 319–363; Richard K. Ashley, "The Geopolitics of Geopolitical Space: Toward a Critical Social Theory of International Politics," *Alternatives*, Vol. 12, No. 4 (October 1987), pp. 403–434; Richard K. Ashley, "The Poverty of Neorealism," *International Organization*, Vol. 38, No. 2 (Spring 1984), pp. 225–286; Jeffrey T. Checkel, "The Constructivist Turn in International Relations Theory: A Review Essay," *World Politics*, Vol. 50, No. 2 (February 1998), pp. 324–348; Robert W. Cox, "Towards a Post-Hegemonic Conceptualization of World Orders: Reflections on the Relevancy of Ibn Khaldun," in James N. Rosenau and Ernst-Otto Czempiel, eds., *Governance Without Government: Order and Change in World Politics* (Cambridge: Cambridge University Press, 1992), chapter 5, pp. 132–159; Martha Finnemore and Kathryin Sikkink, "International Norm Dynamics and Political Change," *International Organization*, Vol. 52, No. 4 (Autumn 1998), pp. 887–917; Stefano Guzzini, "A Reconstruction of Constructivism in International Relations," *European Journal of International Relations*, Vol. 6, No. 2 (June 2000), pp. 147–182; Ted Hopf, "The Promise of Constructivism in International Relations Theory," *International Security*, Vol. 23, No. 1 (Summer 1998), pp. 171–200; Peter J. Katzenstein, ed., *The Culture of National Security: Norms and Identity in World Politics* (New York: Columbia University Press, 1996); Rey Koslowski and Friedrich V. Kratochwil, "Understanding Change in International Politics: The Soviet Empire's Demise and the International System," *International Organization*, Vol. 48, No. 2 (Spring 1994), pp. 215–247; Ruggie, "Continuity and Transformation in the World Polity"; John G. Ruggie, "What Makes the World Hang Together? Neo-Utilitarianism and the Social Constructivist Challenge," *International Organization*, Vol. 52, No. 4 (Autumn 1998), pp. 855–885; John G. Ruggie, *Constructing the World Polity: Essays on International Institutionalization* (New York: Routledge, 1998); Alexander Wendt, "Constructing International Politics," *International Security*, Vol. 20, No. 1 (Summer 1995), pp. 71–81; Wendt, "Anarchy Is What States Make of It"; Alexander Wendt, *Social Theory of International Politics* (Cambridge: Cambridge University Press, 1999).

18. Wendt, "Anarchy Is What States Make of It."

19. Robert Axelrod and Robert O. Keohane, "Achieving Cooperation under Anarchy: Strategies and Institutions," *World Politics*, Vol. 38, No. 1 (October 1985), pp. 226–254; Oye, "Explaining Cooperation under Anarchy."

20. Keohane, *After Hegemony*, chapters 5, 6.

21. Martin Wight, "Why Is There No International Theory?" in James Der Derian, ed., *International Theory: Critical Investigations* (New York: New York University Press, 1995), pp. 15–35. The first edition was published in Herbert Butterfield and Wight Martin, eds., *Diplomatic Investigations: Essays in the Theory of International Politics* (London: George Allen & Unwin, 1966), pp. 17–34.

22. It is very important to make a clear distinction between preferences of countries and their action strategies. Preferences of countries are not affected by changes in their strategic environment, such as change in the distribution of capabilities in the system. Jeffrey W. Legro and Andrew Moravcsik, "Is Anybody Still a Realist?" *International Security*, Vol. 24, No. 2 (Fall 1999), pp. 5–55. Strategies of

countries are subject to changes and include the way in which a nation defines
its interests, the way in which it treats them, and the means that it will use for
contending with threats aimed against it. Melvyn P. Leffler, *A Preponderance of
Power: National Security, the Truman Administration, and the Cold War* (Stanford, CA:
Stanford University Press, 1992), p. ix; John J. Mearsheimer, *Liddell Hart and the
Weight of History* (Ithaca, NY: Cornell University Press, 1988), p. 17; Barry Posen,
The Sources of Military Doctrine: France, Britain, and Germany Between the World Wars
(Ithaca, NY: Cornell University Press, 1984).

23. Hans J. Morgenthau, *Politics Among Nations: The Struggle for Power and Peace*
(New York: Alfred A. Knopf, 1978), pp. 2–12; Waltz, *Theory of International Politics*,
chapter 2.

24. Morgenthau, *Politics Among Nations*, p. 46.

25. A. F. K. Organski and Jacek Kugler, *The War Ledger* (Chicago: University of
Chicago Press, 1980), pp. 19–20, 23.

26. Schweller, "Bandwagoning for Profit," pp. 104–105.

27. Felix Gilbert, *To the Farewell Address: Ideas of Early American Foreign Policy*
(Princeton, NJ: Princeton University Press, 1961), pp. 95–96. Thomas Schelling
argues that this view of the diplomacy of major powers, which he considers
greedy, is a precise picture of interests of countries in the pre-Napoleonic period,
which may be referred to as the *sport of kings' war*. Thomas C. Schelling, *Arms and
Influence* (New Haven, CT: Yale University Press, 1966), pp. 27–28.

28. Morgenthau, *Politics Among Nations*, chapter 1.

29. Schweller, "Bandwagoning for Profit," pp. 100–104. It is important to note
that this statement by Schweller led Legro and Moravcsik to argue that he had
changed realism to idealism because he based himself on the preferences of countries rather than variance in their capabilities for explaining the shift in the polarity
of the system in the interwar period of the 1930s. Legro and Moravcsik, "Is Anybody Still a Realist?"

30. Benjamin Frankel, "Restating the Realist Case: An Introduction," *Security
Studies*, Vol. 5, No. 3 (Spring 1996), pp. ix–xx; Sean M. Lynn-Jones, "Realist and
America's Rise," *International Security*, Vol. 23, No. 2 (Fall 1998), pp. 157–182.

31. Waltz, *Theory of International Politics*.

32. Jervis, "Cooperation under the Security Dilemma."

33. Waltz, *Theory of International Politics*, p. 126.

34. For studies from the defensive realism, see Walt, *The Origins of Alliance*;
Posen, *The Sources of Military Doctrine*; Thomas J. Christensen and Snyder Jack,
"Chain Gangs and Passed Bucks: Predicting Alliance Patterns in Multipolar-
ity," *International Organization*, Vol. 44, No. 2 (Spring 1990), pp. 137–168; Thomas
J. Christensen, "Perceptions and Alliances in Europe, 1865–1940," *International
Organization*, Vol. 51, No. 1 (Winter 1997), pp. 65–97; Van Evera, "Offense, Defense,
and the Causes of War"; Stephen Van Evera, *Causes of War: Power and the Roots of
Conflict* (Ithaca, NY: Cornell University Press, 1999).

35. Mearsheimer, *The Tragedy of Great Power Politics*.

36. By examining six cases of behavior of great powers (Japan 1868–1945, Germany 1862–1945, the Soviet Union 1917–1991, Italy 1861–1943, Britain 1792–1945,
and the United States 1800–1990), Mearsheimer tries to prove that the history of
great powers' politics includes primarily a clash of revisionist countries and that
the only status quo powers that appeared were local hegemons. The cases of Japan,
Germany, the Soviet Union, and Italy strongly support his theory. These countries

have constantly sought opportunities to expand, have exploited these opportunities, and have become more aggressive with increasing power. The examples of nonexpansion were primarily the result of more successful deterrence rather than the disappearance of the expansion motif. For example, Germany in 1871–1900 was a nonaggressive country, but this stemmed from the fact that any further expansion beyond unification of Germany would have led to a war of great powers in which Germany would have lost. Therefore, as the theory expects, Germany accepted the status quo and waited until 1903, in which it became a potential hegemon, upon achieving greater military well-being and power than any other European country and an aggressive policy appeared immediately. The two cases in which democratic powers were involved, the United States and Great Britain, posed a difficult test for Mearsheimer's theory, and it passed it. Mearsheimer argues that the nonexpansion of these two powers to Europe stemmed from the "checking power of the water"—the Atlantic Ocean preventing the United States from expanding to Europe just as the English Channel prevented the expansion of Great Britain to Europe. Mearsheimer, *The Tragedy of Great Power Politics*, chapter 6.

37. Mearsheimer, *The Tragedy of Great Power Politics*, p. 21.

38. For studies from the offensive realism, see Mearsheimer, "Back to the Future"; Mearsheimer, "The False Promise of International Institutions"; Mearsheimer, *The Tragedy of Great Power Politics*; Zakaria, *From Wealth to Power*; Schweller, "Bandwagoning for Profit"; Randall L. Schweller, *Deadly Imbalances: Tripolarity and Hitler's Strategy of World Conquest* (New York: Columbia University Press, 1998); Samuel P. Huntington, "Why International Primacy Matters," *International Security*, Vol. 17, No. 4 (Spring 1993), pp. 68–83; Labs "Beyond Victory."

39. Taliaferro, "Security Seeking under Anarchy," pp. 158–159.

40. Bull, *The Anarchical Society*; Milner, "The Assumption of Anarchy in International Relations Theory."

41. Neorealism argues that the main purpose of countries is to prevent hegemony of other countries and maintain the balance of power in the system. According to this assumption, countries, particularly great powers, will balance against countries that will be the key threat to their interests, particularly against any country that will act to establish a hegemonic status in the system. The theory argues that the balance mechanism usually works successfully in preventing hegemony, whether the reason for this is that potential hegemons are deterred from the formation of military coalitions against them or that the potential hegemons are defeated in war after the failure of deterrence. Levy, "Contending Theories of International Conflict," p. 6.

42. Mearsheimer, *The Tragedy of Great Power Politics*, pp. 34–35.

43. Zakaria presents a similar argument, whereby European state people, under the system of great powers of the 19th century, clearly understood that capabilities shaped intentions. Zakaria, *From Wealth to Power*, p. 5.

44. Zakaria, *From Wealth to Power*; Kennedy, *The Rise and Fall of the Great Powers*.

45. The most significant study of homeostatic and ideas stemming from it remains a book dating from the 1960s. Karl W. Deutsch, *The Nerves of Government: Models of Political Communication and Control* (London: Free Press, 1966), especially chapters 5, 11. Robert Jervis's book of 1997 relating to the term in a number of contexts is also noteworthy. Robert Jervis, *System Effects: Complexity in Political and Social Life* (Princeton, NJ: Princeton University Press, 1997), especially pp. 275–282.

46. Deutsch, *The Nerves of Government*, pp. 79, 184, 187.

47. Pamela B. De Vinne, ed., *The American Heritage: Illustrated Encyclopedic Dictionary* (Boston: Houghton Mifflin Company, 1987), p. 807b.

48. De Vinne, *The American Heritage*, p. 425b.

49. Jervis, *System Effects*, p. 127 fn. 3.

50. Bruce Bueno De Mesquita argues that system-transforming wars can be small. A small event—the Seven Weeks' War of 1866—fundamentally changed the international order by providing the foundation for German hegemony on the European continent. Bruce Bueno De Mesquita, "Pride of Place: The Origins of German Hegemony," *World Politics*, Vol. 43, No. 1 (October 1990), pp. 28–53, at p. 28.

51. Graham Evans and Jeffrey Newnham, *The Penguin Dictionary of International Relations* (London: Penguin Books, 1998), p. 170.

52. Evans and Newnham, *The Penguin Dictionary of International Relations*, p. 170.

53. Arturo Rosenblueth, Norbert Wiener, and Julian Bigelow, "Behavior, Purpose and Theology," *Philosophy of Science*, Vol. 10, No. 1 (January 1943), pp. 18–24, at p. 19.

54. Rosenblueth, Wiener, and Bigelow, "Behavior, Purpose and Theology," p. 19.

55. EAST GERMAN UPRISING (ICB #141); POLAND LIBERALIZATION (ICB #154); HUNGARIAN UPRISING (ICB #155); PRAGUE SPRING (ICB #227); SOLIDARITY (ICB #315).

56. Ofer Israeli, "Did Bush Save America?" *Jerusalem Post*, April 22, 2010.

57. Colin McInnes, "A Different Kind of War? September 11 and the United States' Afghan War," *Review of International Studies*, Vol. 29, No. 2 (2003), pp. 165–184, at p. 170.

58. Legro and Moravcsik, "Is Anybody Still a Realist?" pp. 17–18.

59. Frankel, "Restating the Realist Case," pp. xii–xiv.

60. The current study adopts the argument of Legro and Moravcsik whereby while classic realists have focused on restrictions forced on countries by distribution of material resources and have rejected the influence of democracy, ideology, economic integration, the law, and institutions of the political world, researchers have turned from defensive realism and neoclassic realism to a new definition of realism, which denies these traditional counterarguments. This action has caused them to slide toward liberal, epistemic, and institutional theories. Legro and Moravcsik, "Is Anybody Still a Realist?"

61. Wendt, *Social Theory of International Politics*, p. 9.

62. Robert G. Gilpin, "No One Loves a Political Realist," in Benjamin Frankel, ed., *Realism, Restatements and Renewal* (New York: Frank Cass, 1996), chapter 3, pp. 3–26; Kenneth N. Waltz, "Realist Thought and Neorealist Theory," *Journal of International Affairs*, Vol. 44, No. 1 (Spring/Summer 1990), pp. 21–37, at p. 37.

63. Wendt, *Social Theory of International Politics*, p. 9.

64. Aron, *Peace and War*, p. 6.

65. Francis Fukuyama, "Challenges to World Order After September 11," in William I. Zartman, ed., *Imbalance of Power: US Hegemony and International Order* (Boulder, CO: Lynne Rienner Publishers, 2009).

66. Waltz, *Theory of International Politics*.

67. These hypotheses are controversial and there are other theories of the state system besides Waltz's neorealism. Wendt, for example, offers a theory of a state system that criticizes Waltz's neorealist theory. Wendt, *Social Theory of International Politics*.

68. Thomas L. Friedman, *The Lexus and the Olive Tree: Understanding Globalization* (New York: Farrar, Straus & Giroux, 1999).

69. Fukuyama, "Challenges to World Order After September 11."

70. Schweller defines resources as potential military power. Schweller, "Tripolarity and the Second World War," p. 77.

71. Mearsheimer, "Back to the Future," p. 7.

72. Waltz, *Theory of International Politics*, p. 131.

73. Waltz argues that military power is a product of the six components that he states, so one may conclude that most of his theory assumes that military power is the only capability that is worthy of evaluation for determining the standing of a state as a great power. Waltz, *Theory of International Politics*, p. 98. Ted Hopf expands Waltz's definition slightly to polarity. In addition to measurement of military capabilities by the players in the system, Hopf argues that the size of the population and the revenues of the regime should also form a basis for determining the status of a state as a pole in the system. Ted Hopf, "Polarity, the Offense-Defense Balance, and War," *The American Political Science Review*, Vol. 85, No. 2 (June 1991), pp. 475–493, at pp. 478–479.

74. In support of the argument of the current study, that economic power alone is insufficient for bringing a country to polar power status in the system, two prominent examples may be shown. The first example is Japan, whose enormous economic power is insufficient for promoting it to this status. Yoichi Funabashi, "Japan and the New World Order," *Foreign Affairs*, Vol. 70, No. 5 (Winter 1991–92), pp. 58–74. The second example is the European Union, whose enormous economic power is insufficient to promote it to this status. The person responsible for the European Union's foreign policy, for example, defined the period preceding the Iraq War (2003) as the darkest period in his seven years in office, because it proved the union's limitations. Dan Bilefsky, "Solana, EU's 'Good Cop,' Takes Stage," *International Herald Tribune*, August 11, 2006.

75. The sources of this approach may be found in the geopolitics approach that was formed as a new discipline in the 1880s by a group of German theorists. That discipline presented the principles of geographic and political science for studying the global distribution of political power. By declaring that a state's power and well-being stem from its geopolitical size, these researches expected the great powers of the future to be the countries that would acquire sufficient territory and raw materials to achieve economic self-sufficiency. Hans W. Weigert, *Generals and Geographers: The Twilight of Geopolitics* (New York: Oxford University Press, 1942), p. 15.

76. Alfred T. Mahan, *The Influence of Sea Power upon History: 1660–1783* (Boston: Little, Brown and Company, 1890).

77. Kennedy, "Mission Impossible."

78. The *realist* view of occupation argues that occupation pays well. According to it, the more you conquer, the richer and stronger you get, so rulers have financial and security incentives to expand. In contrast, according to the *liberal* view, occupation does not pay. This is because the more you conquer, the weaker you become, because of entering a larger vortex of costs. Therefore, rulers do not have financial incentive to expand. Peter Liberman, "The Spoils of Conquest," *International Security*, Vol. 18, No. 2 (Fall 1993), pp. 125–153, at p. 125.

79. Liberman, "The Spoils of Conquest."

80. Halford Mackinder, "The Geographical Pivot of History," *The Geographical Journal*, Vol. 23, No. 4 (April 1904), pp. 421–437. Mackinder's ideas had great

influence in the 20th century. To a great extent, these ideas constituted the basis for German attempts to penetrate the heart of Russian territory in both world wars, manifesting in the German aspiration of *lebensraum* (a term that was introduced by Mackinder) in the East. Mackinder's ideas also influenced American geopolitical thinking. Kennedy, "Mission Impossible."

81. Mackinder, "The Geographical Pivot of History," p. 436; Halford Mackinder, *Democratic Ideals and Reality: A Study in the Politics of Reconstruction* (London: Constable, 1919).

82. Nicholas J. Spykman, *The Geography of the Peace*, ed. by Helen R. Nicholl (New York: Harcourt, Brace & Company, 1944), p. 43.

83. Nicholas J. Spykman, *America's Strategy in World Politics: The United States and the Balance of Power* (New York: Harcourt, 1942), p. 24.

84. About at least a year before Pearl Harbor and Hitler's declaration of war, President Roosevelt wanted to join the European struggle, because "if Great Britain falls, the axis countries will control the continents of Europe, Asia, Africa, and Australia and the oceans—and will send enormous military resources and fleets to act against the Western Hemisphere." Alton Frye, *Nazi Germany and the American Hemisphere, 1939–1941* (New Haven, CT: Yale University Press, 1967), p. 190.

85. George F. Kennan, *American Diplomacy 1900–1950* (Chicago: University of Chicago Press, 1951), p. 5.

86. George Bush, *National Security Strategy of the United States, 1990–1991* (Washington, DC: Maxwell Macmillan Pergamon, 1990), p. 5; Melvyn P. Leffler, "The American Conception of National Security and the Beginnings of the Cold War, 1945–48," *The American Historical Review*, Vol. 89, No. 2 (April 1984), pp. 346–381.

87. Adam Smith, *An Inquiry into the Nature and Causes of the Wealth of Nations* (New York: Oxford University Press, 1976—The first edition was published in 1776). Richard Cobden wrote in 1894 that wherever an empire achieves status in neighboring territories by force of arms, the territory seizure will be a source of weakness rather than strength. Richard Cobden, *Speeches on Questions of Public Policy*, ed. by John Bright and James Rogers (London: Macmillan, 1870), Vol. 1; and Richard Cobden, *Political Writings* (New York: D. Appleton, 1867), Vol. 1. Norman Angell argues that European nations do not increase their wealth by enlarging their territory. Norman Angell, *The Great Illusion: A Study of the Relations of Military Power to National Advantage* (New York: G. P. Putnam's Sons, 1910). According to Klaus Knorr, conquest of territories for economic reasons has become out of date. Klaus M. Knorr, *The Power of Nations: The Political Economy of International Relations* (New York: Basic Books, 1975). Carl Kaysen agrees that the question of whether the degree of occupation of a new territory adds to the economic power of the occupier is debatable. Carl Kaysen, "Is War Obsolete? A Review Essay," *International Security*, Vol. 14, No. 4 (Spring 1990), pp. 42–64.

88. Unlike the current standard, Schweller argues that there are good reasons for analyzing tripolarity as a structure separate from a multipolar system in which more than three powers operate. Schweller, *Deadly Imbalances*.

89. It should be noted that each of the three key theoretical paradigms in international relations theory relates differently to the structure of the international system. Constructivism treats it as a distribution of ideas because it has an idealist ontology. Neoliberalism considers it to be material capabilities and institutions because it added to a supra-institutional structure to the material base. Neorealism

considers it a distribution of material capabilities, because of its material attitude to objects. Wendt, *Social Theory of International Politics*, p. 5.

90. A discussion of a system containing five players does not have to lead to the conclusion that the system contains just five independent countries. However, it is not always clear what the distinguishing characteristics of polar powers are from countries that are not considered as players in the balance of power system. In the dispute concerning the relative stability of bipolar or multipolar systems, it is not always clear whether the distinction is between a world of two great powers only or a world of multiple great powers, or between a world of multiple great powers in which two are much stronger than the others, and a world of multiple great powers in which power is divided more equally. According to Wagner, this distinction may also be attributed to the structure of alliances that characterizes the international system. Wagner, "The Theory of Games and the Balance of Power."

91. Waltz, for example, argues that the question of which nations are great powers is an empiric question and one that may be answered using common sense. Waltz, *Theory of International Politics*, p. 131.

92. Edward D. Mansfield, "Concentration, Polarity, and the Distribution of Power," *International Studies Quarterly*, Vol. 37, No. 1 (March 1993), pp. 105–128, at pp. 108–109.

93. Waltz, *Theory of International Politics*, pp. 90–91.

94. Waltz, *Theory of International Politics*, pp. 98–99.

95. Legro and Moravcsik, "Is Anybody Still a Realist?" pp. 12–18.

96. Wendt, *Social Theory of International Politics*, p. 11 fn. 31.

97. The other paradigm is the behavioral paradigm that includes early realists that argue that the behavior of countries is what determines their outcomes in international politics. Waltz, "Evaluating Theories," p. 913.

98. Wendt, "The Agent-Structure Problem in International Relations Theory."

99. Kenneth N. Waltz, "The Origins of War in Neorealist Theory," *Journal of Interdisciplinary History*, Vol. 18, No. 4 (Spring 1988), pp. 615–628, at p. 618.

100. Andrew Moravcsik, "Taking Preferences Seriously: A Liberal Theory of International Politics," *International Organization*, Vol. 51, No. 4 (Autumn 1997), pp. 513–553.

101. Thomas S. Kuhn, *The Structure of Scientific Revolutions* (Chicago: The University of Chicago Press, 1962).

102. Among the earlier and the prominent supporters of the realist theory we can mark Edward H. Carr, *The Twenty Years' Crisis, 1919–1939: An Introduction to the Study of International Relations* (London: Macmillan, 1939); Morgenthau, *Politics Among Nations*; John H. Hertz, *Political Realism and Political Idealism: A Study in Theories and Realities* (Chicago: Chicago University Press, 1951); George F. Kennan, *Realities of American Foreign Policy* (Princeton, NJ: Princeton University Press, 1954); Reinhold Niebuhr, *Moral Man and Immoral Society: A Study in Ethics and Politics* (New York: Charles Scribner's Sons, 1932); George Schwarzenberger, *Power Politics: An Introduction to the Study of International Relations and Post-War Planning* (London: J. Cape, 1941); Spykman, *America's Strategy in World Politics*; Arnold Wolfers, *Discord and Collaboration: Essays on International Politics* (Baltimore: Johns Hopkins University Press, 1962).

103. One may conclude from Waltz's statements that the smallest possible number of powers in a self-help system is two powers and that a unipolar system cannot exist, in his opinion. Waltz, *Theory of International Politics*, p. 136.

104. Miller, *When Opponents Cooperate*, pp. 11–12.

105. Ethan B. Kapstein and Michael Mastanduno, eds., *Unipolar Politics: Realism and State Strategies After the Cold War* (New York: Columbia University Press, 1999); Wohlforth, "The Stability of a Unipolar World"; Ikenberry, *America Unrivaled*.

106. Mearsheimer, "Back to the Future."

CHAPTER 3

1. Wohlforth presents a similar plea. According to him, the 19th century was not a "British peace": in 1815–1853, it was the British and Russian peace; in 1853–1871, it was not peace of any kind; and in 1871–1914, it was the British and German peace; similarly, the Cold War was not the American peace but the American and Soviet peace; he states that today only one power is left, so this period may be called "the American peace." Wohlforth, "The Stability of a Unipolar World," p. 39.

2. Waltz, *Theory of International Politics*, p. 163; Waltz, "The Emerging Structure of International Politics," p. 44.

3. Mearsheimer, *The Tragedy of Great Power Politics*, p. 357.

4. Schweller, "Tripolarity and the Second World War"; Schweller, *Deadly Imbalances*.

5. Waltz, *Theory of International Politics*, p. 162; Mearsheimer, "Back to the Future," p. 5; Mearsheimer, *The Tragedy of Great Power Politics*, p. 357.

6. Mearsheimer, "Back to the Future," pp. 5–7.

7. Huntington, "The Lonely Superpower," p. 36.

8. A number of arguments have been made that the United States, Germany, and Japan are becoming poles, and each of them controls a significant regional block. Schweller, "Tripolarity and the Second World War," p. 99; that a world will be composed of three competing blocks—Europe, East Asia, and the Americans—with the United States heading the weakest and most problematic block. Walter R. Mead, "On the Road to Ruin," in C. W. Kegley and E. R. Wittkopf, eds., *The Future of American Foreign Policy* (New York: St. Martin's Press, 1992), chapter 26, pp. 332–339; that the current international system has become economically tripolar and three powers—the United States, Japan, and Germany—are intertwined in complex relations. L. Silk, "Some Things Are More Vital Than Money When It Comes to Creating the World Anew," *New York Times*, September 22, 1991.

9. Layne, "The Unipolar Illusion"; Wohlforth, "The Stability of a Unipolar World."

10. Stephen G. Brooks and William C. Wohlforth, "American Primacy in Perspective," *Foreign Affairs*, Vol. 81, No. 4 (July/August 2002), pp. 20–33; Huntington, "Why International Primacy Matters"; Huntington, "The Lonely Superpower"; Ikenberry, *America Unrivaled*; Robert Jervis, "International Primacy: Is the Game Worth the Candle?" *International Security*, Vol. 17, No. 4 (Spring 1993), pp. 52–67; Kapstein and Mastanduno, *Unipolar Politics*; Krauthammer, "The Unipolar Moment"; Kupchan, "After Pax Americana"; Kurth, "America's Grand Strategy"; Manstanduno, "Preserving the Unipolar Moment"; Joseph S. Nye Jr., "Limits of American Power," *Political Science Quarterly*, Vol. 117, No. 4 (Winter 2002), pp. 545–559; Barry R. Posen, "Command of the Commons: The Military Foundation of U.S. Hegemony," *International Security*, Vol. 28, No. 1 (Summer 2003), pp. 5–46; Barry R. Posen and Andrew L. Ross, "Competing Visions for U.S. Grand Strategy,"

International Security, Vol. 21, No. 3 (Winter 1996/97), pp. 5–53; Dimitri K. Simes, "America's Imperial Dilemma," *Foreign Affairs*, Vol. 82, No. 6 (November/December 2003), pp. 91–102; Steve Smith, "The End of the Unipolar Moment? September 11 and the Future of World Order," *International Relations*, Vol. 16, No. 2 (2002), pp. 171–183; Charles Krauthammer, "Democratic Realism: An American Foreign Policy for a Unipolar World" (A lecture given by Krauthammer in *American Enterprise Institute for Public Policy Research*, February 2004).

CHAPTER 4

1. Michael Nicholson, *Formal Theories in International Relations* (Cambridge: Cambridge University Press, 1989).

2. Charles Taylor, "Interpretation and the Sciences of Man," in *Philosophical Papers* (Cambridge: Cambridge University Press, 1985), chapter 1, pp. 15–57.

3. According to Stephen Walt, any theory that is not verified by empiric findings has no scientific value and should therefore be rejected. Stephen M. Walt, "Rigor or Rigor Mortis? Rational Choice and Security Studies," *International Security*, Vol. 23, No. 4 (Spring 1999), pp. 5–48, at p. 32.

4. According to Alexander George, one of the main goals of theoretical research in social science is conversion of historical knowledge into a broad comprehensive theory that covers the complexity of phenomena or actions that are asked for achieving this goal. Alexander L. George, "Case Studies and Theory Development: The Method of Structured, Focused Comparison," in Paul Gordon Lauren, ed., *Diplomacy: New Approaches in History, Theory, and Policy* (New York: Free Press, 1979), pp. 43–68, at pp. 44–49. The *International Security Journal* summer of 1997 edition is devoted to examining the feasibility of mutual inspiration between history and political science. Colin Elman and Miriam F. Elman, "Diplomatic History and International Relations Theory: Respecting Difference and Crossing Boundaries," *International Security*, Vol. 22, No. 1 (Summer 1997), pp. 5–21; John L. Gaddis, "History, Theory, and Common Ground," *International Security*, Vol. 22, No. 1 (Summer 1997), pp. 75–85; Alexander L. George, "Knowledge for Statecraft: The Challenge for Political Science and History," *International Security*, Vol. 22, No. 1 (Summer 1997), pp. 44–52; Stephen H. Haber, David M. Kennedy, and Stephen D. Krasner, "Brothers under the Skin: Diplomatic History and International Relations," *International Security*, Vol. 22, No. 1 (Summer 1997), pp. 34–43; Edward Ingram, "The Wonderland of the Political Scientist," *International Security*, Vol. 22, No. 1 (Summer 1997), pp. 53–63; Jack S. Levy, "Too Important to Leave to the Other: History and Political Science in the Study of International Relations," *International Security*, Vol. 22, No. 1 (Summer 1997), pp. 22–33; Paul W. Schroeder, "History and International Relations Theory: Not Use or Abuse, but Fit or Misfit," *International Security*, Vol. 22, No. 1 (Summer 1997), pp. 64–74.

5. According to Walt, the development of useful knowledge for understanding human social behavior and important social problems is the main goal of social science. Achieving this goal requires three objectives to be met: (A) *Development of theories with logical consistency and precision.* Inconsistent theories are problematic because some of their conclusions or expectations may not stem logically from their basic assumptions and they may form a distorted picture of the world. They are also harder to assess because it is difficult to check whether the common

proofs support them; (B) *Development of theories with originality*. Although the measurement of originality may be difficult and debatable, it is still one of the most important characteristics of any scientific theory; and (C) *Development of empirically valid theories*. Theories may be examined by assessing the correlation between the independent variables and dependent variables, or by checking the causative logic directly through following processes. Walt, "Rigor or Rigor Mortis?" p. 13.

6. Stephen Van Evera, *Guide to Methods for Students of Political Science* (Ithaca, NY: Cornell University Press, 1997), pp. 27–30.

7. *Quantitative analysis* attempts to prove correlation between independent variables and dependent variables. It is done by analyzing a large number of test cases, or by statistical analysis of many test cases that are grouped and studied to assess whether the results correspond with the theory's expectations. *Qualitative analysis* attempts to prove causality between independent and dependent variables. Within it, a limited number of test cases are analyzed in order to prove the causality between the explanatory phenomena and the explained ones, in a manner that the theory predicted. Gary King, Robert O. Keohane, and Sidney Verba, *Designing Social Inquiry: Scientific Inference in Qualitative Research* (Princeton, NJ: Princeton University Press, 1994), p. 5.

8. King, Keohane, and Verba, *Designing Social Inquiry*, chapter 6.

9. The test cases approach is one of the best ways of examining the validity of theories in international relations. Most theories that deal with war are examined in the best possible manner through the test cases approach, because the international historical records of politics and diplomacy preceding war that serve as the basis of our data are usually suitable for use for in-depth research of multiple cases more than research of a large number of cases. Van Evera, *Guide to Methods for Students of Political Science*, pp. 27–30.

10. Both *quantitative studies* and *qualitative studies* of social science have a dual goal of describing and explaining. Both are essential because we cannot create a significant causal explanation without a good description of events. A description usually appears first, and it loses most of the interest in it, unless it is associated with a number of causative relations. It is difficult to develop explanations before something is known about the world, but the connection between description and explanation is two-way. Sometimes our explanations lead us to look for descriptions of different parts of the world, and sometimes our descriptions may lead us to new causal explanations. King, Keohane, and Verba, *Designing Social Inquiry*, p. 34.

11. The attempt not to be satisfied with some a posteriori explanations of events but also present an a priori prediction of them draws me into the heart of the existing debate in theoretical research of international relations concerning the importance of observing events compared with explaining them. The theory that has been developed in the current study argues that Waltz is right, and an explanation is a significant component of a theory. However, according to the current study, a theory that cannot predict anything based on its assumptions is an insufficient one. Therefore, the theory that is being developed in the book is not satisfied with describing the events, but also argues that it can offer an explanation as to why events occur in the way they do with regard to the two dependent variables that are being assessed in the study.

12. George, "Case Studies and Theory Development," pp. 44–49; Alexander L. George and Andrew Bennett, *Case Studies and Theory Development in the Social Sciences* (Cambridge, MA: BCSIA Studies in International Security, 2004).

13. According to the *similarity method*, test cases that are different in all variables except for the explanatory variable, which is identical, are chosen. The researcher is left to prove that the explained variable remains identical and unchanged between the test cases. This increases the likelihood that the explanation proposed by him is a good one. According to the *difference method*, most variables become constant, except for the explanatory variable that varies between the test cases assessed by the study. In this case, the difference in the results of the explained variable increases the explanatory power of the study. King, Keohane, and Verba, *Designing Social Inquiry*, chapter 6.

14. Levy, *War in the Modern Great Power System, 1495–1975.*

15. Waltz, *Theory of International Politics.*

16. Mearsheimer, *The Tragedy of Great Power Politics.*

17. Waltz, "The Origins of War in Neorealist Theory," p. 620.

18. Bueno De Mesquita, *The War Trap*; Levy, *War in the Modern Great Power System, 1495–1975*; David J. Singer and Melvin Small, *The Wages of War, 1816–1965: A Statistical Handbook* (New York: John Wiley, 1972); Melvin Small and David J. Singer, *Resort to Arms: International and Civil Wars, 1816–1980* (Beverly Hills, CA: Sage Publications, 1982); Wright, *A Study of War*; Edward D. Mansfield, "The Distribution of Wars over Time," *World Politics*, Vol. 41, No. 1 (October 1988), pp. 21–51.

19. Two wars were fought in the Middle East and were therefore not included in the study: War (#25); War (#31). Four wars were fought in the Western Hemisphere and were therefore not included in the study: War (#40); War (#43); War (#49); War (#52). Two wars that were fought in Eurasia were not included in the assessment because they did not involve any of the five great powers constituting the system: War (#34); War (#37). See Appendix B.

20. War (#100); War (#103); War (#112); War (#115); War (#117); War (#124); War (#125). See Appendix B.

21. A number of historians have argued that the global hostility between Britain and Russia originates from 1815 and even earlier. Edward Ingram, *Commitment to Empire: Prophecies of the Great Game in Asia, 1797–1800* (New York: Oxford University Press, 1981). On Russia as a European hegemon, see Smith M. Anderson, *The Rise of Modern Diplomacy, 1450–1919* (New York: Longman, 1993); Adam Watson, "Russia and the European State System," in Hedley Bull and Watson Adam, eds., *The Expansion of International Society* (Oxford: Oxford University Press, 1984), chapter 4, pp. 61–74. Also see William R. Seton-Watson, *Britain in Europe, 1789–1914: A Survey of Foreign Policy* (Cambridge: Cambridge University Press, 1937).

22. Two wars were fought in the Western Hemisphere and were therefore not included in the study: War (#7); War (#19). Four wars that were fought in Eurasia were not included in the assessment because they did not involve either of the two superpowers constituting the system: War (#1); War (#10); War (#31); War (#16). See Appendix B.

23. Stanley Hoffmann, *Gulliver's Troubles: or, The Setting of American Foreign Policy* (New York: McGraw-Hill, 1968), chapters 2, 3.

24. Six wars were fought in the Western Hemisphere and were therefore not included in the study: War (#60); War (#64); War (#70); War (#79); War (#88); War (#91). Two wars were fought in the Middle East and were therefore not included in the study: War (#65); War (#94). Six wars were fought in Asia and were therefore not included in the study: War (#67); War (#72); War (#73); War (#82); War (#83); War (#85). Two wars that were fought in Europe and the Middle East were not included in the assessment because they did not involve either of the two super-powers constituting the system: War (#61); War (#76). See Appendix B.

25. War (#147); War (#148); War (#157); War (#160); War (#166); War (#169); War (#172); War (#175); War (#178); War (#181); War (#184); War (#187); War (#189); War (#190); War (#193); War (#199); War (#202); War (#205); War (#208). The Afghanistan War, which involved the Soviet Union, was not included in the quantitative exam-ination because that war is defined as an intrastate war. During it, Afghanistan fought rebels and the Soviet Union assisted it. See Appendix B. However, I con-ducted a qualitative assessment of that war.

26. The duration of the Korean War was calculated according to the period only in which the United States was involved and not according to the war's total dur-ation (it lasted 1,130 days in total). This is because the war was defined according to the United States' participation. The number of deaths was calculated according to the number of deaths throughout the war (including the period preceding the United States' intervention) because it was not possible to calculate the number of deaths for the period of the United States' participation only.

27. The duration of the Vietnam War was calculated according to the per-iod only in which the United States was involved and not according to the war's total duration (it lasted 3,735 days in total). This is because the war was defined according to the United States' participation. The number of deaths was calculated according to the number of deaths throughout the war (including the period pre-ceding the United States' intervention) because it was not possible to calculate the number of deaths for the period of the United States' participation only.

28. The duration of the Gulf War was calculated according to the period only in which the United States was involved and not according to the war's total dur-ation (it lasted 253 days in total). This is because the war was defined according to the United States' participation. The number of deaths was calculated according to the number of deaths throughout the war (including the period preceding the United States' intervention) because it was not possible to calculate the number of deaths for the period of the United States' participation only.

29. The duration of the war was calculated in the following manner: the start of the war—the date on which the battles commenced, October 7, 2001. McInnes, "A Different Kind of War?" p. 174; the end of the war—the establishment of the government of Afghanistan, Saturday, July 26, 2003. See http:usinfo.state.govsa Archive2005Sep16-145163.html

30. The duration of the war was calculated in the following manner: the start of the war—the day on which the battles commenced, March 20, 2003; the end of the war—the official date of transfer of sovereignty to Iraq, June 28, 2004. See http://icasualties.org/

31. Alexander L. George, ed., *Avoiding War: Problems of Crisis Management* (Boulder, CO: Westview, 1991).

32. Joseph R. Gochal and Jack S. Levy, "Crisis Mismanagement or Conflict of Interests? A Case Study of the Origins of the Crimean War," in Zeev Maoz et al.,

eds., *Multiple Paths to Knowledge in International Relations: Methodology in the Study of Conflict Management and Conflict Resolution* (New York: Lexington Books, 2004), pp. 309–342, at p. 310.

33. On the security dilemma, see John H. Herz, "Idealist Internationalism and the Security Dilemma," *World Politics*, Vol. 2, No. 2 (January 1950), pp. 157–180; Glaser L. Charles "The Security Dilemma Revisited," *World Politics*, Vol. 50, No. 1 (October 1997), pp. 171–201.

34. Robert Jervis, *Perception and Misperception in International Politics* (Princeton, NJ: Princeton University Press, 1976), chapter 3.

35. Bruce M. Russett, *The Prisoners of Insecurity: Nuclear Deterrence, the Arms Race, and Arms Control* (San Francisco: W. H. Freeman, 1983).

36. Jack S. Levy, "The Role of Crisis Mismanagement in the Outbreak of World War I," in Alexander L. George, ed., *Avoiding War: Problems of Crisis Management* (Boulder, CO: Westview Press, 1991), pp. 62–117.

37. Zeev Maoz, *Paradoxes of War: On the Art of National Self-Entrapment* (Boston: Unwin Hyman, 1990), chapter 4; George, *Avoiding War*.

38. Barbara W. Tuchman, *The Guns of August* (New York: Ballantine Books, 1962); Miles Kahler, "Rumors of War: The 1914 Analogy," *Foreign Affairs*, Vol. 58, No. 2 (Winter 1979/1980), pp. 374–396.

39. During the multipolar system of 1849–1870, a limited number of wars were fought in Europe involving the five great powers that constituted the system. An explanation for this phenomenon at the individual level has been offered by a number of historians. They argue that the major limitation, short duration, and low violence of the wars fought in those years stemmed from the skill and moderation demonstrated by Bismarck and Cavour. The current study denies this argument because like the Prussian leader Bismarck, the Italian leader Cavour acted within a framework of limitations and possibilities within the European system. Paul W. Schroeder, "The 19th-Century International System: Changes in the Structure," *World Politics*, Vol. 39, No. 1 (October 1986), pp. 1–26, at pp. 7–8.

40. Levy, "Theories of General War," p. 346.

41. Ludwig Dehio, *The Precarious Balance: Four Centuries of the European Power Struggle* (New York: Knopf, 1962), chapter 4; David M. Goldfrank, *The Origins of the Crimean War* (London: Longman, 1994); Norman Rich, *Why the Crimean War? A Cautionary Tale* (Hanover, NH: University Press of New England, 1985); David Wetzel, *The Crimean War: A Diplomatic History* (New York: Columbia University Press, 1985).

42. Clive Ponting, *The Crimean War* (London: Chatto & Windus, 2004), p. vii.

43. Ponting, *The Crimean War*, p. 1.

44. Ponting, *The Crimean War*, p. 2 fn. 1.

45. Ponting, *The Crimean War*, p. 3.

46. Smith M. Anderson, *The Eastern Question, 1774–1923: A Study in International Relations* (New York: St. Martin's Publication, 1966), p. 132.

47. Gavin B. Henderson, "The Two Interpretations of the Four Points," *The English Historical Review*, Vol. 52, No. 205 (January 1937), pp. 48–66.

48. Richard Smoke, *War: Controlling Escalation* (Cambridge, MA: Harvard University Press, 1977), p. 193.

49. Jervis, *Perception and Misperception in International Politics*, chapter 1; Jack, S. Levy, "Misperception and the Causes of War: Theoretical Linkages and Analytical Problems," *World Politics*, Vol. 36, No. 1 (October 1983), pp. 76–99.

50. Ponting, *The Crimean War*, pp. 1–3.

51. Ponting, *The Crimean War*, p. viii.

52. James L. Richardson, *Crisis Diplomacy: The Great Powers since the Mid-Nineteenth Century* (Cambridge: Cambridge University Press, 1994), p. 70.

53. Norman Rich, *Great Power Diplomacy, 1814–1914* (New York: McGraw-Hill, 1992), p. 104; Richardson, *Crisis Diplomacy*, p. 84.

54. Richardson, *Crisis Diplomacy*, p. 70.

55. Rich, *Great Power Diplomacy, 1814–1914*, p. 107.

56. Richardson, *Crisis Diplomacy*, p. 71; Rich, *Great Power Diplomacy, 1814–1914*, p. 107.

57. Rich, *Great Power Diplomacy, 1814–1914*, pp. 107–108.

58. Richardson, *Crisis Diplomacy*, p. 70.

59. Ponting, *The Crimean War*, pp. iv, vii.

60. Rich, *Great Power Diplomacy, 1814–1914*, p. 103; Ann Pottinger Saab, *The Origins of the Crimean Alliance* (Charlottesville: University of Virginia Press, 1977), p. 156; Gochal and Levy, "Crisis Mismanagement or Conflict of Interests," p. 332.

61. Gochal and Levy, "Crisis Mismanagement or Conflict of Interests," p. 309 fn. 3.

62. Ponting, *The Crimean War*, p. iv.

63. On the First World War, see Samuel R. Williamson Jr., "The Origins of World War I," *Journal of Interdisciplinary History*, Vol. 18, No. 4 (Spring 1988), pp. 795–818; Michael Howard, "Men Against Fire: Expectations of War in 1914," *International Security*, Vol. 9, No. 1 (Summer 1984), pp. 41–57; Fritz Fischer, *Germany's Aims in the First World War* (New York: W. W. Norton, 1967); Fritz Fischer, *War of Illusions: German Policies from 1911–1914*, translated from Germany by Marian Jackson (New York: Norton, 1975); Fritz Fischer, *World Power or Decline: The Controversy over Germany's Aims in the First World War*, translated from Germany by Lancelot L. Farrar, Robert Kimber, and Rita Kimber (New York: Norton, 1974); David E. Kaiser, "Germany and the Origins of the First World War," *The Journal of Modern History*, Vol. 55, No. 3 (September 1983), pp. 442–474; Wolfgang H. Koch, ed., *The Origins of the First World War: Great Power Rivalry and German War Aims* (New York: Taplinger Publication Co., 1972).

64. In Paul Kennedy's opinion, in the years preceding the First World War, each power had much greater military expenses than in the preceding two to three decades. This phenomenon included remote countries, such as the United States, following its war with Spain, and Japan, following its war with Russia. However, the arms race was definitely centered within Europe. Paul M. Kennedy, "The First World War and the International Power System," *International Security*, Vol. 9, No. 1 (Summer 1984), pp. 7–40, at p. 8 Table 1.

65. During those decades, militarists adopted offensive military doctrines. The civilian elites and the public assumed that attacking would be advantageous in battle and that offensive solutions to security problems were the most effective. Stephen Van Evera, "The Cult of the Offensive and the Origins of the First World War," *International Security*, Vol. 9, No. 1 (Summer 1984), pp. 58–107; Jack Snyder, "Civil-Military Relations and the Cult of the Offensive, 1914 and 1984," *International Security*, Vol. 9, No. 1 (Summer 1984), pp. 108–146.

66. The improvement in the relations between Great Britain and Germany during those years contributed to the outbreak of the war. In Britain, the détente formed the misbelief that the crisis that broke out in July 1914 could be averted through Anglo-German cooperation. The leaders did not wish to provoke Germany

and therefore failed in taking early steps to determine the German actions that led to the war. The détente also contributed to erroneous German hopes that Britain would remain neutral in a land war, and therefore it encouraged Germany to adopt a policy that posed a risk of the awakening of such a conflict. Sean M. Lynn-Jones, "Détente and Deterrence: Anglo-German Relations, 1911–1914," *International Security*, Vol. 11, No. 2 (Fall 1986), pp. 121–150, at p. 124.

67. Schelling, *Arms and Influence*; Jervis, *Perception and Misperception in International Politics*, p. 94; Jervis, "Cooperation under the Security Dilemma," p. 192.

68. Jack S. Levy, "Organizational Routines and the Causes of War," *International Studies Quarterly*, Vol. 30, No. 2 (June 1986), pp. 193–222.

69. According to Jervis, the First World War is an example of the way in which wars can break out owing to hostility cycles of this kind. The cyclic model is characterized by action-reaction processes in which each country considers its own actions to be defensive actions whereas those of its adversaries are considered to be provocations. Hostility also intensifies even if no country wants war. According to him, the First World War provided the inspiration for the model. Jervis, *Perception and Misperception in International Politics*, pp. 58–113.

70. Tuchman, *The Guns of August*; Kahler, "Rumors of War"; Richard N. Lebow, *Nuclear Crisis Management: A Dangerous Illusion* (Ithaca, NY: Cornell University Press, 1987), chapters 2–4; Paul Bracken, *The Command and Control of Nuclear Forces* (New Haven, CT: Yale University Press, 1983), pp. 2–3, 65, 222–223.

71. Jack S. Levy, "Preferences, Constraints, and Choices in July 1914," *International Security*, Vol. 15, No. 3 (Winter 1990–1991), pp. 151–186.

72. Levy, "Preferences, Constraints, and Choices in July 1914."

73. Dickinson, *The European Anarchy*, pp. 14, 101; Lowes G. Dickinson, *The International Anarchy, 1904–1914* (London: G. Allen & Unwin Ltd., 1926).

74. Levy, "Preferences, Constraints, and Choices in July 1914."

75. Harrison R. Wagner, "What Was Bipolarity?" *International Organization*, Vol. 47, No. 1 (Winter 1993), pp. 77–106, at p. 81.

76. Mearsheimer, "Back to the Future," p. 22.

77. The *Entente Cordiale* between Britain and France was signed in London on April 8, 1904. At its time of signing, Britain and France were two adversaries that had fought each other for centuries, and even in the early 20th century, they competed over control of Africa, Asia, and the Middle East. What they had in common was their attitude to Germany, which they suspected of planning to take over Europe. After about two years, German Kaiser Wilhelm II tried to take over Morocco and hoped that the British would fear a confrontation and abandon the French. However, in the end, he led France and Britain to "learn the enemy." France trusted Britain to help it if the Germans started a war. The agreement successfully relieved the colonial adversity between the two and led to formation of an alliance against Germany in both World Wars.

78. Scott D. Sagan, "1914 Revisited: Allies, Offense, and Instability," *International Security*, Vol. 11, No. 2 (Fall 1986), pp. 151–175; Christensen and Snyder, "Chain Gangs and Passed Bucks."

79. COW, Interstate Wars.

80. Cow, State System Membership List.

81. Levy, "Preferences, Constraints, and Choices in July 1914," p. 162.

82. Waltz, *Theory of International Politics*; Posen, *The Sources of Military Doctrine*; Christensen and Snyder, "Chain Gangs and Passed Bucks."

83. Schweller, "Tripolarity and the Second World War," p. 74.

84. Stephen Van Evera, "Primed for Peace: Europe after the Cold War," *International Security*, Vol. 15, No. 3 (Winter 1990–1991), pp. 7–57.

85. Kalevi J. Holsti, *Peace and War: Armed Conflicts and International Order, 1648–1989* (Cambridge: Cambridge University Press, 1991), pp. 224–225.

86. Wagner, "What Was Bipolarity?" p. 81.

87. Mearsheimer, "Back to the Future," p. 22.

88. The Maginot Line was a system of border fornications that the French built after 1929 in order to defend their borders with Germany. The line was completed in 1934. The strategic thinking behind the Maginot Line was a result of French experience in the First World War.

89. Peter Calvocoressi, Guy Wint, and John Pritchard, *Total War: The Causes and Courses of the Second World War*, 2nd ed. (New York: Pantheon, 1989).

90. In the Russo-Finnish War (#142) (11/30/1939–3/12/1940), the death toll was the Soviet Union 126,875 and Finland 24,923.

91. Mearsheimer presented a lot of support for this argument. Mearsheimer, "Back to the Future," pp. 22–24.

92. Waltz, *Theory of International Politics*, especially chapter 8; Dale C. Copeland, "Neorealism and the Myth of Bipolar Stability: Toward a New Dynamic Realist Theory of Major War," *Security Studies*, Vol. 5, No. 3 (Spring 1996), pp. 29–89; Hopf, "Polarity, the Offense-Defense Balance, and War."

93. Mearsheimer, "Back to the Future," p. 20.

94. A. J. P. Taylor, *The Struggle for Mastery in Europe, 1848–1918* (Oxford: Clarendon Press, 1954), pp. xix–xx.

95. Edward V. Gulick, *Europe's Classical Balance of Power: A Case History of the Theory and Practice of One of the Great Concepts of European Statecraft* (Ithaca, NY: Cornell University Press, 1955).

96. F. R. Bridge and Roger Bullen, *The Great Powers and the European States System, 1815–1914* (New York: Longman, 1980).

97. Josef V. Polisensky, *War and Society in Europe, 1618–1648* (Cambridge: Cambridge University Press, 1978); Theodore K. Rabb, *The Struggle for Stability in Early Modern Europe* (New York: Oxford University Press, 1975).

98. Ragnhild Hatton, *George I, Elector and King* (New Haven, CT: Yale University Press, 2001); David B. Horn, *Great Britain and Europe in the Eighteenth Century* (Oxford: Clarendon Press, 1967); Paul Langford, *The Eighteenth Century, 1688–1815* (New York: St. Martin's Press, 1976); Derek McKay and Hamish M. Scott, *The Rise of the Great Powers, 1648–1815* (New York: Longman, 1983).

99. The Holy Alliance was an agreement signed on September 26, 1815, between Russia, Austria, and Prussia as an attempt of conservative leaders to maintain the social order.

100. Schroeder, "The 19th-Century International System," pp. 2, 4.

101. Benjamin Miller asserts that a concert is an international institution, or a security regime, for the highest level of diplomatic cooperation of all great powers at that time. Benjamin Miller, "Explaining the Emergence of Great Power Concerts," *Review of International Studies*, Vol. 20 (October 1994), pp. 327–348.

102. Robert Jervis, "From Balance to Concert: A Study of International Security Cooperation," *World Politics*, Vol. 38, No. 1 (October 1985), pp. 58–79.

103. In times of prosperity, the concert reflected the balance of powers. States did not tend to behave in a way that weakened their relative power, and

maintaining the balance of power remained the main goal of the concert regime of the 19th century. Richard B. Elrod, "The Concert of Europe: A Fresh Look at an International System," *World Politics*, Vol. 28, No. 2 (January 1976), pp. 159–174; Schroeder, "The 19th-Century International System"; Stephen Van Evera, "Why Cooperation Failed in 1914," *World Politics*, Vol. 38, No. 1 (October 1985), pp. 80–117; Wright, *A Study of War*.

104. Mearsheimer, "The False Promise of International Institutions," p. 36.

105. Jervis, "From Balance to Concert," p. 58.

106. Charles A. Kupchan and Clifford A. Kupchan, "A New Concert for Europe," in Graham T. Allison and Gregory F. Treverton, eds., *Rethinking America's Security: Beyond Cold War to New World Order* (New York: W. W. Norton, 1992), pp. 249–266; Charles A. Kupchan and Clifford A. Kupchan, "Concerts, Collective Security, and the Future of Europe," *International Security*, Vol. 16, No. 1 (Summer 1991), pp. 114–161.

107. Elrod, "The Concert of Europe," pp. 160–166.

108. Wohlforth, "The Stability of a Unipolar World," p. 26.

109. In the Soviet Invasion of Hungary (156#) (11/4/1956–11/14/1956) the death toll was Hungary 926 and the Soviet Union 1,500; in the Turco-Cypriot War (184#) (7/20/1974–7/29/1974) the death toll was Turkey 1,000 and Cyprus 500.

110. John L. Gaddis, "The Long Peace: Elements of Stability in the Postwar International System," *International Security*, Vol. 10, No. 4 (Spring 1986), pp. 99–142; Kaysen, "Is War Obsolete?"; John E. Mueller, *Retreat from Doomsday: The Obsolescence of Major War* (New York: Basic Books, 1989); Robert Jervis, "The Political Effects of Nuclear Weapons: A Comment," *International Security*, Vol. 13, No. 2 (Fall 1988), pp. 80–90; Mearsheimer, "Back to the Future."

111. For discussion and criticism of the democratic peace theory, see Michael E. Brown, Sean M. Lynn-Jones, and Steven E. Miller, eds., *Debating the Democratic Peace* (Cambridge, MA: MIT Press, 1996); Michael W. Doyle, "Kant, Liberal Legacies, and Foreign Affairs, Part 2," *Philosophy and Public Affairs*, Vol. 12, No. 4 (Autumn 1983), pp. 323–353; Michael W. Doyle, "Kant, Liberal Legacies, and Foreign Affairs," *Philosophy and Public Affairs*, Vol. 12, No. 3 (Summer 1983), pp. 205–235; Michael W. Doyle, "Liberalism and World Politics," *The American Political Science Review*, Vol. 80, No. 4 (December 1986), pp. 1151–1169; Francis Fukuyama, "The End of History?" *The National Interest*, Vol. 16 (Summer 1989), pp. 3–18; Joanne S. Gowa, "Democratic States and International Disputes," *International Organization*, Vol. 49, No. 3 (Summer 1995), pp. 511–522; Joanne S. Gowa, *Ballots and Bullets: The Elusive Democratic Peace* (Princeton, NJ: Princeton University Press, 1999); Edward D. Mansfield and Jack Snyder, "Democratization and War," *Foreign Affairs*, Vol. 74, No. 3 (May/June 1995), pp. 79–97; Zeev Maoz and Bruce Russett, "Normative and Structural Causes of Democratic Peace, 1946–1986," *The American Political Science Review*, Vol. 87, No. 3 (September 1993), pp. 624–638; John M. Owen, "How Liberalism Produces Democratic Peace," *International Security*, Vol. 19, No. 2 (Fall 1994), pp. 87–125; John M. Owen, *Liberal Peace, Liberal War: American Politics and International Security* (Ithaca, NY: Cornell University Press, 1997); James L. Ray, *Democracy and International Conflict: An Evaluation of the Democratic Peace Proposition* (Columbia: University of South Carolina Press, 1995); Bruce M. Russett, *Grasping the Democratic Peace: Principles for a Post-Cold War World* (Princeton, NJ: Princeton University Press, 1993); Samuel P. Huntington, "No Exit: The Errors of Endism," *The National Interest*, Vol. 17 (Fall 1989), pp. 3–11; Miriam F. Elman, ed.,

Paths to Peace: Is Democracy the Answer? (Cambridge, MA: MIT Press, 1997); Miriam
F. Elman, "The Never-Ending Story: Democracy and Peace," *International Studies
Review*, Vol. 1, No. 3 (Autumn 1999), pp. 87–103.

112. Mueller, *Retreat from Doomsday*; Donald Kagan, Eliot A. Cohen, Charles
F. Doran, and Michael Mandelbaum, "Is Major War Obsolete? An Exchange,"
Survival, Vol. 41, No. 2 (Summer 1999), pp. 139–152; Kaysen, "Is War Obsolete?";
Michael Mandelbaum, "Is Major War Obsolete?" *Survival*, Vol. 40, No. 4 (Winter
1998–1999), pp. 20–38; Peter Wallensteen and Margareta Sollenberg, "The End of
International War? Armed Conflict 1989–95," *Journal of Peace Research*, Vol. 33, No.
3 (August 1996), pp. 353–370.

113. After 1713, Holland was ejected from the great powers system and focused
on commercial and colonial powers. For more than 250 years, Holland tried not to
intervene in international wars in Europe, a modus operandi that may be called
Hollandization. Kaysen, "Is War Obsolete?" p. 44.

114. Kaysen, "Is War Obsolete?"; Waltz, "The Emerging Structure of International Politics," pp. 76–77.

115. Mearsheimer, "Back to the Future," p. 30.

116. Waltz, "Evaluating Theories," pp. 915–916; Layne, "The Unipolar Illusion"; Manstanduno, "Preserving the Unipolar Moment."

117. Kupchan, "After Pax Americana."

118. Sean M. Lynn-Jones and Steven E. Miller, eds., *The Cold War and After:
Prospects for Peace* (Cambridge, MA: MIT Press, 1991); David A. Baldwin, ed., *Neo-
realism and Neoliberalism: The Contemporary Debate* (New York: Columbia University
Press, 1993).

119. John J. Mearsheimer, "Why We Will Soon Miss the Cold War," *The Atlantic*,
Vol. 266, No. 2 (August 1990), pp. 35–42; Mearsheimer, "Back to the Future."

120. Wohlforth, "The Stability of a Unipolar World," p. 23.

121. IRAQ NO-FLY ZONE (ICB #406).

122. IRAQ TROOP DEPLOYMENT-KUWAIT (ICB #412).

123. DESERT STRIKE (ICB #419).

124. UNSCOM I (ICB #422).

125. UNSCOM II OPERATION DESERT FOX (ICB #429).

126. NORTH KOREA NUCLEAR I (ICB #408).

127. AFGHANISTAN-USA (ICB #434); David N. Gibbs, "Realpolitik and
Humanitarian Intervention: The Case of Somalia," *International Politics*, Vol. 37,
No. 1 (March 2000), pp. 41–55.

128. US EMBASSY BOMBINGS (ICB #427).

129. The United States Navy Web site: http://www.navy.mil/

130. AFGHANISTAN-USA (ICB #434).

131. AFGHANISTAN-USA (ICB #434).

132. IRAQ REGIME (ICB #441).

133. Seven wars were not included in the assessment because they did not
involve one of the seven polar powers at least.

134. Paul W. Schroeder, *The Transformation of European Politics, 1763–1848* (New
York: Oxford University Press, 1994); Paul W. Schroeder, *Austria, Great Britain, and
the Crimean War: The Destruction of the European Concert* (Ithaca, NY: Cornell University Press, 1972); Adam Watson, *The Evolution of International Society: A Comparative Historical Analysis* (London: Routledge, 1992); William E. Echard, *Napoleon*

III and the Concert of Europe (Baton Rouge: Louisiana State University Press, 1983), chapters 1–2.

135. Schroeder, *Austria, Great Britain, and the Crimean War*; John S. Curtiss, *Russia's Crimean War* (Durham, NC: Duke University Press, 1979); Rich, *Why the Crimean War?*

136. Schroeder, "The 19th-Century International System," p. 6.

137. Additional noteworthy consequences are Austria was neglected and isolated; Italy, German, and the Balkan question remained unresolved; France won only a prestige victory; the only true victors were those that later exploited the wars for their own individual goals—Sardinia/Piedmont, Prussia, and others. Paul W. Schroeder, "The Lost Intermediaries: The Impact of 1870 on the European System," *The International History Review*, Vol. 6, No. 1 (February 1984), pp. 1–27.

138. On the Seven Weeks' War (1866) between Prussia and Austria, see Gordon A. Craig, *The Battle of Koniggratz: Prussia's Victory over Austria, 1866* (Philadelphia, PA: Lippincott, 1964); Gordon A. Craig, *The Politics of the Prussian Army, 1640–1945* (Oxford: Clarendon Press, 1955); Heinrich Friedjung, *The Struggle for Supremacy in Germany, 1859–1866*, translated from the German by A. J. P. Taylor and William McElwee (New York: Russell, 1966—original edition 1897); Montague H. Hozier, *The Seven Weeks' War: Its Antecedents and Its Incidents* (London: Macmillan, 1871); Geoffrey Wawro, *The Austro-Prussian War: Austria's War with Prussia and Italy in 1866* (Cambridge: Cambridge University Press, 1997); Dennis E. Showalter, *Railroads and Rifles: Soldiers, Technology and the Unification of Germany* (Hamden, CT: Archon Books, 1975).

139. The Gastein Convention was intended to settle the outstanding questions on the sovereignty of Schleswig-Holstein, which stemmed from Denmark's defeat against Austria and Prussia in their war against it in 1864. Alexander Malet, *The Overthrow of the Germanic Confederation by Prussia in 1866* (London: Longmans, Green, 1870), pp. 106–110.

140. On the Franco-Prussian War (July 1870–May 1871), see Richard E. Holmes, *The Road to Sedan: The French Army, 1866–1870* (Atlantic Highlands, NJ: Humanities Press, 1984); Michael Howard, *The Franco-Prussian War: The German Invasion of France, 1870–1871* (London: Rupert Hart-Davis, 1961); Robert Tombs, *The War Against Paris, 1871* (Cambridge: Cambridge University Press, 1981).

141. Mearsheimer argues that great powers tend to prefer the pattern of buck-passing to balancing. Mearsheimer, *The Tragedy of Great Power Politics*, pp. 160–161.

142. Glenn H. Snyder, "Mearsheimer's World—Offensive Realism and the Struggle for Security: A Review Essay," *International Security*, Vol. 27, No. 1 (Summer 2002), pp. 149–173, at p. 163.

143. James Joll, *The Origins of the First World War* (New York: Longman, 1984).

144. Ralph K. White, "Why Aggressors Lose," *Political Psychology*, Vol. 11, No. 2 (1990), pp. 227–242, at pp. 227–228.

145. White, "Why Aggressors Lose," pp. 229–230.

146. Anton W. DePorte, *Europe between the Superpowers: The Enduring Balance*, 2nd ed. (New Haven, CT: Yale University Press, 1986).

147. On the U.S.-Korea War of 1950–1953, see Dean Acheson, *The Korean War* (New York: Norton, 1971); Clay Blair, *The Forgotten War: America in Korea, 1950–1953* (New York: Times Books, 1987); Rosemary Foot, *The Wrong War: American Policy and the Dimensions of the Korean Conflict, 1950–1953* (Ithaca, NY: Cornell University

Press, 1985); Max Hastings, *The Korean War* (New York: Simon and Schuster, 1987); Burton I. Kaufman, *The Korean War: Challenges in Crisis, Credibility, and Command* (Philadelphia, PA: Temple University Press, 1986); Clarence Y. H. Lo, "Civilian Policy Makers and Military Objectives: A Case Study of the U.S. Offensive to Win the Korean War," *Journal of Political and Military Sociology*, Vol. 7 (Fall 1979), pp. 229–242; McCune, "The Thirty-Eighth Parallel in Korea"; Allan R. Millett, "A Reader's Guide to the Korean War," *The Journal of Military History*, Vol. 61, No. 3 (July 1997), pp. 583–597; Michael O'Hanlon, "Stopping a North Korean Invasion: Why Defending South Korea Is Easier Than the Pentagon Thinks," *International Security*, Vol. 22, No, 4 (Spring 1998), pp. 135–170; David Rees, *Korea: The Limited War* (London: Macmillan, 1964); Michael Schaller, "U.S. Policy in the Korean War," *International Security*, Vol. 11, No. 3 (Winter 1986–87), pp. 162–166; James F. Schnable, *Policy and Direction: The First Year* (Washington, DC: Center of Military History, United States Army, 1992); Tucker C. Spencer, ed., *Encyclopedia of the Korean War*, 3 vols. (Santa Barbara, CA: ABC-CLIO, 2000); Richard G. Stilwell, "The United States, Japan and the Security of Korea," *International Security*, Vol. 2, No. 2 (Autumn 1977), pp. 93–95; John G. Stoessinger, *Why Nations Go to War* (New York: St. Martin's Press, 1974), chapter 3, pp. 69–103; John Toland, *In Mortal Combat: Korea, 1950–1953* (New York: Morrow, 1991); Franklin B. Weinstein, "The United States, Japan and the Security of Korea," *International Security*, Vol. 2, No. 2 (Autumn 1977), pp. 68–89; Franklin B. Weinstein, "The Korean Debate, Continued," *International Security*, Vol. 2, No. 3 (Winter 1978), pp. 160–167; I. D. White, "Commentary: The United States, Japan and the Security of Korea," *International Security*, Vol. 2, No. 2 (Autumn 1977), pp. 90–92.

148. Raymond G. O'Connor, "Victory in Modern War," *Journal of Peace Research*, Vol. 6, No. 4 (December 1969), pp. 367–384, at p. 372.

149. Small and Singer, *Resort to Arms*; James F. Dunnigan and William C. Martel, *How to Stop a War: The Lessons on Two Hundred Years of War and Peace* (New York: Doubleday Religious Publishing Group, 1987).

150. Shannon McCune, "The Thirty-Eighth Parallel in Korea," *World Politics*, Vol. 1, No. 2 (January 1949), pp. 223–232.

151. On the U.S.-Vietnam War of 1968–1975, see Jeffrey J. Clarhe, *Advice and Support: The Final Years, 1965–1973, The United States Army in Vietnam* (Washington, DC: U.S. Army Center of Military History, 1988); Phillip B. Davidson, *Vietnam at War: The History, 1946–1975* (Novato, CA: Presidio Press, 1988); Michael Gravel, ed., *The Pentagon Papers: The Defense Department History of United States Decisionmaking on Vietnam*, 5 vols. (Boston, MA: Beacon Press, 1971); George C. Herring, *America's Longest War: The United States and Vietnam, 1950–1975*, 3rd ed. (New York: McGraw-Hill, 1996); George C. Herring, ed., *The Secret Diplomacy of the Vietnam War: The Negotiating Volumes of the Pentagon Papers* (Austin: University of Texas Press, 1983); Stanley Hoffmann et al., "Vietnam Reappraised," *International Security*, Vol. 6, No. 1 (Summer 1981), pp. 3–26; David E. Kaiser, "Vietnam: Was the System the Solution?" *International Security*, Vol. 4, No. 4 (Spring 1980), pp. 199–218; Stanley Karnow, *Vietnam: A History* (New York: Viking Press, 1983); Fredrik Logevall, *Choosing War: The Lost Chance for Peace and the Escalation of War in Vietnam* (Berkeley: University of California Press, 1999); James Nathan, "The New Strategy: Force and Diplomacy in American Foreign Policy," *Defense Analysis*, Vol. 11, No. 2 (August 1995), pp. 121–145; James S. Olson, *Where the Domino Fell: America*

in Vietnam, 1945–1990 (New York: St Martin's Press, 1991); Stephen P. Rosen, "Vietnam and the American Theory of Limited War," *International Security*, Vol. 7, No. 2 (Fall 1982), pp. 83–113; Lewis Sorley, *A Better War: The Unexamined Victories and Final Tragedy of America's Last Years in Vietnam* (New York: Harcourt Brace & Co., 1999); Ronald H. Spector, "U.S. Army Strategy in the Vietnam War," *International Security*, Vol. 11, No. 4 (Spring 1987), pp. 130–134.

152. Kurth, "America's Grand Strategy."

153. Yehoshafat Harkabi, *War and Strategy* (Tel Aviv: Maarachot, 1997) [Hebrew], p. 595.

154. Harry G. Summers, *On Strategy: A Critical Analysis of the Vietnam War* (Novato, CA: Presidio Press, 1982), pp. 1–7.

155. Clausewitz, Carl Von, *On War* (Princeton, NJ: Princeton University Press, 1984); Ashley L. Roger, *A Short Guide to Clausewitz on War* (London: Weidenfeld, 1967).

156. Summers, *On Strategy*, pp. 4–5.

157. On the Gulf War of 1991 between the U.S. and the coalition against Iraq, see Rick Atkinson, *Crusade: The Untold Story of the Persian Gulf War* (Boston, MA: Houghton Mifflin, 1993); Stephen Biddle, "Victory Misunderstood: What the Gulf War Tells Us about the Future of Conflict," *International Security*, Vol. 21, No. 2 (Fall 1996), pp. 139–179; Anthony H. Cordesman and Abraham R. Wagner, *The Gulf War (The Lessons of Modern War)*, (Boulder, CO: Westview Press, 1996); Lawrence Freedman and Efraim Karsh, *The Gulf Conflict, 1990–1991: Diplomacy and War in the New World Order* (Princeton, NJ: Princeton University Press, 1993); Norman Friedman, *Desert Victory: The War for Kuwait* (Annapolis, MD: Naval Institute Press, 1991); Michael R. Gordon and Bernard E. Trainor, *The Generals' War: The Inside Story of the Conflict in the Gulf* (Boston, MA: Little Brown, 1995); Mohamed Heikal, *Illusions of Triumph: An Arab View of the Gulf War* (London: HarperCollins, 1992); Thomas G. Mahnken and Barry D. Watts, "What the Gulf War Can (and Cannot) Tell Us about the Future of Warfare," *International Security*, Vol. 22, No. 2 (Fall 1997), pp. 151–162.

158. Graham E. Fuller and Ian O. Lesser, "Persian Gulf Myths," *Foreign Affairs*, Vol. 76, No. 3 (May–June 1997), pp. 42–52.

159. George, "Case Studies and Theory Development," pp. 43–44.

160. Sarah O'Hara and Michael Heffernan, "From Geo-Strategy to Geo-Economics: The 'Heartland' and British Imperialism Before and After MacKinder," *Geopolitics*, Vol. 11, No. 1 (Spring 2006), pp. 54–73, at p. 54; Michael G. Partem, "The Buffer System in International Relations," *The Journal of Conflict Resolution*, Vol. 27, No. 1 (March 1983), pp. 3–26; Trygve Mathison, *The Function of Small States in the Strategies of Great Powers* (Oslo: Scandinavian University Books, 1971).

161. Edward Ingram, *The Beginning of the Great Game in Asia, 1828–1834* (New York: Oxford University Press, 1979), pp. 74–117; David Gillard, *The Struggle for Asia, 1828–1914: A Study in British and Russian Imperialism* (London: Methuen, 1977), pp. 26–31, 34–35, 46–53; James A. Norris, *The First Afghan War, 1838–1842* (Cambridge: Cambridge University Press, 1967), pp. 22–47; G. J. Alder, "The Key to India? Britain and the Herat Problem, 1830–1863—Part I," *Middle Eastern Studies*, Vol. 10, No. 1 (1974), pp. 186–209, at pp. 186–190.

162. Schroeder, *The Transformation of European Politics, 1763–1848*, p. 757.

163. M. E. Yapp, *Strategies of British India: Britain, Iran, and Afghanistan, 1798–1850* (Oxford: Oxford University Press, 1980), pp. 129–150; Norris, *The First Afghan*

War, 1838–1842, pp. 82–84; G. J. Alder, "The Key to India? Britain and the Herat problem, 1830–1863—Part II," *Middle Eastern Studies*, Vol. 10, No. 3 (October 1974), pp. 287–384, at pp. 300–307.

164. Yapp, *Strategies of British India*, pp. 160–172; Ingram, *The Beginning of the Great Game in Asia, 1828–1834*, pp. 124–178; Robert A. Huttenback, *British Relations with Sind, 1799–1843: An Anatomy of Imperialism* (Berkeley: University of California Press, 1962).

165. Robert Strausz-Hupe, "The Anglo-Afghan War of 1919," *Military Affairs*, Vol. 7, No. 2 (Summer 1943), pp. 89–96, at p. 90.

166. Bruce R. Kuniholm, "The Geopolitics of the Caspian Basin," *The Middle East Journal*, Vol. 54, No. 4 (Autumn 2000), pp. 546–571.

167. Senzil Nawid, "The State, the Clergy, and British Imperial Policy in Afghanistan during the 19th and Early 20th Centuries," *International Journal of Middle East Studies*, Vol. 29, No. 4 (November 1997), pp. 581–605.

168. Yapp, *Strategies of British India*, p. 290.

169. Schroeder, *The Transformation of European Politics, 1763–1848*, p. 759.

170. Nawid, "The State, the Clergy, and British Imperial Policy in Afghanistan during the 19th and Early 20th Centuries," p. 587.

171. Nawid, "The State, the Clergy, and British Imperial Policy in Afghanistan during the 19th and Early 20th Centuries," p. 587.

172. Nawid, "The State, the Clergy, and British Imperial Policy in Afghanistan during the 19th and Early 20th Centuries," pp. 587–588.

173. Yapp, *Strategies of British India*, pp. 267–271, 308–361.

174. Schroeder, *The Transformation of European Politics, 1763–1848*, p. 761.

175. Nawid, "The State, the Clergy, and British Imperial Policy in Afghanistan during the 19th and Early 20th Centuries," pp. 587–588.

176. Yapp, *Strategies of British India*, pp. 340–347, 419–439; Norris, *The First Afghan War, 1838–1842*, pp. 364–416.

177. Nawid, "The State, the Clergy, and British Imperial Policy in Afghanistan during the 19th and Early 20th Centuries," pp. 587–588.

178. Yapp, *Strategies of British India*, pp. 482–591.

179. Nawid, "The State, the Clergy, and British Imperial Policy in Afghanistan during the 19th and Early 20th Centuries," p. 589.

180. Ronald Quinault, "Afghanistan and Gladstone's Moral Foreign Policy," *History Today*, Vol. 52, No. 12 (December 2002), pp. 28–34, at p. 29.

181. Nawid, "The State, the Clergy, and British Imperial Policy in Afghanistan during the 19th and Early 20th Centuries," p. 589.

182. Nawid, "The State, the Clergy, and British Imperial Policy in Afghanistan during the 19th and Early 20th Centuries," p. 589.

183. India Office Records, LP&S10125, 3082, A.165, confidential document, 1907. In: Nawid, "The State, the Clergy, and British Imperial Policy in Afghanistan during the 19th and Early 20th Centuries," p. 590 fn. 31.

184. Nawid, "The State, the Clergy, and British Imperial Policy in Afghanistan during the 19th and Early 20th Centuries," p. 681.

185. Nawid, "The State, the Clergy, and British Imperial Policy in Afghanistan during the 19th and Early 20th Centuries," pp. 586–587.

186. Strausz-Hupe, "The Anglo-Afghan War of 1919," p. 89.

187. Strausz-Hupe, "The Anglo-Afghan War of 1919," p. 91.

188. Strausz-Hupe, "The Anglo-Afghan War of 1919," pp. 91–92.

189. Strausz-Hupe, "The Anglo-Afghan War of 1919," p. 92.

190. Charles G. Cogan, "Partners in Time: The CIA and Afghanistan since 1979," *World Policy Journal*, Vol. 10, No. 2 (Summer 1993), pp. 73–82, at p. 81.

191. A. Z. Hilali, "China's Response to the Soviet Invasion of Afghanistan," *Central Asian Survey*, Vol. 20, No. 3 (September 2001), pp. 323–351.

192. S. A. Yetiv, "How the Soviet Military Intervention in Afghanistan Improved the U.S. Strategic Position in the Persian Gulf," *Asian Affairs*, Vol. 17, No. 2 (Summer 1990), pp. 62–81.

193. Yetiv, "How the Soviet Military Intervention in Afghanistan Improved the U.S. Strategic Position in the Persian Gulf."

194. Yetiv, "How the Soviet Military Intervention in Afghanistan Improved the U.S. Strategic Position in the Persian Gulf."

195. Yetiv, "How the Soviet Military Intervention in Afghanistan Improved the U.S. Strategic Position in the Persian Gulf."

196. Cogan, "Partners in Time," p. 75.

197. Cogan, "Partners in Time," p. 74.

198. Steve Coll, "Anatomy of a Victory: CIA's Covert Afghan War," *Washington Post*, July 19, 1992.

199. George Lardner Jr., "Afghan, Cambodia Aid Cut: Conferees' Report Sets Out New Rules for CIA Operations," *Washington Post*, October 24, 1990.

200. Bill McCollum, "Afghan Endgame: The CIA Has Bungled It," *Washington Post*, September 10, 1989.

201. CNN chronology: http://cnn.com/2001/US/09/11/chronology.attack

202. Michael Cox, "American Power Before and After 11 September: Dizzy with Success?" *International Affairs*, Vol. 78, No. 2 (2002), pp. 261–276; John G. Ikenberry, "American Grand Strategy in the Age of Terror," *Survival*, Vol. 43, No. 4 (Winter 2001), pp. 19–34; Steve Smith, "The United States Will Emerge from this as a More Dominant World Power," *The Times*, September 19, 2001; Stanley Hoffman, "On the War," *New York Review of Books*, November 1, 2001.

203. Steven Simon and Daniel Benjamin, "The Terror," *Survival*, Vol. 43, No. 4 (Winter 2001), pp. 5–18, at p. 5; Lawrence Freedman, "The Third World War?" *Survival*, Vol. 43, No. 4 (Winter 2001–2002), pp. 61–88, at pp. 66–67, 85–86.

204. McInnes, "A Different Kind of War?" p. 170.

205. McInnes, "A Different Kind of War?" p. 170 fn. 30.

206. McInnes, "A Different Kind of War?" p. 172 fn. 34.

207. Inderjeet Parmar, "Catalysing Events, Think Thanks and American Foreign Policy Shifts: A Comparative Analysis of the Impacts of Pearl Harbor 1941 and 11 September 2001," *Government and Opposition*, Vol. 40, No. 1 (Winter 2005), pp. 1–25, at p. 1.

208. McInnes, "A Different Kind of War?" p. 175.

209. Shahram Akbarzadeh, "Keeping Central Asia Stable," *The World Quarterly*, Vol. 25, No. 4 (2004), pp. 689–705, at p. 689.

210. Akbarzadeh, "Keeping Central Asia Stable," p. 699.

211. Akbarzadeh, "Keeping Central Asia Stable," pp. 700–701.

212. Akbarzadeh, "Keeping Central Asia Stable," p. 703.

213. Parmar, "Catalysing Events, Think Thanks and American Foreign Policy Shifts," p. 1.

214. John G. Ikenberry, "America's Imperial Ambition," *Foreign Affairs*, Vol. 81, No. 5 (September–October 2002), pp. 44–60.

215. Brookings Institution Press Briefing, Repairing the Rift: The United States and *Europe After Iraq*, 3 April 2003. In: Parmar, "Catalysing Events, Think Thanks and American Foreign Policy Shifts," p. 7 fn. 25.

216. Kirk Spitzer, "Green Berets Outfought, Out Thought Taliban," *USA Today*, January 7, 2002.

217. John Moore, "International Red Cross Visits Taliban Prisoners Held by Marines at Kandahar Base," *Associated Press*, December 29, 2001; Matt Kelley, "Twenty More Suspected al-Qaida Fighters Sent to U.S. Marine Base in Afghanistan," *Associated Press*, December 27, 2001; Deborah Hastings, Associated Press writer, "7,000 Taliban, al-Qaida Being Held," *Washington Post*, December 21, 2001.

218. James Risen, "Taliban Chiefs Prove Elusive, Americans Say," *New York Times*, December 20, 2001; Pauline Jelinek, "U.S. Keeps Lists for Afghan War," *AP Online*, November 30, 2001; Rowan Scarborough, "Probers Told of Taliban Deaths," *Washington Times*, January 12, 2002.

219. Bradley Graham, "Strikes Level Al Qaeda Camp," *Washington Post*, January 8, 2002.

220. Carl Conetta, "Strange Victory: A Critical Appraisal of Operation Enduring Freedom and the Afghanistan War," Cambridge, MA: Commonwealth Institute Project on Defense Alternatives Research Monograph #6, 30 January 2002, pp. 4–5.

221. Conetta, "Strange Victory," pp. 5–6.

CHAPTER 5

1. The section is based on Ofer Israeli. "A New World Order," *Jerusalem Post*, January 24, 2017. Used by permission.

2. Fukuyama, "The End of History?"; Francis Fukuyama, *The End of History and the Last Man* (New York: Avon Books, 1992).

3. Samuel P. Huntington, "The Clash of Civilizations?" *Foreign Affairs*, Vol. 72, No. 3 (Summer 1993), pp. 22–49; Samuel P. Huntington, *The Clash of Civilizations and the Remaking of World Order* (New York: Simon & Schuster, 1996).

4. Elspeth Reeve, "Obama Foreign Policy: 'Leading from Behind'," *The Atlantic*, April 25, 2011.

5. Israeli, "A New World Order."

References

Ablowitz, Reuben, "The Theory of Emergence," *Philosophy of Science*, Vol. 6, No. 1 (January 1939), pp. 1–16.

Acheson, Dean, *The Korean War* (New York: Norton, 1971).

Adler, Emanuel, "Seizing the Middle Ground: Constructivism in World Politics," *European Journal of International Relations*, Vol. 3, No. 3 (September 1997), pp. 319–363.

Akbarzadeh, Shahram, "Keeping Central Asia Stable," *The World Quarterly*, Vol. 25, No. 4 (2004), pp. 689–705.

Alder, G. J., "The Key to India? Britain and the Herat Problem, 1830–1863—Part I," *Middle Eastern Studies*, Vol. 10, No. 1 (1974), pp. 186–209.

Alder, G. J., "The Key to India? Britain and the Herat Problem, 1830–1863—Part II," *Middle Eastern Studies*, Vol. 10, No. 3 (October 1974), pp. 287–384.

Anderson, M. Smith, *The Eastern Question, 1774–1923: A Study in International Relations* (New York: St. Martin's Publication, 1966).

Anderson, M. Smith, *The Rise of Modern Diplomacy, 1450–1919* (New York: Longman, 1993).

Angell, Norman, *The Great Illusion: A Study of the Relations of Military Power to National Advantage* (New York: G. P. Putnam's Sons, 1910).

Aron, Raymond, *Peace and War: A Theory of International Relations*, translated from the French by Richard Howard and Annette Baker Fox, Abridged by Remy Inglis Hall (Garden City, NY: Anchor Press, 1973).

Ashley, K. Richard, "The Geopolitics of Geopolitical Space: Toward a Critical Social Theory of International Politics," *Alternatives*, Vol. 12, No. 4 (October 1987), pp. 403–434.

Ashley, K. Richard, "The Poverty of Neorealism," *International Organization*, Vol. 38, No. 2 (Spring 1984), pp. 225–286.

Atkinson, Rick, *Crusade: The Untold Story of the Persian Gulf War* (Boston, MA: Houghton Mifflin, 1993).

Axelrod, Robert, and Robert O. Keohane, "Achieving Cooperation under Anarchy: Strategies and Institutions," *World Politics*, Vol. 38, No. 1 (October 1985), pp. 226–254.

Baldwin, A. David, ed., *Neorealism and Neoliberalism: The Contemporary Debate* (New York: Columbia University Press, 1993).

Bergeson, Albert, "Cycles of War in the Reproduction of the World Economy," paper presented at the Annual Meeting of the International Studies Association, Atlanta, GA, March 27–31, 1984.

Biddle, Stephen, "Victory Misunderstood: What the Gulf War Tells Us about the Future of Conflict," *International Security*, Vol. 21, No. 2 (Fall 1996), pp. 139–179.

Bilefsky, Dan, "Solana, EU's 'Good Cop,' Takes Stage," *International Herald Tribune*, August 11, 2006.

Blair, Clay, *The Forgotten War: America in Korea, 1950–1953* (New York: Times Books, 1987).

Bousquet, Nicole, "From Hegemony to Competition: Cycles of the Core?" in Terence K. Hopkins and Immanuel Wallerstein, eds., *Processes of the World System* (Beverly Hills, CA: Sage Publications, 1980), chapter 2, pp. 46–100.

Bracken, Paul, *The Command and Control of Nuclear Forces* (New Haven, CT: Yale University Press, 1983).

Bridge, F. R., and Roger Bullen, *The Great Powers and the European States System, 1815–1914* (New York: Longman, 1980).

Brooks, G. Stephen, and William C. Wohlforth, "American Primacy in Perspective," *Foreign Affairs*, Vol. 81, No. 4 (July/August 2002), pp. 20–33.

Brooks, G. Stephen, and William C. Wohlforth, "Power, Globalization, and the End of the Cold War: Reevaluating a Landmark Case for Ideas," *International Security*, Vol. 25, No. 3 (Winter 2000–2001), pp. 5–53.

Brown, E. Michael, Sean M. Lynn-Jones, and Steven E. Miller, eds., *Debating the Democratic Peace* (Cambridge, MA: MIT Press, 1996).

Bueno De Mesquita, Bruce, "Pride of Place: The Origins of German Hegemony," *World Politics*, Vol. 43, No. 1 (October 1990), pp. 28–53.

Bueno De Mesquita, Bruce, *The War Trap* (New Haven, CT: Yale University Press, 1981).

Bukey, Evan Burr, *Hitler's Hometown: Linz, Austria, 1908–1945* (Bloomington: Indiana University Press, 1986).

Bull, Hedley, *The Anarchical Society: A Study of Order in World Politics* (New York: Columbia University Press, 2002).

Bush, George, *National Security Strategy of the United States, 1990–1991* (Washington, DC: Maxwell Macmillan Pergamon, 1990).

Buszynski, Leszek, "Russia and the CIS in 2003: Regional Reconstruction," *Asian Survey*, Vol. 44, No. 1 (January–February 2004), pp. 158–167.

Calvocoressi, Peter, Guy Wint, and John Pritchard, *Total War: The Causes and Courses of the Second World War*, 2nd ed. (New York: Pantheon, 1989).

Carlton, Eric, *Occupation: The Policies and Practice of Military Conquerors* (New York: Routledge, 1992).

Carr, H. Edward, *The Twenty Years' Crisis, 1919–1939: An Introduction to the Study of International Relations* (London: Macmillan, 1939).

Checkel, T. Jeffrey, "The Constructivist Turn in International Relations Theory: A Review Essay," *World Politics*, Vol. 50, No. 2 (February 1998), pp. 324–348.

Christensen, J. Thomas, "Perceptions and Alliances in Europe, 1865–1940," *International Organization*, Vol. 51, No. 1 (Winter 1997), pp. 65–97.

Christensen, J. Thomas, and Snyder Jack, "Chain Gangs and Passed Bucks: Predicting Alliance Patterns in Multipolarity," *International Organization*, Vol. 44, No. 2 (Spring 1990), pp. 137–168.

Clarhe, J. Jeffrey, *Advice and Support: The Final Years, 1965–1973, The United States Army in Vietnam* (Washington, DC: U.S. Army Center of Military History, 1988).

Clausewitz, Carl Von, *On War* (Princeton, NJ: Princeton University Press, 1984).

Cobden, Richard, *Political Writings* (New York: D. Appleton, 1867), Vol. 1.

Cobden, Richard, *Speeches on Questions of Public Policy*, ed. By John Bright and James Rogers (London: Macmillan, 1870), Vol. 1.

Cogan, G. Charles, "Partners in Time: The CIA and Afghanistan since 1979," *World Policy Journal*, Vol. 10, No. 2 (Summer 1993), pp. 73–82.

Coll, Steve, "Anatomy of a Victory: CIA's Covert Afghan War," *Washington Post*, July 19, 1992.

Conetta, Carl, "Strange Victory: A Critical Appraisal of Operation Enduring Freedom and the Afghanistan War," Cambridge, MA: Commonwealth Institute Project on Defense Alternatives Research Monograph #6, 30 January 2002. http://www.comw.org/pda/0201strangevic.pdf

"Cooperation under Anarchy," special Volume of *World Politics*, Vol. 38, No. 1 (October 1985), edited by Oye.

Copeland, C. Dale, "Neorealism and the Myth of Bipolar Stability: Toward a New Dynamic Realist Theory of Major War," *Security Studies*, Vol. 5, No. 3 (Spring 1996), pp. 29–89.

Copeland, C. Dale, *The Origins of Major War* (Ithaca, NY and London: Cornell University Press, 2000).

Cordesman, H. Anthony, and Abraham R. Wagner, *The Gulf War (The Lessons of Modern War)* (Boulder, CO: Westview Press, 1996).

Cox, Michael, "American Power Before and After 11 September: Dizzy with Success?" *International Affairs*, Vol. 78, No. 2 (2002), pp. 261–276.

Cox, W. Robert, "Towards a Post-Hegemonic Conceptualization of World Orders: Reflections on the Relevancy of Ibn Khaldun," in James N. Rosenau and Ernst-Otto Czempiel, eds., *Governance Without Government: Order and Change in World Politics* (Cambridge: Cambridge University Press, 1992), chapter 5, pp. 132–159.

Craig, A. Gordon, *The Battle of Koniggratz: Prussia's Victory over Austria, 1866* (Philadelphia, PA: Lippincott, 1964).

Craig, A. Gordon, *The Politics of the Prussian Army, 1640–1945* (Oxford: Clarendon Press, 1955).

Curtiss, S. John, *Russia's Crimean War* (Durham, NC: Duke University Press, 1979).

Davidson, B. Phillip, *Vietnam at War: The History, 1946–1975* (Novato, CA: Presidio Press, 1988).

De Vinne, B. Pamela, ed., *The American Heritage: Illustrated Encyclopedic Dictionary* (Boston, MA: Houghton Mifflin Company, 1987).

Dehio, Ludwig, *The Precarious Balance: Four Centuries of the European Power Struggle* (New York: Knopf, 1962).

DePorte, W. Anton, *Europe between the Superpowers: The Enduring Balance*, 2nd ed. (New Haven, CT: Yale University Press, 1986).

Deutsch, W. Karl, *The Nerves of Government: Models of Political Communication and Control* (London: Free Press, 1966).

Dickinson, G. Lowes, *The European Anarchy* (New York: The Macmillan Company, 1916).

Dickinson, G. Lowes, *The International Anarchy, 1904–1914* (London: G. Allen & Unwin Ltd., 1926).

Dow, Mark, "Occupying and Obscuring Haiti," *New Politics*, Vol. 5, No. 2 (Winter 1995), pp. 12–26.

Doyle, W. Michael, "Kant, Liberal Legacies, and Foreign Affairs, Part 1," *Philosophy and Public Affairs*, Vol. 12, No. 3 (Summer 1983), pp. 205–235.

Doyle, W. Michael, "Kant, Liberal Legacies, and Foreign Affairs, Part 2," *Philosophy and Public Affairs*, Vol. 12, No. 4 (Autumn 1983), pp. 323–353.

Doyle, W. Michael, "Liberalism and World Politics," *The American Political Science Review*, Vol. 80, No. 4 (December 1986), pp. 1151–1169.

Dunn, S. Frederick, "The Scope of International Relations," *World Politics*, Vol. 1, No. 1 (October 1948), pp. 142–146.

Dunnigan, F. James, and William C. Martel, *How to Stop a War: The Lessons on Two Hundred Years of War and Peace* (New York: Doubleday Religious Publishing Group, 1987).

Durkheim, Emile, *The Division of Labor in Society*, translated by George Simpson (New York: Free Press, 1964).

Durkheim, Emile, *The Rules of Sociological Method* (New York: Free Press, 1982).

Echard, E. William, *Napoleon III and the Concert of Europe* (Baton Rouge: Louisiana State University Press, 1983).

Edelstein, M. David, "Occupational Hazards: Why Military Occupations Succeed or Fail," *International Security*, Vol. 29, No. 1 (Summer 2004), pp. 49–91.

Elman, Colin, "Cause, Effect, and Consistency: A Response to Kenneth Waltz," *Security Studies*, Vol. 6, No. 1 (Autumn 1996), pp. 58–61.

Elman, Colin, "Horses for Courses: Why *Not* Neorealist Theories of Foreign Policy?" *Security Studies*, Vol. 6, No. 1 (Autumn 1996), pp. 7–53.

Elman, Colin, and Miriam F. Elman, "Diplomatic History and International Relations Theory: Respecting Difference and Crossing Boundaries," *International Security*, Vol. 22, No. 1 (Summer 1997), pp. 5–21.

Elman, F. Miriam, "The Never-Ending Story: Democracy and Peace," *International Studies Review*, Vol. 1, No. 3 (Autumn 1999), pp. 87–103.

Elman, F. Miriam, ed., *Paths to Peace: Is Democracy the Answer?* (Cambridge, MA: MIT Press, 1997).

Elrod, B. Richard, "The Concert of Europe: A Fresh Look at an International System," *World Politics*, Vol. 28, No. 2 (January 1976), pp. 159–174.

Evans, Graham, and Newnham Jeffrey, *The Penguin Dictionary of International Relations* (London: Penguin Books, 1998).

Ferguson, Niall, *Colossus: The Price of America's Empire* (New York: Penguin Press, 2004).

Finnemore, Martha, and Kathryin Sikkink, "International Norm Dynamics and Political Change," *International Organization*, Vol. 52, No. 4 (Autumn 1998), pp. 887–917.

Fischer, Fritz, *Germany's Aims in the First World War* (New York: W. W. Norton, 1967).

Fischer, Fritz, *War of Illusions: German Policies from 1911–1914*, translated from Germany by Marian Jackson (New York: Norton, 1975).

Fischer, Fritz, *World Power or Decline: The Controversy over Germany's Aims in the First World War*, translated from Germany by Lancelot L. Farrar, Robert Kimber, and Rita Kimber (New York: Norton, 1974).

Foot, Rosemary, *The Wrong War: American Policy and the Dimensions of the Korean Conflict, 1950–1953* (Ithaca, NY: Cornell University Press, 1985).

Frankel, Benjamin, "Restating the Realist Case: An Introduction," *Security Studies*, Vol. 5, No. 3 (Spring 1996), pp. ix–xx.

Freedman, Lawrence, "The Third World War?" *Survival*, Vol. 43, No. 4 (Winter 2001–2002), pp. 61–88.

Freedman, Lawrence, and Efraim Karsh, *The Gulf Conflict, 1990–1991: Diplomacy and War in the New World Order* (Princeton, NJ: Princeton University Press, 1993).

Friedjung, Heinrich, *The Struggle for Supremacy in Germany, 1859–1866*, translated from the German by A. J. P. Taylor and William McElwee (New York: Russell, 1966—original edition 1897).

Friedman, L. Thomas, *The Lexus and the Olive Tree: Understanding Globalization* (New York: Farrar, Straus & Giroux, 1999).

Friedman, Norman, *Desert Victory: The War for Kuwait* (Annapolis, MD: Naval Institute Press, 1991).

Frye, Alton, *Nazi Germany and the American Hemisphere, 1939–1941* (New Haven, CT: Yale University Press, 1967).

Fukuyama, Francis, "Challenges to World Order after September 11," in William I. Zartman, ed., *Imbalance of Power: US Hegemony and International Order* (Boulder, CO: Lynne Rienner Publishers, 2009).

Fukuyama, Francis, "The End of History?" *The National Interest*, Vol. 16 (Summer 1989), pp. 3–18.

Fukuyama, Francis, *The End of History and the Last Man* (New York: Avon Books, 1992).

Fuller, E. Graham, and Ian O. Lesser, "Persian Gulf Myths," *Foreign Affairs*, Vol. 76, No. 3 (May–June 1997), pp. 42–52.

Funabashi, Yoichi, "Japan and the New World Order," *Foreign Affairs*, Vol. 70, No. 5 (Winter 1991–92), pp. 58–74.

Gaddis, L. John, "History, Theory, and Common Ground," *International Security*, Vol. 22, No. 1 (Summer 1997), pp. 75–85.

Gaddis, L. John, "The Long Peace: Elements of Stability in the Postwar International System," *International Security*, Vol. 10, No. 4 (Spring 1986), pp. 99–142.

Gelb, H. Leslie, "Vietnam: The System Worked," *Foreign Policy*, No. 3 (Summer 1971), pp. 140–167.

Gelb, H. Leslie, and Richard K. Betts, *The Irony of Vietnam: The System Worked* (Washington, DC: The Brookings Institution, 1979).

George, L. Alexander, ed., *Avoiding War: Problems of Crisis Management* (Boulder, CO: Westview, 1991).

George, L. Alexander, "Case Studies and Theory Development: The Method of Structured, Focused Comparison," in Paul Gordon Lauren, ed., *Diplomacy: New Approaches in History, Theory, and Policy* (New York: Free Press, 1979), pp. 43–68.

George, L. Alexander, "Knowledge for Statecraft: The Challenge for Political Science and History," *International Security*, Vol. 22, No. 1 (Summer 1997), pp. 44–52.

George, L. Alexander, and Andrew Bennett, *Case Studies and Theory Development in the Social Sciences* (Cambridge, MA: BCSIA Studies in International Security, 2004).

Gibbs, N. David, "Realpolitik and Humanitarian Intervention: The Case of Somalia," *International Politics*, Vol. 37, No. 1 (March 2000), pp. 41–55.

Gilbert, Felix, *To the Farewell Address: Ideas of Early American Foreign Policy* (Princeton, NJ: Princeton University Press, 1961).

Gillard, David, *The Struggle for Asia, 1828–1914: A Study in British and Russian Imperialism* (London: Methuen, 1977).

Gilpin, G. Robert, "No One Loves a Political Realist," in Benjamin Frankel, ed., *Realism, Restatements and Renewal* (New York: Frank Cass, 1996), chapter 3, pp. 3–26.

Gilpin, G. Robert, *War and Change in World Politics* (Cambridge: Cambridge University Press, 1981).

Glaser, L. Charles, "The Security Dilemma Revisited," *World Politics*, Vol. 50, No. 1 (October 1997), pp. 171–201.

Gochal, R. Joseph, and Jack S. Levy, "Crisis Mismanagement or Conflict of Interests? A Case Study of the Origins of the Crimean War," in Zeev Maoz et al., eds., *Multiple Paths to Knowledge in International Relations: Methodology in the Study of Conflict Management and Conflict Resolution* (New York: Lexington Books, 2004), pp. 309–342.

Goldfrank, M. David, *The Origins of the Crimean War* (London: Longman, 1994).

Gordon, R. Michael, and Bernard E. Trainor, *The Generals' War: The Inside Story of the Conflict in the Gulf* (Boston, MA: Little Brown, 1995).

Gowa, S. Joanne, *Ballots and Bullets: The Elusive Democratic Peace* (Princeton, NJ: Princeton University Press, 1999).

Gowa, S. Joanne, "Democratic States and International Disputes," *International Organization*, Vol. 49, No. 3 (Summer 1995), pp. 511–522.

Graham, Bradley, "Strikes Level Al Qaeda Camp," *Washington Post*, January 8, 2002.

Gravel, Michael, ed., *The Pentagon Papers: The Defense Department History of United States Decisionmaking on Vietnam*, 5 vols. (Boston, MA: Beacon Press, 1971).

Gulick, V. Edward, *Europe's Classical Balance of Power: A Case History of the Theory and Practice of One of the Great Concepts of European Statecraft* (Ithaca, NY: Cornell University Press, 1955).

Guzzini, Stefano, "A Reconstruction of Constructivism in International Relations," *European Journal of International Relations*, Vol. 6, No. 2 (June 2000), pp. 147–182.

Haber, H. Stephen, David M. Kennedy, and Stephen D. Krasner, "Brothers under the Skin: Diplomatic History and International Relations," *International Security*, Vol. 22, No. 1 (Summer 1997), pp. 34–43.

Harkabi, Yehoshafat, *War and Strategy* (Tel Aviv: Maarachot, 1997) [Hebrew].

Hastings, Deborah, Associated Press writer, "7,000 Taliban, al-Qaida Being Held," *Washington Post*, December 21, 2001.

Hastings, Max, *The Korean War* (New York: Simon and Schuster, 1987).

Hatton, Ragnhild, *George I, Elector and King* (New Haven, CT: Yale University Press, 2001).

Heikal, Mohamed, *Illusions of Triumph: An Arab View of the Gulf War* (London: HarperCollins, 1992).

Henderson, B. Gavin, "The Two Interpretations of the Four Points," *The English Historical Review*, Vol. 52, No. 205 (January 1937), pp. 48–66.

Herring, C. George, *America's Longest War: The United States and Vietnam, 1950–1975*, 3rd ed. (New York: McGraw-Hill, 1996).

Herring, C. George, ed., *The Secret Diplomacy of the Vietnam War: The Negotiating Volumes of the Pentagon Papers* (Austin: University of Texas Press, 1983).

Herz, H. John, "Idealist Internationalism and the Security Dilemma," *World Politics*, Vol. 2, No. 2 (January 1950), pp. 157–180.

Herz, H. John, *Political Realism and Political Idealism: A Study in Theories and Realities* (Chicago: Chicago University Press, 1951).

Hilali, A. Z., "China's Response to the Soviet Invasion of Afghanistan," *Central Asian Survey*, Vol. 20, No. 3 (September 2001), pp. 323–351.

Hoffmann, Stanley, *Gulliver's Troubles: or, The Setting of American Foreign Policy* (New York: McGraw-Hill, 1968).

Hoffmann, Stanley, "On the War," *New York Review of Books*, November 1, 2001.

Hoffmann, Stanley, Samuel P. Huntington, Ernest R. May, Richard N. Neustadt, and Thomas C. Schelling, "Vietnam Reappraised," *International Security*, Vol. 6, No. 1 (Summer 1981), pp. 3–26.

Holmes, E. Richard, *The Road to Sedan: The French Army, 1866–1870* (Atlantic Highlands, NJ: Humanities Press, 1984).

Holsti, J. Kalevi, *Peace and War: Armed Conflicts and International Order, 1648–1989* (Cambridge: Cambridge University Press, 1991).

Hopf, Ted, "Polarity, the Offense-Defense Balance, and War," *The American Political Science Review*, Vol. 85, No. 2 (June 1991), pp. 475–493.

Hopf, Ted, "The Promise of Constructivism in International Relations Theory," *International Security*, Vol. 23, No. 1 (Summer 1998), pp. 171–200.

Horn, B. David, *Great Britain and Europe in the Eighteenth Century* (Oxford: Clarendon Press, 1967).

Howard, Michael, *The Franco-Prussian War: The German Invasion of France, 1870–1871* (London: Rupert Hart-Davis, 1961).

Howard, Michael, "Men Against Fire: Expectations of War in 1914," *International Security*, Vol. 9, No. 1 (Summer 1984), pp. 41–57.

Hozier, H. Montague, *The Seven Weeks' War: Its Antecedents and Its Incidents* (London: Macmillan, 1871).

Huntington, P. Samuel, "The Clash of Civilizations?" *Foreign Affairs*, Vol. 72, No. 3 (Summer 1993), pp. 22–49.

Huntington, P. Samuel, *The Clash of Civilizations and the Remaking of World Order* (New York: Simon & Schuster, 1996).

Huntington, P. Samuel, "The Lonely Superpower," *Foreign Affairs*, Vol. 78, No. 2 (March 1999), pp. 35–49.

Huntington, P. Samuel, "No Exit: The Errors of Endism," *The National Interest*, Vol. 17 (Fall 1989), pp. 3–11.

Huntington, P. Samuel, *Who Are We? The Challenges to America's National Identity* (New York: Simon & Schuster, 2004).

Huntington, P. Samuel, "Why International Primacy Matters," *International Security*, Vol. 17, No. 4 (Spring 1993), pp. 68–83.

Huttenback, A. Robert, *British Relations with Sind, 1799–1843: An Anatomy of Imperialism* (Berkeley: University of California Press, 1962).

Ikenberry, G. John, ed., *America Unrivaled: The Future of the Balance of Power* (Ithaca,
NY: Cornell University Press, 2002).

Ikenberry, G. John, "American Grand Strategy in the Age of Terror," *Survival*, Vol.
43, No. 4 (Winter 2001), pp. 19–34.

Ikenberry, G. John, "America's Imperial Ambition," *Foreign Affairs*, Vol. 81, No.
5 (September–October 2002), pp. 44–60.

Ingram, Edward, *The Beginning of the Great Game in Asia, 1828–1834* (New York:
Oxford University Press, 1979).

Ingram, Edward, *Commitment to Empire: Prophecies of the Great Game in Asia, 1797–
1800* (New York: Oxford University Press, 1981).

Ingram, Edward, "The Wonderland of the Political Scientist," *International Security*,
Vol. 22, No. 1 (Summer 1997), pp. 53–63.

Israeli, Ofer, "Did Bush Save America?" *Jerusalem Post*, April 22, 2010.

Israeli, Ofer, "An Israeli Perspective on the Russian Chess Game in Syria." Unpublished: Prepared for "The Russian Foreign Policy in the Middle East," University of Haifa, June 8, 2015 [Hebrew].

Israeli, Ofer, "The Necessary Russian Involvement within the Disintegrated Middle East," *Maariv*, August 2, 2015 [Hebrew].

Israeli, Ofer, "A New World Order," *The Jerusalem Post*, January 25, 2017.

Israeli, Ofer, "The Unipolar Trap," *American Diplomacy* (April 2013), pp. 1–8.

Jelinek, Pauline, "U.S. Keeps Lists for Afghan War," *AP Online*, November 30, 2001.

Jentleson, W. Bruce, and Christopher A. Whytock, "Who 'Won' Libya? The Force-
Diplomacy Debate and Its Implications for Theory and Policy," *International
Security*, Vol. 30, No. 3 (Winter 2005/06), pp. 47–86.

Jervis, Robert, "Cooperation under the Security Dilemma," *World Politics*, Vol. 30,
No. 2 (January 1978), pp. 167–214.

Jervis, Robert, "From Balance to Concert: A Study of International Security Cooperation," *World Politics*, Vol. 38, No. 1 (October 1985), pp. 58–79.

Jervis, Robert, "International Primacy: Is the Game Worth the Candle?" *International Security*, Vol. 17, No. 4 (Spring 1993), pp. 52–67.

Jervis, Robert, *Perception and Misperception in International Politics* (Princeton, NJ:
Princeton University Press, 1976).

Jervis, Robert, "The Political Effects of Nuclear Weapons: A Comment," *International Security*, Vol. 13, No. 2 (Fall 1988), pp. 80–90.

Jervis, Robert, *System Effects: Complexity in Political and Social Life* (Princeton, NJ:
Princeton University Press, 1997).

Joll, James, *The Origins of the First World War* (New York: Longman, 1984).

Kagan, Donald, Eliot A. Cohen, Charles F. Doran, and Michael Mandelbaum,
"Is Major War Obsolete? An Exchange," *Survival*, Vol. 41, No. 2 (Summer
1999), pp. 139–152.

Kahler, Miles, "Rumors of War: The 1914 Analogy," *Foreign Affairs*, Vol. 58, No. 2
(Winter 1979/1980), pp. 374–396.

Kaiser, E. David, "Germany and the Origins of the First World War," *The Journal of
Modern History*, Vol. 55, No. 3 (September 1983), pp. 442–474.

Kaiser, E. David, "Vietnam: Was the System the Solution?" *International Security*,
Vol. 4, No. 4 (Spring 1980), pp. 199–218.

Kaplan, A. Morton, "Some Problems of International Systems Research," in *International Political Communities: An Anthology* (Garden City, NY: Doubleday and Company, 1966), pp. 469–501.

Kapstein, B. Ethan, and Michael Manstanduno, eds., *Unipolar Politics: Realism and State Strategies after the Cold War* (New York: Columbia University Press, 1999).

Karnow, Stanley, *Vietnam: A History* (New York: Viking Press, 1983).

Katzenstein, J. Peter, ed., *The Culture of National Security: Norms and Identity in World Politics* (New York: Columbia University Press, 1996).

Kaufman, I. Burton, *The Korean War: Challenges in Crisis, Credibility, and Command* (Philadelphia, PA: Temple University Press, 1986).

Kaysen, Carl, "Is War Obsolete? A Review Essay," *International Security*, Vol. 14, No. 4 (Spring 1990), pp. 42–64.

Kelley, Matt, "Twenty More Suspected al-Qaida Fighters Sent to U.S. Marine Base in Afghanistan," *Associated Press*, December 27, 2001.

Kennan, F. George, *American Diplomacy 1900–1950* (Chicago: University of Chicago Press, 1951).

Kennan, F. George, *Realities of American Foreign Policy* (Princeton, NJ: Princeton University Press, 1954).

Kennedy, M. Paul, "The First World War and the International Power System," *International Security*, Vol. 9, No. 1 (Summer 1984), pp. 7–40.

Kennedy, M. Paul, "Mission Impossible?" *New York Review of Books*, Vol. LI, No. 10 (June 10, 2004), pp. 16–19.

Kennedy, M. Paul, *The Rise and Fall of the Great Powers: Economic Change and Military Conflict from 1500 to 2000* (New York: Random House, 1987).

Keohane, O. Robert, *After Hegemony: Cooperation and Discord in the World Political Economy* (Princeton, NJ: Princeton University Press, 1984).

Keohane, O. Robert, "Institutionalist Theory and the Realist Challenge after the Cold War," in David A. Baldwin, ed., *Neorealism and Neoliberalism: The Contemporary Debate* (New York: Columbia University Press, 1993), chapter 11, pp. 269–300.

Keohane, O. Robert, ed., *Neorealism and Its Critics* (New York: Columbia University Press, 1986).

Keohane, O. Robert, and Joseph S. Nye, *Power and Interdependence: World Politics in Transition* (Boston: Little Brown, 1977).

King, Gary, Robert O. Keohane, and Sidney Verba, *Designing Social Inquiry: Scientific Inference in Qualitative Research* (Princeton, NJ: Princeton University Press, 1994).

Knorr, M. Klaus, *The Power of Nations: The Political Economy of International Relations* (New York: Basic Books, 1975).

Koch, H. Wolfgang, ed., *The Origins of the First World War: Great Power Rivalry and German War Aims* (New York: Taplinger Publication Co., 1972).

Koslowski, Rey, and Friedrich V. Kratochwil, "Understanding Change in International Politics: The Soviet Empire's Demise and the International System," *International Organization*, Vol. 48, No. 2 (Spring 1994), pp. 215–247.

Krauthammer, Charles, "Democratic Realism: An American Foreign Policy for a Unipolar World" (A lecture given by Krauthammer in *American Enterprise Institute for Public Policy Research*, February 2004).

Krauthammer, Charles, "The Unipolar Moment," *Foreign Affairs*, Vol. 70, No. 1 (1990–1991), pp. 23–33.

Kuhn, S. Thomas, *The Structure of Scientific Revolutions* (Chicago: The University of Chicago Press, 1962).

Kuniholm, R. Bruce, "The Geopolitics of the Caspian Basin," *The Middle East Journal*, Vol. 54, No. 4 (Autumn 2000), pp. 546–571.

Kupchan, A. Charles, "After Pax Americana: Benign Power, Regional Integration, and the Sources of Stable Multipolarity," *International Security*, Vol. 23, No. 2 (Fall 1998), pp. 40–79.

Kupchan, A. Charles, "Rethinking Europe," *The National Interest*, Vol. 56 (Summer 1999), pp. 73–79.

Kupchan, A. Charles, and Clifford A. Kupchan, "Concerts, Collective Security, and the Future of Europe," *International Security*, Vol. 16, No. 1 (Summer 1991), pp. 114–161.

Kupchan, A. Charles, and Clifford A. Kupchan, "A New Concert for Europe," in Graham T. Allison and Gregory F. Treverton, eds., *Rethinking America's Security: Beyond Cold War to New World Order* (New York: W. W. Norton, 1992), pp. 249–266.

Kurth, James, "America's Grand Strategy: A Pattern of History," *The National Interest*, Vol. 43 (Spring 1996), pp. 3–19.

Labs, J. Eric, "Beyond Victory: Offensive Realism and the Expansion of War Aims," *Security Studies*, Vol. 6, No. 4 (December 1997), pp. 1–49.

Langford, Paul, *The Eighteenth Century, 1688–1815* (New York: St. Martin's Press, 1976).

Lardner, George, Jr., "Afghan, Cambodia Aid Cut: Conferees' Report Sets Out New Rules for CIA Operations," *Washington Post*, October 24, 1990.

Layne, Christopher, "The Unipolar Illusion: Why New Great Powers Will Rise," *International Security*, Vol. 17, No. 4 (Spring 1993), pp. 5–51.

Lebow, N. Richard, *Nuclear Crisis Management: A Dangerous Illusion* (Ithaca, NY: Cornell University Press, 1987).

Leffler, P. Melvyn, "The American Conception of National Security and the Beginnings of the Cold War, 1945–48," *The American Historical Review*, Vol. 89, No. 2 (April 1984), pp. 346–381.

Leffler, P. Melvyn, *A Preponderance of Power: National Security, the Truman Administration, and the Cold War* (Stanford, CA: Stanford University Press, 1992).

Legro, W. Jeffrey, and Andrew Moravcsik, "Is Anybody Still a Realist?" *International Security*, Vol. 24, No. 2 (Fall 1999), pp. 5–55.

Lerman, A. Katharine, "Bismarckian Germany and the Structure of the German Empire," in Mary Fulbrook, ed., *German History since 1800* (London: Arnold, 1997), chapter 8, pp. 147–167.

Levy, S. Jack, "Contending Theories of International Conflict: A Levels-of-Analysis Approach," in Chester A. Crocker, and Fen O. Hampson, eds., *Managing Global Chaos: Sources of and Responses to International Conflict* (Washington, DC: United States Institute of Peace, 1996), pp. 3–24.

Levy, S. Jack, "Misperception and the Causes of War: Theoretical Linkages and Analytical Problems," *World Politics*, Vol. 36, No. 1 (October 1983), pp. 76–99.

Levy, S. Jack, "Organizational Routines and the Causes of War," *International Studies Quarterly*, Vol. 30, No. 2 (June 1986), pp. 193–222.

Levy, S. Jack, "Preferences, Constraints, and Choices in July 1914," *International Security*, Vol. 15, No. 3 (Winter 1990–1991), pp. 151–186.

Levy, S. Jack, "The Role of Crisis Mismanagement in the Outbreak of World War I," in Alexander L. George, ed., *Avoiding War: Problems of Crisis Management* (Boulder, CO: Westview Press, 1991), pp. 62–117.

Levy, S. Jack, "Theories of General War," *World Politics*, Vol. 37, No. 3 (April 1985), pp. 344–374.

Levy, S. Jack, "Too Important to Leave to the Other: History and Political Science in the Study of International Relations," *International Security*, Vol. 22, No. 1 (Summer 1997), pp. 22–33.

Levy, S. Jack, *War in the Modern Great Power System, 1495–1975* (Lexington: University Press of Kentucky, 1983).

Liberman, Peter, *Does Conquest Pay? The Exploitation of Occupied Industrial Societies* (Princeton, NJ: Princeton University Press, 1996).

Liberman, Peter, "The Spoils of Conquest," *International Security*, Vol. 18, No. 2 (Fall 1993), pp. 125–153.

Lo, Y. H. Clarence, "Civilian Policy Makers and Military Objectives: A Case Study of the U.S. Offensive to Win the Korean War," *Journal of Political and Military Sociology*, Vol. 7 (Fall 1979), pp. 229–242.

Logevall, Fredrik, *Choosing War: The Lost Chance for Peace and the Escalation of War in Vietnam* (Berkeley, CA: University of California Press, 1999).

Lynn-Jones, M. Sean, "Détente and Deterrence: Anglo-German Relations, 1911–1914," *International Security*, Vol. 11, No. 2 (Fall 1986), pp. 121–150.

Lynn-Jones, M. Sean, "Realist and America's Rise," *International Security*, Vol. 23, No. 2 (Fall 1998), pp. 157–182.

Lynn-Jones, M. Sean, and Steven E. Miller, eds., *The Cold War and After: Prospects for Peace* (Cambridge, MA: MIT Press, 1991).

Mackinder, Halford, *Democratic Ideals and Reality: A Study in the Politics of Reconstruction* (London: Constable, 1919).

Mackinder, Halford, "The Geographical Pivot of History," *The Geographical Journal*, Vol. 23, No. 4 (April 1904), pp. 421–437.

Mahan, T. Alfred, *The Influence of Sea Power upon History: 1660–1783* (Boston: Little, Brown and Company, 1890).

Mahnken, G. Thomas, and Barry D. Watts, "What the Gulf War Can (and Cannot) Tell Us about the Future of Warfare," *International Security*, Vol. 22, No. 2 (Fall 1997), pp. 151–162.

Malet, Alexander, *The Overthrow of the Germanic Confederation by Prussia in 1866* (London: Longmans, Green, 1870).

Mandelbaum, Michael, "Is Major War Obsolete?" *Survival*, Vol. 40, No. 4 (Winter 1998–1999), pp. 20–38.

Mansfield, D. Edward, "Concentration, Polarity, and the Distribution of Power," *International Studies Quarterly*, Vol. 37, No. 1 (March 1993), pp. 105–128.

Mansfield, D. Edward, "The Distribution of Wars over Time," *World Politics*, Vol. 41, No. 1 (October 1988), pp. 21–51.

Manstanduno, Michael, "Preserving the Unipolar Moment: Realist Theories and U.S. Grand Strategy after the Cold War," *International Security*, Vol. 21, No. 4 (Spring 1997), pp. 49–88.

Maoz, Zeev, *Paradoxes of War: On the Art of National Self-Entrapment* (Boston, MA: Unwin Hyman, 1990).

Maoz, Zeev, and Bruce Russett, "Normative and Structural Causes of Democratic Peace, 1946–1986," *The American Political Science Review*, Vol. 87, No. 3 (September 1993), pp. 624–638.

Mathison, Trygve, *The Function of Small States in the Strategies of Great Powers* (Oslo: Scandinavian University Books, 1971).

McCollum, Bill, "Afghan Endgame: The CIA Has Bungled It," *Washington Post*, September 10, 1989.

McCune, Shannon, "The Thirty-Eighth Parallel in Korea," *World Politics*, Vol. 1, No. 2 (January 1949), pp. 223–232.

McInnes, Colin, "A Different Kind of War? September 11 and the United States' Afghan War," *Review of International Studies*, Vol. 29, No. 2 (2003), pp. 165–184.

McKay, Derek, and Hamish M. Scott, *The Rise of the Great Powers, 1648–1815* (New York: Longman, 1983).

Mead, R. Walter, "On the Road to Ruin," in C. W. Kegley and E. R. Wittkopf, eds., *The Future of American Foreign Policy* (New York: St. Martin's Press, 1992), chapter 26, pp. 332–339.

Mearsheimer, J. John, "Back to the Future: Instability in Europe after the Cold War," *International Security*, Vol. 15, No. 1 (Summer 1990), pp. 5–56.

Mearsheimer, J. John, "The False Promise of International Institutions," *International Security*, Vol. 19, No. 3 (Winter 1994/95), pp. 5–49.

Mearsheimer, J. John, *Liddell Hart and the Weight of History* (Ithaca, NY: Cornell University Press, 1988).

Mearsheimer, J. John, *The Tragedy of Great Power Politics* (New York: W. W. Norton & Company, 2001).

Mearsheimer, J. John, "Why We Will Soon Miss the Cold War," *The Atlantic*, Vol. 266, No. 2 (August 1990), pp. 35–42.

Miller, Benjamin, "Explaining the Emergence of Great Power Concerts," *Review of International Studies*, Vol. 20 (October 1994), pp. 327–348.

Miller, Benjamin, *When Opponents Cooperate: Great Power Conflict and Collaboration in World Politics* (Ann Arbor: The University of Michigan Press, 2002).

Millett, R. Allan, "A Reader's Guide to the Korean War," *The Journal of Military History*, Vol. 61, No. 3 (July 1997), pp. 583–597.

Milner, Helen, "The Assumption of Anarchy in International Relations Theory: A Critique," *Review of International Studies*, Vol. 17, No. 1 (January 1991), pp. 67–85.

Moore, John, "International Red Cross Visits Taliban Prisoners Held by Marines at Kandahar Base," *Associated Press*, December 29, 2001.

Moravcsik, Andrew, "Taking Preferences Seriously: A Liberal Theory of International Politics," *International Organization*, Vol. 51, No. 4 (Autumn 1997), pp. 513–553.

Morgenthau, J. Hans, *Politics Among Nations: The Struggle for Power and Peace* (New York: Alfred A. Knopf, 1978).

Mueller, E. John, *Retreat from Doomsday: The Obsolescence of Major War* (New York: Basic Books, 1989).

Munro, H. Ross, "The Asian Interior: China's Waxing Spheres of Influence," *Orbis*, Vol. 38, No. 4 (Fall 1994), pp. 585–605.

Nathan, James, "The New Strategy: Force and Diplomacy in American Foreign Policy," *Defense Analysis*, Vol. 11, No. 2 (August 1995), pp. 121–145.

Nawid, Senzil, "The State, the Clergy, and British Imperial Policy in Afghanistan during the 19th and Early 20th Centuries," *International Journal of Middle East Studies*, Vol. 29, No. 4 (November 1997), pp. 581–605.

Nicholson, Michael, *Formal Theories in International Relations* (Cambridge: Cambridge University Press, 1989).

Niebuhr, Reinhold, *Moral Man and Immoral Society: A Study in Ethics and Politics* (New York: Charles Scribner's Sons, 1932).

Norris, A. James, *The First Afghan War, 1838–1842* (Cambridge: Cambridge University Press, 1967).

Nye, S. Joseph, Jr., "Limits of American Power," *Political Science Quarterly*, Vol. 117, No. 4 (Winter 2002), pp. 545–559.

O'Connor, G. Raymond, "Victory in Modern War," *Journal of Peace Research*, Vol. 6, No. 4 (December 1969), pp. 367–384.

O'Hanlon, Michael, "Stopping a North Korean Invasion: Why Defending South Korea Is Easier Than the Pentagon Thinks," *International Security*, Vol. 22, No, 4 (Spring 1998), pp. 135–170.

O'Hara, Sarah, and Michael Heffernan, "From Geo-Strategy to Geo-Economics: The 'Heartland' and British Imperialism Before and After MacKinder," *Geopolitics*, Vol. 11, No. 1 (Spring 2006), pp. 54–73.

Olson, S. James, *Where the Domino Fell: America in Vietnam, 1945–1990* (New York: St Martin's Press, 1991).

Onuf, G. Nicholas, *World of Our Making: Rules and Rule in Social Theory and International Relations* (Columbia: University of South Carolina Press, 1989).

Organski, A. F. K., *World Politics* (New York: Knopf, 1968).

Organski, A. F. K., and Jacek Kugler, *The War Ledger* (Chicago: University of Chicago Press, 1980).

Owen, M. John, "How Liberalism Produces Democratic Peace," *International Security*, Vol. 19, No. 2 (Fall 1994), pp. 87–125.

Owen, M. John, *Liberal Peace, Liberal War: American Politics and International Security* (Ithaca, NY: Cornell University Press, 1997).

Oye, A. Kenneth, "Explaining Cooperation under Anarchy: Hypotheses and Strategies," *World Politics*, Vol. 38, No. 1 (October 1985), pp. 1–24.

Parkinson, F., ed., *Conquering the Past: Austrian Nazism Yesterday and Today* (Detroit: Wayne State University Press, 1989).

Parmar, Inderjeet, "Catalysing Events, Think Thanks and American Foreign Policy Shifts: A Comparative Analysis of the Impacts of Pearl Harbor 1941 and 11 September 2001," *Government and Opposition*, Vol. 40, No. 1 (Winter 2005), pp. 1–25.

Partem, G. Michael, "The Buffer System in International Relations," *The Journal of Conflict Resolution*, Vol. 27, No. 1 (March 1983), pp. 3–26.

Pauley, F. Bruce, *Hitler and the Forgotten Nazis: A History of Austrian National Socialism* (Chapel Hill, NC: University of North Carolina Press, 1981).

Pei, Minxin, and Sara Kasper, *Lessons from the Past: The American Record of Nation Building* (Washington, DC: Carnegie Endowment for International Peace, 2003).

Polisensky, V. Josef, *War and Society in Europe, 1618–1648* (Cambridge: Cambridge University Press, 1978).

Ponting, Clive, *The Crimean War* (London: Chatto & Windus, 2004).

Posen, R. Barry, "Command of the Commons: The Military Foundation of U.S. Hegemony," *International Security*, Vol. 28, No. 1 (Summer 2003), pp. 5–46.

Posen, R. Barry, *The Sources of Military Doctrine: France, Britain, and Germany Between the World Wars* (Ithaca, NY: Cornell University Press, 1984).

Posen, R. Barry, and Andrew L. Ross, "Competing Visions for U.S. Grand Strategy," *International Security*, Vol. 21, No. 3 (Winter 1996/97), pp. 5–53.

Powell, Robert, "Anarchy in International Relations Theory: The Neorealist-Neoliberal Debate," *International Organization*, Vol. 48, No. 2 (Spring 1994), pp. 313–344.

Quinault, Ronald, "Afghanistan and Gladstone's Moral Foreign Policy," *History Today*, Vol. 52, No. 12 (December 2002), pp. 28–34.

Rabb, K. Theodore, *The Struggle for Stability in Early Modern Europe* (New York: Oxford University Press, 1975).

Ray, L. James, *Democracy and International Conflict: An Evaluation of the Democratic Peace Proposition* (Columbia, SC: University of South Carolina Press, 1995).

Rees, David, *Korea: The Limited War* (London: Macmillan, 1964).

Reeve, Elspeth, "Obama Foreign Policy: 'Leading from Behind'," *The Atlantic*, April 25, 2011.

Rich, Norman, *Great Power Diplomacy, 1814–1914* (New York: McGraw-Hill, 1992).

Rich, Norman, *Why the Crimean War? A Cautionary Tale* (Hanover, NH: University Press of New England, 1985).

Richardson, L. James, *Crisis Diplomacy: The Great Powers since the Mid-Nineteenth Century* (Cambridge: Cambridge University Press, 1994).

Risen, James, "Taliban Chiefs Prove Elusive, Americans Say," *New York Times*, December 20, 2001.

Rivkin, B. David, Jr., and Darin R. Bartram, "Military Occupation: Legally Ensuring a Lasting Peace," *The Washington Quarterly*, Vol. 26, No. 3 (Summer 2003), pp. 87–103.

Roger, L. Ashley, *A Short Guide to Clausewitz on War* (London: Weidenfeld, 1967).

Rose, Gideon, "Neoclassical Realism and Theories of Foreign Policy," *World Politics*, Vol. 51, No. 1 (October 1998), pp. 144–172.

Rosen, P. Stephen, "Vietnam and the American Theory of Limited War," *International Security*, Vol. 7, No. 2 (Fall 1982), pp. 83–113.

Rosenblueth, Arturo, Norbert Wiener, and Julian Bigelow, "Behavior, Purpose and Theology," *Philosophy of Science*, Vol. 10, No. 1 (January 1943), pp. 18–24.

Ruggie, G. John, *Constructing the World Polity: Essays on International Institutionalization* (New York: Routledge, 1998).

Ruggie, G. John, "Continuity and Transformation in the World Polity: Toward a Neorealist Synthesis," *World Politics*, Vol. 35, No. 2 (January 1983), pp. 261–285.

Ruggie, G. John, "What Makes the World Hang Together? Neo-Utilitarianism and the Social Constructivist Challenge," *International Organization*, Vol. 52, No. 4 (Autumn 1998), pp. 855–885.

Russett, M. Bruce, *Grasping the Democratic Peace: Principles for a Post-Cold War World* (Princeton, NJ: Princeton University Press, 1993).

Russett, M. Bruce, *The Prisoners of Insecurity: Nuclear Deterrence, the Arms Race, and Arms Control* (San Francisco, CA: W. H. Freeman, 1983).

Saab, Ann Pottinger, *The Origins of the Crimean Alliance* (Charlottesville, VA: University of Virginia Press, 1977).

Sagan, D. Scott, "1914 Revisited: Allies, Offense, and Instability," *International Security*, Vol. 11, No. 2 (Fall 1986), pp. 151–175.

Scarborough, Rowan, "Probers Told of Taliban Deaths," *Washington Times*, January 12, 2002.

Schaller, Michael, "U.S. Policy in the Korean War," *International Security*, Vol. 11, No. 3 (Winter 1986–87), pp. 162–166.

Schelling, C. Thomas, *Arms and Influence* (New Haven, CT: Yale University Press, 1966).

Schnable, F. James, *Policy and Direction: The First Year* (Washington, DC: Center of Military History, United States Army, 1992).

Schroeder, W. Paul, "The 19th-Century International System: Changes in the Structure," *World Politics*, Vol. 39, No. 1 (October 1986), pp. 1–26.

Schroeder, W. Paul, *Austria, Great Britain, and the Crimean War: The Destruction of the European Concert* (Ithaca, NY: Cornell University Press, 1972).

Schroeder, W. Paul, "History and International Relations Theory: Not Use or Abuse, but Fit or Misfit," *International Security*, Vol. 22, No. 1 (Summer 1997), pp. 64–74.

Schroeder, W. Paul, "The Lost Intermediaries: The Impact of 1870 on the European System," *The International History Review*, Vol. 6, No. 1 (February 1984), pp. 1–27.

Schroeder, W. Paul, *The Transformation of European Politics, 1763–1848* (New York: Oxford University Press, 1994).

Schuschnigg, Kurt, *The Brutal Takeover: The Austrian Ex-Chancellor's Account of the Anschluss of Austria by Hitler* (London: Weidenfeld and Nicolson, 1971).

Schwarzenberger, George, *Power Politics: An Introduction to the Study of International Relations and Post-War Planning* (London: J. Cape, 1941).

Schweller, L. Randall, "Bandwagoning for Profit: Bringing the Revisionist State Back In," *International Security*, Vol. 19, No. 1 (Summer 1994), pp. 72–107.

Schweller, L. Randall, *Deadly Imbalances: Tripolarity and Hitler's Strategy of World Conquest* (New York: Columbia University Press, 1998).

Schweller, L. Randall, "Neorealism's Status-Quo Bias: What Security Dilemma?" *Security Studies*, Vol. 5, No. 3 (Spring 1996), pp. 90–121.

Schweller, L. Randall, "Tripolarity and the Second World War," *International Studies Quarterly*, Vol. 37, No. 1 (March 1993), pp. 73–103.

Schweller, L. Randall, and William C. Wohlforth, "Power Test: Evaluating Realism in Response to the End of the Cold War," *Security Studies*, Vol. 9, No. 3 (Spring 2000), pp. 60–107.

Seton-Watson, R. William, *Britain in Europe, 1789–1914: A Survey of Foreign Policy* (Cambridge: Cambridge University Press, 1937).

Sharif, Ismail, "Growing Discontent with Globalization," *World Affairs*, Vol. 7, No. 3 (July–September 2003), pp. 14–27.

Showalter, E. Dennis, *Railroads and Rifles: Soldiers, Technology and the Unification of Germany* (Hamden, CT: Archon Books, 1975).

Silk, L., "Some Things Are More Vital Than Money When It Comes to Creating the World Anew," *New York Times*, September 22, 1991.

Simes, K. Dimitri, "America's Imperial Dilemma," *Foreign Affairs*, Vol. 82, No. 6 (November/December 2003), pp. 91–102.

Simon, Steven, and Daniel Benjamin, "The Terror," *Survival*, Vol. 43, No. 4 (Winter 2001), pp. 5–18.

Singer, J. David, and Melvin Small, *The Wages of War, 1816–1965: A Statistical Handbook* (New York: John Wiley, 1972).

Small, Melvin, and David J. Singer, *Resort to Arms: International and Civil Wars, 1816–1980* (Beverly Hills, CA: Sage Publications, 1982).

Smith, Adam, *An Inquiry into the Nature and Causes of the Wealth of Nations* (New York: Oxford University Press, 1976—The first edition was published in 1776).

Smith, Steve, "The End of the Unipolar Moment? September 11 and the Future of World Order," *International Relations*, Vol. 16, No. 2 (2002), pp. 171–183.

Smith, Steve, "The United States Will Emerge from this as a More Dominant World Power," *The Times*, September 19, 2001.

Smoke, Richard, *War: Controlling Escalation* (Cambridge, MA: Harvard University Press, 1977).

Snyder, H. Glenn, *Alliance Politics* (Ithaca, NY: Cornell University Press, 1997).

Snyder, H. Glenn, "Mearsheimer's World—Offensive Realism and the Struggle for Security: A Review Essay," *International Security*, Vol. 27, No. 1 (Summer 2002), pp. 149–173.

Snyder, Jack, "Civil-Military Relations and the Cult of the Offensive, 1914 and 1984," *International Security*, Vol. 9, No. 1 (Summer 1984), pp. 108–146.

Snyder, Jack, *Myths of Empire: Domestic Politics and International Ambition* (Ithaca, NY: Cornell University Press, 1991).

Sorley, Lewis, *A Better War: The Unexamined Victories and Final Tragedy of America's Last Years in Vietnam* (New York: Harcourt Brace & Co., 1999).

Spector, H. Ronald, "U.S. Army Strategy in the Vietnam War," *International Security*, Vol. 11, No. 4 (Spring 1987), pp. 130–134.

Spencer, C. Tucker, ed., *Encyclopedia of the Korean War*, 3 vols. (Santa Barbara, CA: ABC-CLIO, 2000).

Spitzer, Kirk, "Green Berets Outfought, Out Thought Taliban," *USA Today*, January 7, 2002.

Spykman, J. Nicholas, *America's Strategy in World Politics: The United States and the Balance of Power* (New York: Harcourt, 1942).

Spykman, J. Nicholas, *The Geography of the Peace*, ed. by Helen R. Nicholl (New York: Harcourt, Brace & Company, 1944).

Stilwell, G. Richard, "The United States, Japan and the Security of Korea," *International Security*, Vol. 2, No. 2 (Autumn 1977), pp. 93–95.

Stoessinger, G. John, *Why Nations Go to War* (New York: St. Martin's Press, 1974).

Strausz-Hupe, Robert, "The Anglo-Afghan War of 1919," *Military Affairs*, Vol. 7, No. 2 (Summer 1943), pp. 89–96.

Summers, G. Harry, *On Strategy: A Critical Analysis of the Vietnam War* (Novato, CA: Presidio Press, 1982).

Taliaferro, W. Jeffrey, "Security Seeking under Anarchy: Defensive Realism Revisited," *International Security*, Vol. 25, No. 3 (Winter 2000/01), pp. 128–161.

Taylor, A. J. P., *The Struggle for Mastery in Europe, 1848–1918* (Oxford: Clarendon Press, 1954).

Taylor, Charles, "Interpretation and the Sciences of Man," in *Philosophical Papers* (Cambridge: Cambridge University Press, 1985), chapter 1, pp. 15–57.

Thayer, A. Bradley, "The *Pax Americana* and the Middle East: U.S. Grand Strategic Interests in the Region after September 11," *Mideast Security and Policy Studies*, No. 56 (December 2003), pp. 1–56.

Thucydides, *The History of Peloponnesian War* (Franklin Center, PA: Franklin Library, 1978).

Thucydides, *The Peloponnesian War* (New York: Penguin, 1978).

Toland, John, *In Mortal Combat: Korea, 1950–1953* (New York: Morrow, 1991).

Tombs, Robert, *The War Against Paris, 1871* (Cambridge: Cambridge University Press, 1981).

Tuchman, W. Barbara, *The Guns of August* (New York: Ballantine Books, 1962).

Tucker, W. Robert, *The Inequality of Nations* (New York: Basic Books, 1977).

Turchin, Peter, *Historical Dynamics: Why States Rise and Fall* (Princeton, NJ: Princeton University Press, 2003).

Turchin, Peter, *War and Peace and War: The Life Cycles of Imperial Nations* (New York: Penguin Group, 2007).

Turchin, Peter, *War and Peace and War: The Rise and Fall of Empires* (New York: A Plum Book, 2007).

Tzu, Sun, *The Art of War*, translated by Ralph Sawyer (New York: Basic Books, 1994).

Van Evera, Stephen, *Causes of War: Power and the Roots of Conflict* (Ithaca, NY: Cornell University Press, 1999).

Van Evera, Stephen, "The Cult of the Offensive and the Origins of the First World War," *International Security*, Vol. 9, No. 1 (Summer 1984), pp. 58–107.

Van Evera, Stephen, *Guide to Methods for Students of Political Science* (Ithaca, NY: Cornell University Press, 1997).

Van Evera, Stephen, "Offense, Defense, and the Causes of War," *International Security*, Vol. 22, No. 4 (Spring 1998), pp. 5–43.

Van Evera, Stephen, "Primed for Peace: Europe after the Cold War," *International Security*, Vol. 15, No. 3 (Winter 1990–1991), pp. 7–57.

Van Evera, Stephen, "Why Cooperation Failed in 1914," *World Politics*, Vol. 38, No. 1 (October 1985), pp. 80–117.

Wagner, R. Harrison, "The Theory of Games and the Balance of Power," *World Politics*, Vol. 38, No. 4 (July 1986), pp. 546–576.

Wagner, R. Harrison, "What Was Bipolarity?" *International Organization*, Vol. 47, No. 1 (Winter 1993), pp. 77–106.

Wallensteen, Peter, and Margareta Sollenberg, "The End of International War? Armed Conflict 1989–95," *Journal of Peace Research*, Vol. 33, No. 3 (August 1996), pp. 353–370.

Wallerstein, Immanuel, *Historical Capitalism* (London: Verso, 1983).

Wallerstein, Immanuel, *The Modern World System II: Mercantilism and the Consolidation of the European World Economy, 1600–1750* (New York: Academic Press, 1980).

Wallerstein, Immanuel, *The Politics of the World-Economy: The States, The Movements, and the Civilizations* (Cambridge: Cambridge University Press, 1984).

Walt, M. Stephen, *The Origins of Alliances* (Ithaca, NY: Cornell University Press, 1987).

Walt, M. Stephen, "Rigor or Rigor Mortis? Rational Choice and Security Studies," *International Security*, Vol. 23, No. 4 (Spring 1999), pp. 5–48.

Waltz, N. Kenneth, "The Emerging Structure of International Politics," *International Security*, Vol. 18, No. 2 (Fall 1993), pp. 44–79.

Waltz, N. Kenneth, "Evaluating Theories," *American Political Science Review*, Vol. 91, No. 4 (December 1997), pp. 913–917.

Waltz, N. Kenneth, "International Politics Is Not Foreign Policy," *Security Studies*, Vol. 6, No. 1 (Autumn 1996), pp. 54–57.

Waltz, N. Kenneth, "The Origins of War in Neorealist Theory," *Journal of Interdisciplinary History*, Vol. 18, No. 4 (Spring 1988), pp. 615–628.

Waltz, N. Kenneth, "Realist Thought and Neorealist Theory," *Journal of International Affairs*, Vol. 44, No. 1 (Spring/Summer 1990), pp. 21–37.

Waltz, N. Kenneth, "The Stability of a Bipolar World," *Daedalus*, Vol. 93, No. 3 (Summer 1964), pp. 881–909.

Waltz, N. Kenneth, *Theory of International Politics* (Reading, MA: Addison-Wesley, 1979).

Watson, Adam, *The Evolution of International Society: A Comparative Historical Analysis* (London: Routledge, 1992).

Watson, Adam, "Russia and the European State System," in Hedley Bull and Watson Adam, eds., *The Expansion of International Society* (Oxford: Oxford University Press, 1984), chapter 4, pp. 61–74.

Wawro, Geoffrey, *The Austro-Prussian War: Austria's War with Prussia and Italy in 1866* (Cambridge: Cambridge University Press, 1997).

Weigert, W. Hans, *Generals and Geographers: The Twilight of Geopolitics* (New York: Oxford University Press, 1942).

Weinstein, B. Franklin, "The Korean Debate, Continued," *International Security*, Vol. 2, No. 3 (Winter 1978), pp. 160–167.

Weinstein, B. Franklin, "The United States, Japan and the Security of Korea," *International Security*, Vol. 2, No. 2 (Autumn 1977), pp. 68–89.

Wendt, Alexander, "The Agent-Structure Problem in International Relations Theory," *International Organization*, Vol. 41, No. 3 (Summer 1987), pp. 335–370.

Wendt, Alexander, "Anarchy Is What States Make of It: The Social Construction of Power Politics," *International Organization*, Vol. 46, No. 2 (Spring 1992), pp. 391–425.

Wendt, Alexander, "Constructing International Politics," *International Security*, Vol. 20, No. 1 (Summer 1995), pp. 71–81.

Wendt, Alexander, *Social Theory of International Politics* (Cambridge: Cambridge University Press, 1999).

Wetzel, David, *The Crimean War: A Diplomatic History* (New York: Columbia University Press, 1985).

White, I. D., "Commentary: The United States, Japan and the Security of Korea," *International Security*, Vol. 2, No. 2 (Autumn 1977), pp. 90–92.

White, K. Ralph, "Why Aggressors Lose," *Political Psychology*, Vol. 11, No. 2 (1990), pp. 227–242.

Wight, Martin, *Power Politics* (London: Harmondsworth, 1978).

Wight, Martin, "Why Is There No International Theory?" in James Der Derian, ed., *International Theory: Critical Investigations* (New York: New York

University Press, 1995), pp. 15–35. The first edition was published in Herbert Butterfield and Wight Martin, eds., *Diplomatic Investigations: Essays in the Theory of International Politics* (London: George Allen & Unwin, 1966), pp. 17–34.

Williamson, R. Samuel, Jr., "The Origins of World War I," *Journal of Interdisciplinary History*, Vol. 18, No. 4 (Spring 1988), pp. 795–818.

Wohlforth, C. William, "Realism and the End of the Cold War," *International Security*, Vol. 19, No. 3 (Winter 1994/1995), pp. 91–129.

Wohlforth, C. William, "Reality Check: Revising Theories of International Politics in Response to the End of the Cold War," *World Politics*, Vol. 50, No. 4 (July 1998), pp. 650–680.

Wohlforth, C. William, "The Stability of a Unipolar World," *International Security*, Vol. 24, No. 1 (Summer 1999), pp. 5–41.

Wolfers, Arnold, *Discord and Collaboration: Essays on International Politics* (Baltimore: Johns Hopkins University Press, 1962).

Wright, Quincy, *A Study of War* (Chicago: The University of Chicago Press, 1942).

Yapp, M. E., *Strategies of British India: Britain, Iran, and Afghanistan, 1798–1850* (Oxford: Oxford University Press, 1980).

Yetiv, S. A., "How the Soviet Military Intervention in Afghanistan Improved the U.S. Strategic Position in the Persian Gulf," *Asian Affairs*, Vol. 17, No. 2 (Summer 1990), pp. 62–81.

Zakaria, Fareed, *From Wealth to Power: The Unusual Origins of America's World Role* (Princeton, NJ: Princeton University Press, 1998).

Ecclesiastes.

The United States Navy Web site: http://www.navy.mil/

CNN chronology: http://cnn.com/2001/US/09/11/chronology.attack

http://www.globalsecurity.org/military/ops/desert_fox.htm

http://pubpages.unh.edu/%7Emwherold/

http://icasualties.org/

http://www.defenselink.mil/transcripts/2004/tr20040419-secdef1362.html

THE CORRELATES OF WAR PROJECT (COW):

COW, General: The Correlates of War Project (COW). http://correlatesofwar.org

- The COW Typology of War: Defining and Categorizing Wars. http://cow.dss.ucdavis.edu/data-sets/COW-war/the-cow-typology-of-war-defining-and-categorizing-wars/view:
  - COW, Interstate Wars
  - COW, Extrastate War
  - COW, Intrastate Wars
- COW National Material Capabilities
- Territorial Change, 1816–2008 (v4.01). http://cow.la.psu.edu/COW2%20Data/TerrChange/terrchange.html
- COW, State System Membership List
- COW, Major Powers

INTERNATIONAL CRISIS BEHAVIOR PROJECT (ICB):

International Crisis Behavior Project (ICB): http://www.icb.umd.edu/dataviewer/

- EAST GERMAN UPRISING (ICB #141)
- POLAND LIBERALIZATION (ICB #154)
- HUNGARIAN UPRISING (ICB #155)
- PRAGUE SPRING (ICB #227)
- SOLIDARITY (ICB #315)
- IRAQ NO-FLY ZONE (ICB #406)
- NORTH KOREA NUCLEAR I (ICB #408)
- IRAQ TROOP DEPLOYMENT-KUWAIT (ICB #412)
- DESERT STRIKE (ICB #419)
- UNSCOM I (ICB #422)
- US EMBASSY BOMBINGS (ICB #427)
- UNSCOM II OPERATION DESERT FOX (ICB #429)
- AFGHANISTAN-USA (ICB #434)
- IRAQ REGIME (ICB #441)

Index

Page numbers followed by an italicized "t" refer to tables.

About the Author

DR. OFER ISRAELI is a geostrategist, international security policy, and Middle East expert. He is a lecturer and a senior research fellow in the Institute for Policy and Strategy (IPS) (https://www.idc.ac.il/en/research/ips/Documents/staff/Ofer-IsraeliE.pdf) at the Interdisciplinary Center (IDC) Herzliya, Israel, and a research fellow at the National Security Studies Center (NSSC) (http://nssc.haifa.ac.il/index.php/en/nssc-staff/academic-staff), University of Haifa, Israel. Dr. Israeli teaches National Security and Strategy at the Israel Defense Forces (IDF) Academy for Strategy. He also teaches International Relations Theory, Foreign Policy Decision Making, Middle East, and Diplomacy and Crisis Management at the Interdisciplinary Center (IDC), Herzliya (http://portal.idc.ac.il/faculty/en/pages/profile.aspx?username=oisraeli); the University of Haifa; the Ben-Gurion University of the Negev; Tel Aviv University; the Open University of Israel; the Israel Defense Forces (IDF) Academy for Tactic Commanders; the Israeli Air Force (IAF) College for Military Flights; and the Israel Defense Forces (IDF) Naval Academy.

His postdoctoral research (2009–2011) at the Center for Peace and Security Studies (cPASS), Georgetown University's School of Foreign Service (SFS), is on *Complexity of International Relations*. His PhD dissertation in International Relations is "Realist Theory of International Outcomes," the University of Haifa's President PhD program for honor students. His MA thesis in International Relations is "The Relation between Military Results & Political Outcomes," the Hebrew University of Jerusalem.

He has written extensively about International Security, with many articles published in academic journals, such as *Israel Affairs*, *Middle East*

Policy, and *Middle Eastern Studies,* as well as popular academic magazines including *American Diplomacy.* His first book, *Theory of War: System Stability and Territorial Outcomes* (Tel Aviv, Israel: Resling, 2017; http://www.resling.co.il/book.asp?book_id=974 [Hebrew]), is a 2017–18 Winner of *Chaikin Prize in Geostrategy,* University of Haifa. His second book is *International Relations Theory of War* (Santa Barbara, CA: Praeger, 2019; https://abc-clio.com/ABC-CLIOCorporate/product.aspx?pc=A6099C). His third book is *Complex Effects of International Relations: Intended and Unintended Consequences of Intentional Human Actions* (Albany, NY: State University of New York Press, forthcoming).

Dr. Israeli often appears as a special International Affairs and Middle East commentator on national and international TV. His articles, op-ed pieces, and TV and radio interviews deal with topics including Israel's Security and Foreign Policy, the Middle East and the Arab world, Iran Nuclear Program, and the U.S. Global Foreign Policy with a focus on its involvement in the Middle East and in the Far East.

In 2008, Dr. Israeli participated in the special program on "U.S. National Security Policymaking in the Twenty-First Century," sponsored by Fulbright and managed by the U.S. Department of State. He also received grants and fellowships from the Leonard Davis Institute for International Relations, the Hebrew University of Jerusalem, and the University of Haifa, Israel.

As part of his security duties, Dr. Israeli deals with issues of strategic planning and national security policy.